ALBUM ART

ART

NEW
MUSIC
GRAPHICS

JOHN FOSTER

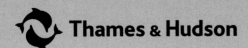
Thames & Hudson

On the cover: (Clockwise from top left) The Flaming Lips, *With A Little Help From My Fwends*;
Matthew Dear, *Beams*; Frank Ocean, *Lens*; Adasiewicz/Erb/Roebke, *Yuria's Dream*; Ambivalent,
Daylights; Grizzly Bear, *Painted Ruins*; Bon Iver, *22, A Million*; Father John Misty, *I Love You,
Honeybear*; Young Magic, *MELT*; The Shins, *Heartworms*; Tame Impala, *Currents*; Nonkeen, *Oddments
Of The Gamble*; Crossfaith, *Freedom* EP; Bartellow, *Panokorama*

Pages 6–7: Tame Impala, *Currents*
Pages 70–71: David Bowie, *The Next Day* (seen on a billboard)
Pages 128–129: Norma Jean, *O'God, The Aftermath*
Pages 194–195: Lykke Li, *Wounded Rhymes*
Pages 254–255: Rihanna, *Unapologetic*

First published in the United Kingdom in 2018 by
Thames & Hudson Ltd, 181A High Holborn, London WC1V 7QX

© 2018 Quarto Publishing plc

This book was designed and produced by
Quid Publishing, an imprint of the Quarto Group
The Old Brewery, 6 Blundell Street, London N7 9BH

British Library Cataloguing-in-Publication Data
A catalogue record for this book is available from the British Library

ISBN 978-0-500-29415-4

Printed and bound in China

Book design: John Foster at badpeoplegoodthings.com

To find out about all our publications, please visit **www.thamesandhudson.com**.
There you can subscribe to our e-newsletter, browse or download our current
catalogue, and buy any titles that are in print.

CONTENTS

INTRODUCTION

It doesn't make sense. Music was supposed to transform into something that only existed in little file formats flying through the air, and yet we find ourselves square in the middle of one of the greatest periods in music packaging. Our desire for something tangible to hold in our hands and fill up our shelves is overwhelming at times. The more this has been taken away from us, thanks to advances in technology, the more we have held tight to the things that mattered. For many people, it was a surprise to discover that one of the things that mattered most was a place for their music to live. They longed for the record sleeve. They even longed for the CD and cassette, practically willing them back into existence, pulling them back from the brink of oblivion. Numerous independent record labels had continued carrying the flag for quality record packaging, and were at the ready when the marketplace responded. Deluxe editions and box sets sprang up as the major labels and big artists took note. Soon, the music industry would see events like Record Store Day pushing collectable packaging back to the forefront in a way that hadn't been seen since the novelty craze of the sixties. Then, the tipping point arrived. Kids started buying physical records. Music packaging became important to a new generation and soon hip clothing outlets began devoting space to racks of LPs and displaying record players. Buying music became special again, and a wave of designers set out to make sure that it stayed that way.

The designers collected here are at the forefront of that movement. Some have been working in the music industry for decades, while others are fresh on the scene. They all share a desire to elevate the simple record cover and the wrapping that surrounds these products into something more, something special, something unique, something memorable. Lifelong music fans, they pour every ounce of creative energy into coming up with solutions worthy of the music inside. They also need to be inventive in how they accomplish this. Coming up with a great concept in a sketch during a meeting and actually seeing it brought to fruition and sitting on a shelf in a record store are two different things. As Paula Scher details in her interview, today's designers are faced with a very different task from the record sleeve designers of the past. Leaving aside the megastars, budgets are tight, yet the pressure to deliver something jaw-dropping and mind-blowing remains.

Nearly everyone interviewed for this book had one firm at the top of their list of all-time album art masters. That firm was Hipgnosis. The draw is not just the brilliant concepts surrounding the work, but equally their ability to convince both the artist and the label that they should invest time, money and resources in executing some of these complicated images. It is a lineage that extends to Stefan Sagmeister, who talked clients into sealing cigarettes into their packaging and creating little plastic worlds that just so happened to have a CD inside them. In his interview, you can see how he finds it difficult to compare the days of jetting off to meet with The Rolling Stones and the complications today's designers must face.

In a lot of ways, the patron saint of today's designers is someone who managed to create an incredibly sophisticated body of work with tiny budgets and very limited resources, and little to help him other than a sharp eye, a lot of hustle, and a gnawing desire to create something special. Vaughan Oliver's celebrated work at v23 served as the inspiration for many of the people here (myself included) entering the design field. (His equally inspiring old v23

running mate Chris Bigg is featured here.) Oliver's work is undeniably arty and delicate and mysterious, yet he often pulled his designs together from meagre beginnings. Even Reid Miles at Blue Note had decent photos of the artists to work from. Oliver would do whatever it took to get the images he needed, lack of budget be damned. Sometimes this meant leaning on existing images and often it meant creating something entirely new, sometimes using himself as the model. The one place where Oliver and Sagmeister intersect is in their willingness to use their own bodies if needed to get the results desired. The designers here are willing to give everything to their projects, regardless of budget, and that becomes evident in their work, from Michael Cina's exquisite paintings to the hundreds of paper cuttings from Jad Fair, to Hvass&Hannibal's woodland photoshoots or Mario Hugo's constructions. They do it because they have to.

The gauge for my love of other designers has always had two levels. The first is a simple appreciation for craft and solid thinking, but also an acknowledgment that, given time and resources, I could have pulled off something pretty similar. The second, far more exclusive level, is work that there is no way in a million years I could have ever dreamed of coming up with, much less made a reality. It was really crystallized for me while talking with Brian Roettinger, a man who has taken up the mantle of Hipgnosis and Sagmeister with a new spin and persuaded one of the biggest stars in the world to promote a record solely around a single colour. We drifted into a discussion about who you could get to do which part of a big project, before circling back to designer/illustrator Robert Beatty. For his project with Kesha, Roettinger had to get Beatty. 'There is only one person on the face of the earth that can deliver that kind of a record cover,' he said, 'and that's Robert Beatty.' Such one-of-a-kind designers are the ones gathered in the pages that await you.

BRAULIO AMADO

PORTUGUESE POWERHOUSE

 There is a special group of people that just make everything that they touch better. Braulio Amado is most definitely one of that select group. This is a man who once made *Bloomberg Businessweek* a must-read for the design community. His unique perspective and colour sense mixes with a deceptively sophisticated illustration style that bridges fifty years of design masters. After stints at heavyweights such as Pentagram and Wieden+Kennedy, Amado finally committed to working solely with clients where he could really use all of his talents. It should come as no surprise that those talents shine brightest when wrapped around music projects. Growing up in Portugal, he became a big part of the Lisbon hardcore scene, playing in bands and promoting shows. Music quickly became an integral part of his life. When he moved to the US to finish his studies, he made opportunities for that love to find a visual outlet by doing gig posters around New York City. These soon became a place for his typographic explorations and skewed sense of humour to flourish. The poster work quickly morphed into more packaging work as artists longed to have his sensibility applied to their albums. The style that emerged was fun but serious. Seriously fun! With each project he manages to challenge the format in bold ways, often pushing his type to the edges and playing with white space until the viewer seriously questions his intentions. His solutions are electric on every level, leaving the rest of us catching our breath trying to play catch-up.

The music business has shifted in a million directions just in the short period between Amado's days as a young promoter and today. 'Things have gotten more digital, that's for sure,' he observes. 'But funnily enough, I design more vinyl packages than CDs now, which is way more fun. It's also the only physical format I listen to. My computer doesn't even have a CD player any more.' He smiles.

The change in how music is displayed for most consumers has opened up a lot of possibilities for Amado. 'With digital covers, you have the name of the artist/record next to the image normally, so it's fun to sometimes make covers without any type on them,' he explains. 'Physical covers allow you to play with the package itself and how you interact with the cover. But, ultimately, I try to get to a strong idea that works no matter what.' It is this drive that makes his work so strong; whether it exists as a postage stamp or plastered across a wall, it is always bold and visually arresting.

'I have a little vinyl collection, so the physical thing definitely has more value to me,' he admits. 'But I normally listen to music through my computer or phone, so when I go to the record store nowadays I buy a record because I really love the band, and a nicely designed cover with inserts and extra content inside definitely makes the whole thing more precious and worthy,' he adds. That feeling is what he wants fans and consumers to get when they interact with a package he is involved with, which means that he is often pushing the artists and labels he works with to provide as much bang per buck as is possible. But once the release is out into the world, the one place he avoids that kind of push and pull in the digital age is on social media. 'I try to not read the comments at all,' he confesses, sheepishly.

FILTERING THE VISUAL NOISE
'My friend Manuel Donada, from Spain, had a record label called Gssh! Gssh!, and all the stuff he put out was the reason that made me want to become a graphic designer and make designs for bands in the early 2000s,' Amado explains. 'It was fun, it was weird, some covers were screen-printed onto odd paper stocks or plastics, and they always had some crazy inserts inside.' The energy inherent in those releases, and the scene surrounding them, would stay with the young Portuguese as he began to find his own creative voice. 'I wish he did more covers nowadays,' he laments.

Detailing all of the other inspirations isn't an easy task for Amado. 'Just so many influences, it's too hard to name them,' he admits. 'I get easily tired of "my style" so I try to do different stuff as often as possible, and that's definitely a product of loving so many different things. But also, with the Internet these days, it's just an overwhelming mix of content that ends up being hard to understand who did it. I'm OK with it, I like the visual confusion, it's exciting.' You can feel that rush of influences and sense of chaos being distilled down to a single gut punch in each of his record covers.

Amado finds that he approaches all of his design and illustration projects in a similar fashion, but designing for music clients requires a little twist. 'Honestly, it's not that different. Music packaging can have a bit of everything – logos, typography, photos, illustration – so I feel like sometimes designing just a logo for a non-music client can be easier,' he explains. 'But also, with covers, you are translating music into something visual, so that on its own requires a different way of solving problems,' he adds.

The fundamental part of that approach is also his favourite part. 'Sketches!' he exclaims. 'I try to always do three very different approaches, and once one of the directions is picked it's like an entire universe was opened up for me to play around and explore.' Working things out by hand also creates a quality that carries all the way through to the final product, with so many of his covers having illustrations or type that have come directly from his pen or pencil.

He also loves that he gets to 'work with punk, rap, rock and electronic bands, so it's always different the way things work and how my work gets influenced,' he adds. It is all a long way from the days of hardcore bands, or even shaking up the business pages. When asked for one quality that he feels makes his work successful, he doesn't hesitate in saying, 'Fun! It has to be fun.'

TITLE: Frank Ocean, *Lens*

(Clockwise from top left) TITLE: Sam O.B., *Common Ground*; TITLE: A$AP Rocky, *RAF*
TITLE: The Space Merchants, *Kiss The Dirt*; TITLE: Poolside, *And The Sea*

TITLE: Crime Department, *Navel-Gazing*

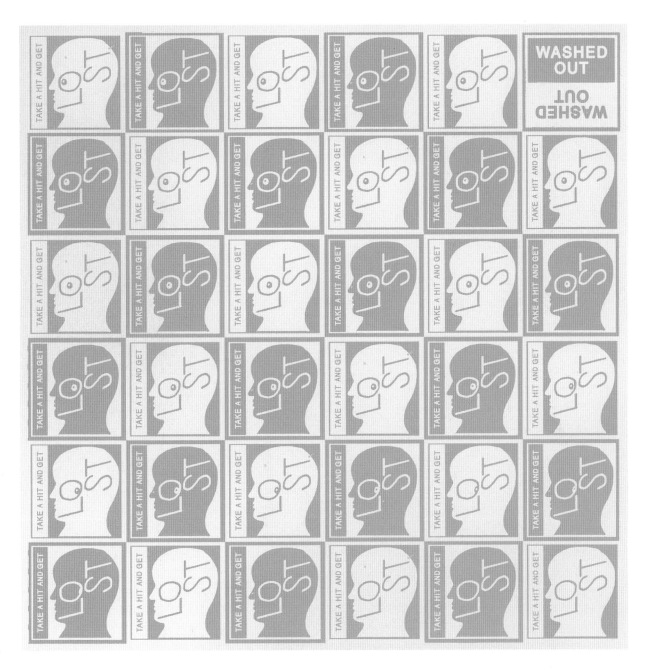

TITLE: Washed Out, *Get Lost*

TITLE: Moullinex, *Hypersex*

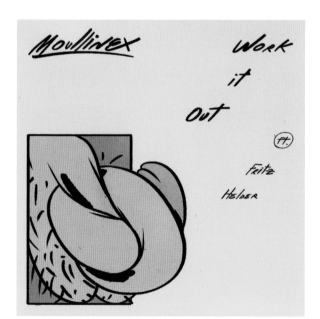

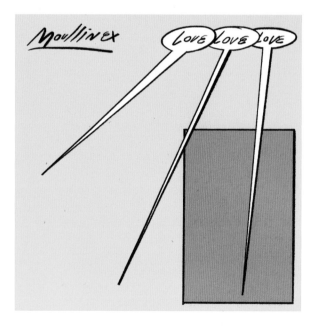

(Clockwise from top left) TITLE: Moullinex, *Open House*; TITLE: Moullinex, *Build A Wall?*
TITLE: Moullinex, *Love Love Love*; TITLE: Moullinex, *Work It Out*

TITLE: Frank Ocean, *Lens*
CLIENT: Blonded Radio
SIZE: 30.4 x 30.4 cm (12 x 12 in.)
PRINTING PROCESS: Digital
INKS: Digital
COMPS PRESENTED: 20
REVISIONS: 2 rounds
APPROVAL: Frank Ocean, Thomas Mastorakos
INVOLVEMENT WITH FINAL PRINTING: N/A

'One day I got a call out of nowhere from Thomas Mastorakos asking if I wanted to do some designs for Frank Ocean,' Amado explains. 'I'm a huge fan and of course I said yes right away. Definitely the biggest thing I ever worked on, so surreal, and I was super excited about it and sketched a LOT of ideas. Frank wanted a little hidden reference to a Kerry James Marshall painting, and while I was sketching stuff I got to the "lens" letters, creating a nose, an eye and ear. It was definitely my favourite version and I'm really glad it was the chosen one.'

TITLE: Sam O.B., *Common Ground*
CLIENT: Lucky Me Records
SIZE: 30.4 x 30.4 cm (12 x 12 in.)
PRINTING PROCESS: Digital
INKS: Digital
COMPS PRESENTED: 3
REVISIONS: 1 round
APPROVAL: Lucky Me Records
INVOLVEMENT WITH FINAL PRINTING: N/A

With so many amazing alterations to both the image and type, creating a skewed reality where some parts are stretched and others are condensed, this simple cover subtly showcases a lot of the playful aspects of Amado's design work. However, he doesn't have playful memories of it in the end. 'I never got paid for my work on this cover,' he says ruefully.

TITLE: A$AP Rocky, *RAF*
CLIENT: Blonded Radio
SIZE: 30.4 x 30.4 cm (12 x 12 in.)
PRINTING PROCESS: Digital
INKS: Digital
COMPS PRESENTED: 3
REVISIONS: 1 round
APPROVAL: Thomas Mastorakos
INVOLVEMENT WITH FINAL PRINTING: N/A

'I was asked to design some stuff for a new Frank Ocean Blonded Radio episode, which I thought would just end up being a promotional image. Suddenly, when it came out, this was the cover. Surreal!' explains Amado. The standout track, featuring Frank Ocean, Lil Uzi Vert and Quavo, quickly took the radio and the pop world by storm, spreading the cover image far and wide.

TITLE: The Space Merchants, *Kiss The Dirt*
CLIENT: Aqualamb
SIZE: 30.4 x 30.4 cm (12 x 12 in.)
PRINTING PROCESS: Offset
INKS: 2 spot PMS + 1 spot metallic
COMPS PRESENTED: 1
REVISIONS: None
APPROVAL: Space Merchants, Aqualamb
INVOLVEMENT WITH FINAL PRINTING: Proofs

'Space Merchants are my friends,' Amado says, 'so I was extremely excited to design their new LP.' He took this opportunity to experiment on the printing and production side. 'I never really get a chance to use metallic inks, but I have been waiting to design something trippy where I could try some of that stuff, and then this project appeared and it finally happened!'

TITLE: Poolside, *And The Sea*
CLIENT: Poolside
SIZE: 30.4 x 30.4 cm (12 x 12 in.)
PRINTING PROCESS: Digital
INKS: Digital
COMPS PRESENTED: 1
REVISIONS: 1 round
APPROVAL: Poolside
INVOLVEMENT WITH FINAL PRINTING: N/A

You never know who might see your work and really like it. Sometimes an indirect job for a client turns into a direct job for said client. Such was the case when Amado did a poster for Poolside's show at a local venue. 'They saw it and emailed me asking if it could also be the cover of their new single, and we were quickly back to work,' he laughs.

TITLE: Crime Department, *Navel-Gazing*
CLIENT: Muzzle Records
SIZE: 30.4 x 30.4 cm (12 x 12 in.)
PRINTING PROCESS: Digital
INKS: Digital
COMPS PRESENTED: 1
REVISIONS: None
APPROVAL: Self
INVOLVEMENT WITH FINAL PRINTING: N/A

Despite his design career taking off, Amado hasn't given up playing music himself, making for a pretty funny client with a wish to be blunt with his own record cover. 'I play in this band so ... I was trying to make something sexual and stupid.'

TITLE: Washed Out, *Get Lost*
CLIENT: Stones Throw Records
SIZE: 30.4 x 30.4 cm (12 x 12 in.)
PRINTING PROCESS: Digital
INKS: Digital
COMPS PRESENTED: 3
REVISIONS: 2 rounds
APPROVAL: Washed Out
INVOLVEMENT WITH FINAL PRINTING: N/A

'Ernest Greene, the main man behind Washed Out, had a very clear idea as to how he wanted the cover to feel,' Amado explains. 'So, I sketched out some weird and trippy stuff and put them in front of him. I actually did this cover around the same time I worked on the Frank Ocean "Lens" cover, and both have faces with letters,' he adds. 'I kind of think that I did it on purpose.'

TITLE: Moullinex, *Hypersex*
CLIENT: Luis Clara Gomes
SIZE: 30.4 x 30.4 cm (12 x 12 in.)
PRINTING PROCESS: Offset
INKS: CMYK
COMPS PRESENTED: 5
REVISIONS: 1 round
APPROVAL: Luis Clara Gomes
INVOLVEMENT WITH FINAL PRINTING: Proof

'I have been working with Luis/Moullinex for years and I think this is his best record,' Amado exclaims. 'It is also the most fun one, so I wanted to make it look fun.' To make that happen, he ended up flipping the design around. 'Initially this was the back cover and the front was just type,' he explains, 'but we decided to switch it at the last minute. The CD version has an alternative cover where all of these things break out of the boxes – but we only decided to do that because it didn't look very good printed smaller.'

TITLE: Moullinex, *Open House*
CLIENT: Luis Clara Gomes
SIZE: 30.4 x 30.4 cm (12 x 12 in.)
PRINTING PROCESS: Digital
INKS: Digital
COMPS PRESENTED: 5
REVISIONS: 2 rounds
APPROVAL: Luis Clara Gomes
INVOLVEMENT WITH FINAL PRINTING: N/A

'This was the first single for the record, as well as the first thing I designed for the Hypersex universe,' Amado explains. 'The cover was initially a really big illustration, and as I worked on it I thought it would be cool to have the small squares with a big splash of yellow, and have all the next singles follow that structure loosely.' That change, and long-range planning, would make the most out of everything that would follow on during the record's campaign.

TITLE: Moullinex, *Build A Wall?*
CLIENT: Luis Clara Gomes
SIZE: 30.4 x 30.4 cm (12 x 12 in.)
PRINTING PROCESS: Digital
INKS: Digital
COMPS PRESENTED: 1
REVISIONS: None
APPROVAL: Luis Clara Gomes
INVOLVEMENT WITH FINAL PRINTING: N/A

This song is not part of the *Hypersex* album, but since Luis worked on the song while he was working on the record, 'it made sense to have the same style as all of the other singles,' Amado explains, before adding a stern 'Fuck Trump!'

TITLE: Moullinex, *Work It Out*
CLIENT: Luis Clara Gomes
SIZE: 30.4 x 30.4 cm (12 x 12 in.)
PRINTING PROCESS: Digital
INKS: Digital
COMPS PRESENTED: 1
REVISIONS: None
APPROVAL: Luis Clara Gomes
INVOLVEMENT WITH FINAL PRINTING: N/A

'This was my first sketch and I told Luis it had to be a penis.' Amado says with a smile. 'Once I finished the cover I was afraid iTunes would censor it, but I am not sure if we have been lucky or the folks over there are giving a critique on my penis illustration skills.'

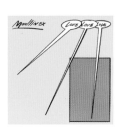

TITLE: Moullinex, *Love Love Love*
CLIENT: Luis Clara Gomes
SIZE: 30.4 x 30.4 cm (12 x 12 in.)
PRINTING PROCESS: Digital
INKS: Digital
COMPS PRESENTED: 2
REVISIONS: None
APPROVAL: Luis Clara Gomes
INVOLVEMENT WITH FINAL PRINTING: N/A

'This cover was actually plan B,' Amado points out. 'Plan A ended up being used for the insert of the *Hypersex* album, but I like how simple this one is,' he adds.

BAD PEOPLE GOOD THINGS

FRONT ROW AT THE ALL-AGES SHOW

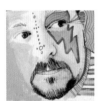 As a young teen, John Foster was incredibly lucky in that he happened to live in a city that not only had a burgeoning music scene, but also one that was tailored towards kids his age. 'It was incredibly important that before I was even old enough to drive, I could go see bands at the 930 Club and weird little places in town,' Foster adds. 'Not only were these shows put on with the explicit decree that they be all ages, but the people on stage were often my age, or close to it. That was really eye-opening, and in so many ways it was creatively empowering. In Washington, DC, during the eighties under Reagan, local teens felt a sense of dread and hopelessness as we practised hiding under desks for a potential nuclear war that we knew was bombing our neighbourhood first, while also trying our best not to contract AIDS,' he explains. Foster was finding refuge in his record collection, carefully studying the liner notes and design credits on his favourite sleeves, but seeing it raw and in person literally blew the doors open on the possibilities. 'The Dischord bands provided such a physical release, while also showing us that we could be involved with the business of music on our own terms,' he underlines. 'Soon after, the bands around Teenbeat and Simple Machines would further that message, championing both the too-well-read and certifiably insane outsider artists, while putting out manuals on how to release records and showing that literally everyone could have a voice. Anyone could do this,' he adds. 'I never forgot that.'

Profile completed with assistance from Emily Potts

'By the time I was in college, I was kicking around the music scene, playing in bands, but not really taking it seriously. I soon realized that I was better off helping more talented musicians promote their bands and music through design,' Foster explains. That meant designing lots of local CD releases and gig posters, and supporting artists that he believed in. 'I even got to be one of a select few to design a Teenbeat release, which is crazy, as Mark Robinson is one of my favourite designers and I can't imagine doing a better job than he could,' he says with a shake of the head.

As his design career began to take off, Foster spent nearly a decade as VP Creative for a nationally known studio. It was there that he worked intensely with the entertainment industry, launching cable networks, blockbuster movies and television shows, and even redesigning cans for Coca-Cola. 'Looking back, it was such a crazy time as far as budgets were concerned,' he marvels. 'We were stretching things to the limit, but we still managed to arrange a photoshoot of a stock car's engine for one project where the disc sat as the top of the air filter.' In doing huge box sets for Warner Bros. and Universal, 'we put collections of surf music in working coolers for the beach. We built custom foam cases of manhole covers. I even went on a shopping spree with the in-house art director on a Tom Jones project, buying up loads of women's underwear for a photoshoot,' he says, adding, 'Maybe it was a sign to stop the madness when Jones's daughter/manager nixed [vetoed] the panties images in the design.'

The one thing that had been missing was working on vinyl packaging. When he set up his own studio, Foster made a concerted effort to seek out those jobs where the format was the one that had served as his primary inspiration for becoming a designer. 'I found myself at the first wave of this vinyl resurgence, and I pinch myself every day that I have spent most of this last decade designing record sleeves,' he adds.

He also took an unusual step and began consulting with record labels – but on the business side, not the design side. 'My past work meant that I had extensive experience in licensing and synchronizations, or commercial placements for music, not to mention contract negotiation,' he explains. 'I also had accumulated a large network of artists over the years, so when it was first proposed by a UK label, it sounded crazy, but I quickly realized that I was well suited for the other side of the music business.' The result was that Foster would find catalogues for the label to buy or license, which then grew into finding new emerging artists. Soon, he was entrenched in all aspects of the business, acting as A&R and helping negotiate contracts and publishing deals, along with high-profile commercial placements. 'It seemed inevitable,

as I became so invested in the artists, and so integrated into their day-to-day business dealings, that I would want them to have the best possible packaging as well,' he admits. 'So one day I might be working to get an ESG song in a huge Xbox commercial for Christmas, the next I am interviewing Renee Scroggins so I can write the liner notes for her reissues, and the day after that I am designing the packaging,' he explains. 'That wasn't the case with every artist I signed, as some had their own creative teams, but I think you can see the results when we are all committed.'

I'M NOT DIFFICULT, I'M MISUNDERSTOOD

With a long history of working with some of the most difficult characters in the music business, Foster credits his even-keeled nature as much as any design talent for getting the projects where they need to be. 'You have to really be off the rails with your behaviour to push me off a project,' he laughs. 'I also find that a lot of these artists aren't nearly as difficult as their reputations would lead you to believe. They just feel like their past labels or designers weren't listening to them, and in many cases they weren't,' he adds. 'I always put the needs of the client first, so there is no way that the solution for them could look exactly like the solution for someone else. In fact, it should be radically different.' For instance, his hand-drawn type for ESG is wildly different than the type for Noveller, because those artists, and their needs, are wildly different. As long as he creates the best possible visual solution for the artist, Foster finds that these so-called cantankerous artists are wonderful to work with. 'They are so happy to actually see a visual interpretation of what they have been asking for – sometimes for decades – that they quicky become lifelong friends and trusted collaborators, and embarrass you with praise from the stage in the middle of their concerts,' he says with a smile.

'I have found that I am more inspired by my favourite designers by how they work, rather than what their work looks like,' Foster explains. 'The common thread, for me, between Vaughan Oliver and David Carson is that both designers are incredible at taking the meagre materials they are given for a project and turning them into complete and utter magic. Carson might rip things apart and make a crazy crop on a boring photograph, or pull one word out of a thousand words of dull copy, and Oliver would go so far as to strap on a belt of eels or make a plaster cast of his own head so that he could get the photograph that he needed. Now that is inspiring!' he exclaims. 'I don't pretend to have the talents of those guys, but I do hope that I share the willingness to experiment and push my resources, so that my clients know that when they give me a blurry photograph to start a project, three days later I will have been to the hardware store, the used bookshop, and have broken both a hacksaw and an old fax machine in delivering something amazing to them.'

(Above and opposite) TITLE: ESG (various releases)

TITLE: Mission Of Burma, *Unsound*

TITLE: Noveller, *A Pink Sunset For No One*

MISSION OF BURMA WHAT THEY TELL ME

WILD FLAG
BOOM

BOOM
WILD FLAG

MISSION OF BURMA
WHAT THEY TELL ME

TITLE: Mission Of Burma / Wild Flag, *What They Tell Me / Boom*

(Clockwise from top left) **TITLE:** The Jean-Paul Sartre Experience, *I Like Rain / Fish In The Sea*; **TITLE:** Cardinal, *Hymns*
TITLE: Deleted Scenes, *Young People's Church Of The Air*; **TITLE:** Pigbag, *Volume One*

(Above and opposite) **TITLE:** Chuck Prophet, *Night Surfer*

TITLE: ESG (various releases)
CLIENT: ESG
SIZE: 30.4 x 30.4 cm (12 x 12 in.)
PRINTING PROCESS: Offset
INKS: CMYK
COMPS PRESENTED: Multiple
REVISIONS: Multiple rounds
APPROVAL: Renee Scroggins
INVOLVEMENT WITH FINAL PRINTING: Proof

'ESG is possibly my favourite band of all time, so getting to work on this series of reissues with Renee Scroggins was a massive honour,' Foster explains. 'I even interviewed Renee and wrote the liner notes, as well as added in a timeline for the band's career for the Best Of collection.' The original sleeves drastically changed styles with each release. 'I wanted to bring everything together with a cohesive aesthetic, so I drew from the NYC graffitti artists from that time period, particularly Keith Haring, for an illustration style that I also applied to the typography,' he adds. 'ESG stands for Emerald, Sapphire and Gold, so that was a jumping-off point, with the other colours for each sleeve referencing the originals.' Foster is also quick to add that 'the swirl in Gina Franklyn's sleeve for their first EP is amazing, so that is referenced here in the more frenzied versions as well.'

TITLE: Mission of Burma, *Unsound*
CLIENT: Mission of Burma
SIZE: 30.4 x 30.4 cm (12 x 12 in.)
PRINTING PROCESS: Offset, die-cut
INKS: Black + spot fluorescent
COMPS PRESENTED: 6
REVISIONS: 5 rounds
APPROVAL: Mission of Burma
INVOLVEMENT WITH FINAL PRINTING: Proof

'I had tried a number of ideas out, with all of them wanting some form of deconstruction, but it just wasn't connecting,' Foster explains. Working with the band and their management, he was getting stacks of photos that he wasn't sure were cover-worthy. 'I then got stuck on this idea of a speaker exploding and being put back together,' he adds, 'which resulted in this simple graphic that I printed out, then manipulated in an old broken scanner, and then took that and ripped it apart, taped it back up, and photographed that. I kept that process going with the credits and photos inside as well.' Taking custom type and using a laser die-cut to show through the fluorescent ink booklet inside sealed the deal.

TITLE: Noveller, *A Pink Sunset For No One*
CLIENT: Noveller
SIZE: 30.4 x 30.4 cm (12 x 12 in.)
PRINTING PROCESS: Offset
INKS: CMYK
COMPS PRESENTED: 3
REVISIONS: 2 rounds
APPROVAL: Sarah Lipstate
INVOLVEMENT WITH FINAL PRINTING: Proof

'I was initially drawn to the evocative title Sarah/Noveller had chosen for her new record,' Foster details, 'and she had to steer me away from pushing for an all-pink cover.' Luckily, Foster had been involved throughout the making of the album, and was acutely aware of what Lipstate had been going through while creating these songs. 'There was an especially poignant moment when Sarah and her sister were going through the dresses they wore as kids for Mardi Gras that had been ruined in the flood that devastated her grandmother's house that really haunted me,' he explains. Turning to his paintbrush, Foster soon created both the type and a unique 'flood dress'.

TITLE: Mission of Burma / Wild Flag, *What They Tell Me / Boom*
CLIENT: Mission of Burma / Wild Flag
SIZE: 17.7 x 17.7 cm (7 x 7 in.)
PRINTING PROCESS: Offset
INKS: CMYK
COMPS PRESENTED: 1
REVISIONS: 2 rounds
APPROVAL: Mission of Burma / Wild Flag
INVOLVEMENT WITH FINAL PRINTING: Proof

Once it was announced that Mission of Burma and Wild Flag would be playing a special concert under the Brooklyn Bridge in Prospect Park together, the idea was hatched to do a split seven-inch, both to sell at the show, and also to celebrate it. 'I was hoping to tie in to the most-recent releases from both artists with the black for Mission of Burma and pink for Wild Flag,' Foster explains. 'I then went quickly to a big hand grenade to match the explosiveness of the artists and the songs they selected. Boom!'

TITLE: The Jean-Paul Sartre Experience,
I Like Rain / Fish In The Sea
CLIENT: The Jean-Paul Sartre Experience
SIZE: 30.4 x 30.4 cm (12 x 12 in.)
PRINTING PROCESS: Digital
INKS: Digital
COMPS PRESENTED: 1
REVISIONS: 1 round
APPROVAL: The Jean-Paul Sartre Experience
INVOLVEMENT WITH FINAL PRINTING: N/A

Foster had been helping reissue the catalogue of The Jean-Paul Sartre Experience for nearly seven years, so when it came time to design the first single for the campaign, it was an understatement to say that he was ready. The box set and individual records were all tied to a consistent design system and look, 'so it was a nice burst of freedom to design something that only needed to relate to the two songs, but it was still a lot of pressure as this was going to be the first thing anyone saw relating to what was to come with the reissues.' He went about pushing and pulling the type to get the desired water streak feeling, making you think that the words are slowly sinking to the depths.

TITLE: Cardinal, *Hymns*
CLIENT: Cardinal
SIZE: 30.4 x 30.4 cm (12 x 12 in.)
PRINTING PROCESS: Offset, die-cut
INKS: CMYK
COMPS PRESENTED: 5
REVISIONS: 2 rounds
APPROVAL: Cardinal
INVOLVEMENT WITH FINAL PRINTING: Proof

'For their return record, Richard Davies and Eric Matthews both sent me piles of photos,' Foster explains. 'With the album titled *Hymns*, the photo with the word on it almost seemed too obvious,' he admits. That was quickly solved with the introduction of a cross die-cut covered in a rich 'cardinal' red, playing up the multiple meanings.

TITLE: Pigbag, *Volume One*
CLIENT: Pigbag
SIZE: 30.4 x 30.4 cm (12 x 12 in.)
PRINTING PROCESS: Offset, die-cut
INKS: CMYK
COMPS PRESENTED: 6
REVISIONS: 3 rounds
APPROVAL: Pigbag
INVOLVEMENT WITH FINAL PRINTING: Proof

'I love the post-funk music of Pigbag, but the sleeve to their first record had almost nothing to work from,' Foster laments. He jumped on the monkey that was on a person's back on that sleeve, played up the Dr Jekyll refence, and created a Day-Glo monkey wearing spectacles and a goatee inside. 'That image peeked through a blitz of playful handmade type that I put together to try to feed off of the funky energy.'

TITLE: Deleted Scenes, *Young People's Church Of The Air*
CLIENT: Deleted Scenes
SIZE: 30.4 x 30.4 cm (12 x 12 in.)
PRINTING PROCESS: Screen-print
INKS: 2 spot inks
COMPS PRESENTED: 5
REVISIONS: 4 rounds
APPROVAL: Deleted Scenes
INVOLVEMENT WITH FINAL PRINTING: Proof

'This was a record for one of my favourite local bands, as well as one of my favourite local labels, so I really wanted it to cut through the visual noise,' Foster says. 'Dan Scheuerman has an innocence at the heart of so many of his songs, as they seem to be stories of kids who get damaged in peculiar ways, but still strive to make the best of their early adult years as they awkwardly find themselves,' he explains. 'When I started to dress up this image I had made of the perfect kid that just can't help but get into trouble with a mask, it all fell into place.'

TITLE: Chuck Prophet, *Night Surfer*
CLIENT: Chuck Prophet
SIZE: 30.4 x 30.4 cm (12 x 12 in.)
PRINTING PROCESS: Offset
INKS: CMYK
COMPS PRESENTED: 12
REVISIONS: 10 rounds
APPROVAL: Chuck Prophet
INVOLVEMENT WITH FINAL PRINTING: Proof

Singer-songwriter Chuck Prophet knew he wanted to wrap his most recent collection of songs around the fallout of a post-traumatic event, leaving people to rely on their survivalist skills. 'Chuck brought these cool shots of himself on the salt flats, almost like he was on another planet, and then I just went crazy gathering up images of medical instruments, and flashlights, and tools and weapons,' Foster explains. 'As I got even more inspired talking with Chuck about it, I started making these background images and painting this crazy type,' he adds. Soon, they had so much material that it formed a huge fold-out poster and they hatched a plan to create a box set of the record where it was all seven-inch discs with a song and unique cover on each side. 'When we really got out of control was when we made the box set 3D and even made custom 3D glasses for it,' Foster smiles.

JONATHAN BARNBROOK

I GUESS I'M JUST A LITTLE TOO SENSITIVE

 Few designers have both the skills and the temperament to work with fine artists at the highest level like Jonathan Barnbrook does. His studio's output can easily be viewed as both the first and last word in cutting-edge refinement, balancing the challenging needs inherent in a client base that sweeps from Art Basel to Damien Hirst to the departed David Bowie. Working on projects that range from massive environmental graphics to tiny postage stamps, the area where you can always feel Barnbrook's love is in his music packaging. Having started the firm right after finishing his studies, and intentionally keeping the studio small, he is fortunate enough to be able to choose what projects he works on and is always careful to make sure that a music packaging project is in that mix. Looking back on his old school books, 'I was intrigued by all the graffiti I had drawn on them. It was the time of punk and new wave, and I had written the names of the bands I liked, as any teenager would – only I had copied all the typefaces perfectly. It seemed that it was really important for me to get this right. Looking back, I saw it was because the typestyle of the band's name expressed the ideology and the atmosphere of the band's music, so I was already very sensitive to that kind of thing,' he explains. It was the perfect marriage of his two passions: music and typography. Those passions would only intensify for a man creating innovative typefaces through his Virus Fonts outlet and releasing music via his Fragile Self collaboration on the very day that I am writing this profile. Can't stop. Won't stop.

'I have said many times that I don't believe your work is separate from your life; it's part of it. So I regard what I do in design as an extension of my philosophy in the way I live my life rather than the other way around,' Barnbrook explains. 'So, in short, although I am not perfect, I do try to practise what I preach. We don't work with companies we don't agree with, which has cost us a lot of money. I live in a modest flat and get to work by bicycle or subway; I don't have a car because I don't want to make the world a worse place with it. We do charity work, but not as often as we would like. I also try and consume responsibly, which is a pain for the people around me when I can't just go to Starbucks or drink Coca-Cola when it is offered, but I think it's worth the effort as it does make a difference. I probably travel on aeroplanes more than I should. However, what we say is not a pose to get more publicity or anything like that. If anything it creates a lot of problems because many clients do not like designers with opinions. Ninety per cent of clients want designers to show them "how", not to ask why they want to do that in the first place,' he admits. Applying that across the board has seen Barnbrook do a lot of explicitly political work from his personal perspective, but also means that he backs musical artists he truly respects and believes in.

SCEPTICAL CONVERSATIONS

'My major influences are not from design or other designers,' he explains. 'My main influence is politics and philosophy and literature, through reading or just being engaged in what is going on in the world. I think it's incredibly important to read, so I constantly have a number of books that I am reading. A few favourite authors would be Hermann Hesse, J. G. Ballard and Samuel Beckett.' Barnbrook adds that he is 'also a big fan of comedy; the way a serious situation can be commented on with humour can be better than any long political critique,' he adds. There is a playfulness that Barnbrook hopes 'people can see, finding some humour in my work, also'.

'I don't follow design that much,' he admits. 'I don't know if that seems a bad thing to do, but I spend my life trying to avoid it,' he says with a wry smile. 'I either understand the thought process or often find design for the sake of it quite irritating. Sometimes design can happen without the intervention of a designer, through a natural process of function and circumstance; that is a fair way to create design, too. There are people I hugely respect, but even then I rarely collect their work. I feel like I spend my life trying to rid myself of possessions rather than gain them,' he laughs. He does find himself drawn to the type design of Eric Gill. 'He worked in several disciplines and produced unique work in each area. I don't think I am in any way as good as him but I hope that when you look at one of my typefaces it looks like my "handwriting", that it could only be done by me. I think the same about Eric Gill – his lettering is a product of his mind with a singular vision which is simply beautiful.'

Barnbrook soaks up inspiration in unlikely areas. It is the things that make him question, as well as take various cultures into consideration, that prove to be the source of much of his thinking. 'Twentieth to twenty-first-century history and contemporary politics are a fountain of endless inspiration. This just comes from learning that the history that we are taught at school and hear about from news, etc. is in fact a very opinionated view. These interpretations and my understanding of them have made me very sceptical about the idea of the truth or what is right, no matter what source it comes from – from politicians to advertising agencies. I think this is one of the reasons I became a typographer – it was a chance to tell the truth through printed words or at least to interject between them and the viewer. When you are a graphic designer, you are at the centre of putting out propaganda for somebody, and it seems impossible not to question this.'

ON THE INSIDE

One of the hallmarks of Barnbrook's career has been his ability to establish long relationships with challenging artists, and it was through one of those relationships that he began another. 'I first met David Bowie through Damien Hirst. Bowie phoned me up out of the blue and asked to pop around to our studio. He knew Hirst and liked the work I was doing for him. He was seeing a number of studios for a book about his wife Iman, and I was lucky enough to be chosen out of them,' he explains. 'So I had had various conversations with him already before the point I started working for him on his covers, although it was something I had been hoping for because I loved his music,' adds. 'The relationship continued for fifteen years where I was lucky enough to do the album covers *Heathen*, *Reality*, *The Next Day*, as well as work extensively on the *David Bowie Is* exhibition. I actually was quite surprised that he kept so loyal to me, because he was known for changing his music so much and he could have his pick of the world's graphic designers, but then I could see he would always stick with a core of people he trusted, that were on his wavelength. So it was an honour to be thought of as part of them.'

In working with Bowie, Barnbrook found every tiny fragment of the design work analysed to the same degree as the music within. In a way, it became the ultimate test for how he works, and who he works with. 'It was fascinating and something I was very aware of as I designed. People would make all of these interesting connections and meanings. To me, it is wonderful because this is one of the best things about the human mind. It is infinitely creative and constructs meaning and will make stories wherever it finds the opportunity.'

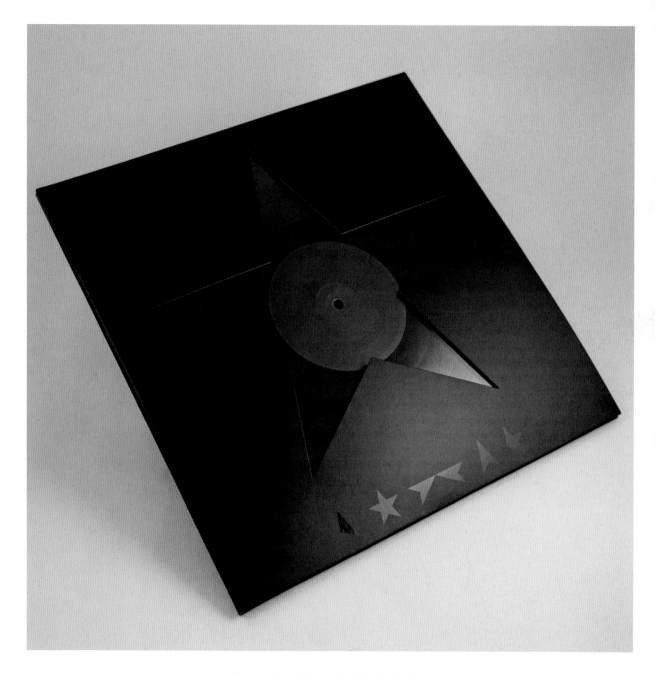

(Above and opposite) **TITLE:** David Bowie, *Blackstar*

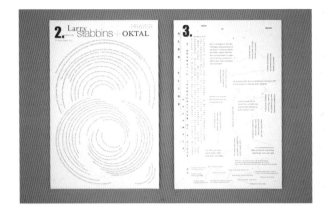

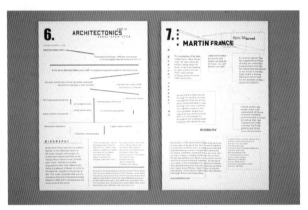

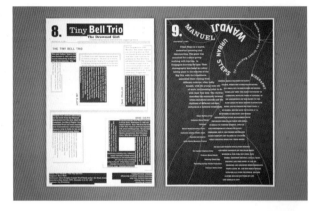

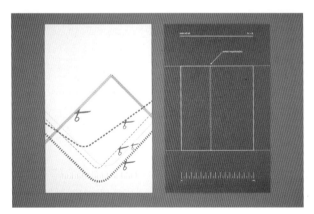

(Above and opposite) **TITLE:** *Unknown Public Volume Twelve*

(Above and opposite) **TITLE**: David Bowie, *The Next Day*

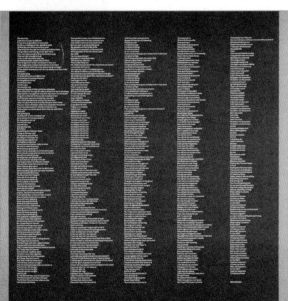

Artist: David Bowie. Album title: The Next Day. Produced by David Bowie and Tony Visconti. Mixed by Tony Visconti. Recorded at The Magic Shop and Human, New York. Engineers: Mario McNulty and Tony Visconti. Assistant Engineers: Brian Thorn and Kabir Hermon. Mastered by Dave McNair. Vinyl Mastered by Alex De Turk at Masterdisk. Cover Design: Barnbrook. Photo credits: Portrait of David Bowie on "Heroes" by Sukita. Inner portrait of David Bowie by Jimmy King. Side One, Song One: The Next Day. Writing credit: David Bowie. Musicians – David Bowie: Vocals and Guitar. Gerry Leonard: Guitar. David Torn: Guitar. Gail Ann Dorsey: Bass. Zachary Alford: Drums. Antoine Silverman, Maxim Moston, Hiroko Taguchi, Anja Wood: Strings. David Bowie and Tony Visconti: String Arrangement. Time taken: Three minutes twenty six seconds. Side One, Song Two: Dirty Boys. Writing credit: David Bowie. Musicians – David Bowie: Vocals, Gerry Leonard: Guitar. Earl Slick: Guitar. Tony Visconti: Guitar. Tony Levin: Bass. Zachary Alford: Drums. Steve Elson: Baritone Sax. Time taken: Two minutes fifty eight seconds. Side One, Song Three: The Stars (Are Out Tonight). Writing credit: David Bowie. Musicians – David Bowie: Vocals and Acoustic Guitar. Gerry Leonard: Guitar. David Torn: Guitar. Gail Ann Dorsey: Bass. Zachary Alford: Drums. Steve Elson: Baritone Sax and Contrabass Clarinet. Tony Visconti: Recorder. Antoine Silverman, Maxim Moston, Hiroko Taguchi, Anja Wood: Strings. David Bowie and Tony Visconti: String Arrangement. Gail Ann Dorsey and Janice Pendarvis: Backing Vocals. Time taken: Three minutes fifty six seconds. Side One, Song Four: Love Is Lost. Writing credit: David Bowie. Musicians – David Bowie: Vocals and Keyboards. Gerry Leonard: Guitars. Gail Ann Dorsey: Bass. Zachary Alford: Drums. Time taken: Three minutes fifty seven seconds. Side Two, Song One: Where Are We Now? Writing credit: David Bowie. Musicians – David Bowie: Vocals and Keyboards. Gerry Leonard: Guitar. Tony Levin: Bass. Zachary Alford: Drums. Henry Hey: Piano. Tony Visconti: Strings. Time taken: Four minutes eight seconds. Side Two, Song Two: Valentine's Day. Writing credit: David Bowie. Musicians – David Bowie: Vocals. Earl Slick: Guitars. Tony Visconti: Bass. Sterling Campbell: Drums. Time taken: Three minutes one second. Side Two, Song Three: If You Can See Me. Writing credit: David Bowie. Musicians – David Bowie: Vocals and Keyboards. Gerry Leonard: Guitar. David Torn: Bass. Tony Levin: Bass. Zachary Alford: Drums and Percussion. Gail Ann Dorsey: Backing Vocals. Time taken: Three minutes sixteen seconds. Side Two, Song Four: I'd Rather Be High. Writing credit: David Bowie. Musicians – David Bowie: Vocals. Gerry Leonard: Guitars. Tony Levin: Bass. Zachary Alford: Drums. Henry Hey: Piano. Tony Visconti: Strings. Time taken: Three minutes forty four seconds. Side Three, Song One: Boss Of Me* Writing credit: David Bowie / Gerry Leonard. Musicians – David Bowie: Vocals. Gerry Leonard: Guitars. Tony Levin: Bass. Zachary Alford: Drums. Steve Elson: Baritone Sax. Tony Visconti: Recorder. Gail Ann Dorsey and Janice Pendarvis: Backing Vocals. Time taken: Four minutes nine seconds. Side Three, Song Two: Dancing Out In Space. Writing credit: David Bowie. Musicians – David Bowie: Vocals and Keyboards. Gerry Leonard: Guitar. David Torn: Guitar. Gail Ann Dorsey: Bass. Zachary Alford: Drums. Time taken: Three minutes twenty four seconds. Side Three, Song Three: How Does The Grass Grow?** Writing credit: David Bowie / Jerry Lordan. Musicians – David Bowie: Vocals and Keyboards. Gerry Leonard: Guitar. David Torn: Guitar. Gail Ann Dorsey: Bass. Zachary Alford: Drums. Gail Ann Dorsey: Backing Vocals. Time taken: Four minutes thirty three seconds. Side Three, Song Four: (You Will) Set The World On Fire. Writing credit: David Bowie. Musicians – David Bowie: Vocals. Earl Slick: Guitar. Gerry Leonard: Guitar. Tony Visconti: Bass. Sterling Campbell: Drums and Tambourine. Gail Ann Dorsey and Janice Pendarvis: Backing Vocals. Time taken: Three minutes thirty seconds. Side Four, Song One: You Feel So Lonely You Could Die. Writing credit: David Bowie. Musicians – David Bowie: Vocals and Acoustic Guitar. Gerry Leonard: Guitar. David Torn: Guitar. Tony Visconti: Guitar. Gail Ann Dorsey: Bass. Zachary Alford: Drums. Henry Hey: Piano. Antoine Silverman, Maxim Moston, Hiroko Taguchi, Anja Wood: Strings. Tony Visconti: String Arrangement. Gail Ann Dorsey and Janice Pendarvis: Backing Vocals. Time taken: Four minutes forty one seconds. Side Four, Song Two: Heat. Writing credit: David Bowie. Musicians – David Bowie: Vocals and Acoustic Guitar. Gerry Leonard: Guitar. David Torn: Guitar. Gail Ann Dorsey: Bass. Zachary Alford: Drums. Antoine Silverman, Maxim Moston, Hiroko Taguchi, Anja Wood: Strings. David Bowie and Tony Visconti: String Arrangement. Time taken: Four minutes twenty five seconds. Side Four, Song Three: So She. Writing credit: David Bowie. Musicians – David Bowie: Vocals, Keyboards and Acoustic Guitar. Gerry Leonard: Guitar and Keyboards. David Torn: Guitar. Tony Visconti: Guitar and Bass. Zachary Alford: Drums. Antoine Silverman, Maxim Moston, Hiroko Taguchi, Anja Wood: Strings. David Bowie and Tony Visconti: String Arrangement. Time taken: Two minutes thirty one seconds. Side Four, Song Four: Plan. Writing credit: David Bowie. Musicians – David Bowie: Keyboards, Guitars, Percussion. Zachary Alford: Drums. Note: this is an Instrumental. Time taken: Two minutes two seconds. Side Four, Song Five: I'll Take You There* Writing credit: David Bowie / Gerry Leonard. Musicians – David Bowie: Vocals, Keyboards and Acoustic Guitar. Gerry Leonard: Guitar. David Torn: Guitar. Tony Visconti: Guitar. Gail Ann Dorsey: Bass. Zachary Alford: Drums. Alex Alexander: Percussion. Gail Ann Dorsey and Janice Pendarvis: Backing Vocals. Time taken: Two minutes forty four seconds. All Songs by David Bowie except where indicated. All songs published by Nipple Music (BMI) administered by RZO Music, Inc. * "Boss Of Me" and "I'll Take You There" by David Bowie/Gerry Leonard. Published by Nipple Music (BMI) administered by RZO Music, Inc. and Cecil Na Phuca (ASCAP) ** "How Does The Grass Grow" by David Bowie/Jerry Lorden. Published by Nipple Music (BMI) administered by RZO Music, Inc. and Regent Music Corp. and Francis, Day & Hunter. Contains an interpolation of "Apache" written by Jerry Lordan and published by Regent Music Corp. and Francis, Day and Hunter. ℗ & © 2013 ISO Records, under exclusive license to Columbia Records, a Division of Sony Music Entertainment. Distributed by Sony Music Entertainment. All trademarks and logos are protected. Made in the EU. LC00162. Columbia is the exclusive trademark of Sony Music Entertainment. 88765461861.

SONY MUSIC

(Above and opposite) **TITLE:** David Bowie, *The Next Day Extra*

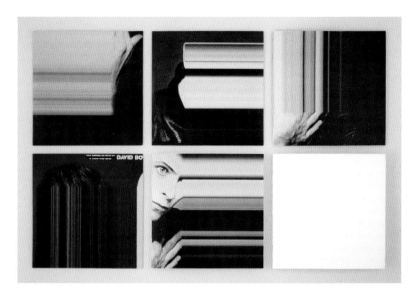

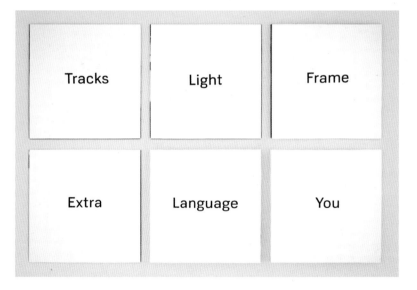

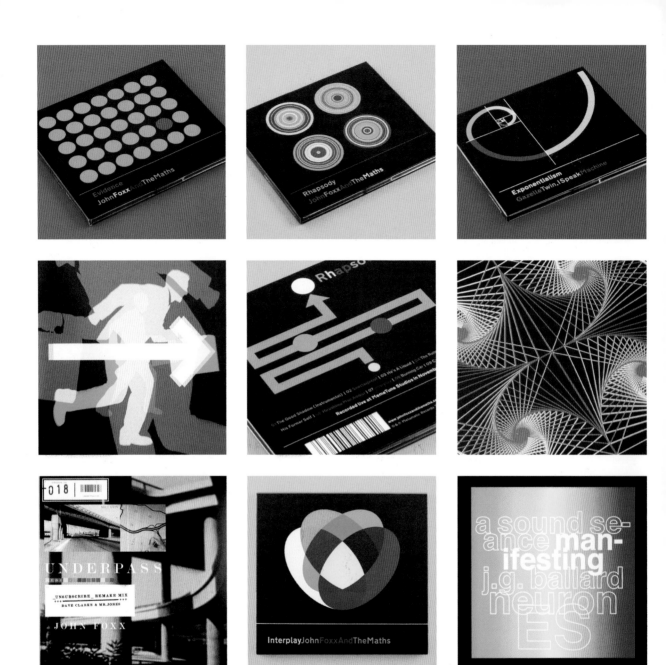

TITLE: John Foxx and the Maths (various releases)

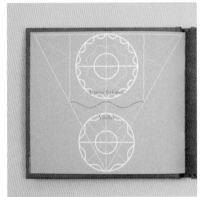

(From top to bottom) **TITLE:** John Foxx & Jori Hulkkonen, *European Splendour*; **TITLE:** Ghost Harmonic, *Codex*
TITLE: Tuxedomoon, *7707 Tm*

TITLE: David Bowie, *Blackstar*
CLIENT: David Bowie
SIZE: 30.4 x 30.4 cm (12 x 12 in.)
PRINTING PROCESS: Offset
INKS: CMYK
COMPS PRESENTED: Multiple
REVISIONS: Multiple rounds
APPROVAL: David Bowie
INVOLVEMENT WITH FINAL PRINTING: None

'This was the first album Bowie had done where there's not a picture of him on the front,' says Jonathan. 'The use of basic shapes is partly about the union of archetypes, but it's also about cutting through the visual noise. There's so much visual clutter around now that I wanted to be simple to the point of excluding all other elements,' he explains. 'While working on this record David talked a lot about the "honesty" of the album without directly stating what he was honest about. Looking back, it was a way of me dealing with and talking about the heaviness of the subjects without directly referring to him, and for David, it was a way of being honest in his comments about the design without burdening me with the heaviness of what I was doing.'

TITLE: *Unknown Public Volume Twelve*
CLIENT: Unknown Public
SIZE: 30.4 x 30.4 cm (12 x 12 in.)
PRINTING PROCESS: Offset
INKS: CMYK
COMPS PRESENTED: Multiple
REVISIONS: Multiple rounds
APPROVAL: John L. Walters
INVOLVEMENT WITH FINAL PRINTING: None

For volume twelve of *Unknown Public*, Barnbrook continued a long line of talented designers. *Unknown Public* is an audio journal devised by John L. Walters, known for his writing for the *Guardian*, and editorial talent for *Eye Magazine*, along with publisher Laurence Aston.

TITLE: David Bowie, *The Next Day*
CLIENT: David Bowie
SIZE: 30.4 x 30.4 cm (12 x 12 in.)
PRINTING PROCESS: Offset
INKS: CMYK
COMPS PRESENTED: Multiple
REVISIONS: Multiple rounds
APPROVAL: David Bowie
INVOLVEMENT WITH FINAL PRINTING: None

'I feel so bloody lucky that I was able to be part of the life of someone who was one of the greatest creative figures of the past one-hundred years, but then when I was working with him I had to get over that sort of thing because it interferes with the creative process,' admits Barnbrook. 'So really I just tried to do my absolute best, because I knew he demanded it and because the music was worthy of it.' The packaging and campaign they would create for *The Next Day* would manage to leverage all of Bowie's work, while also being shockingly modern.

TITLE: David Bowie, *The Next Day Extra*
CLIENT: David Bowie
SIZE: 30.4 x 30.4 cm (12 x 12 in.)
PRINTING PROCESS: Offset
INKS: CMYK
COMPS PRESENTED: Multiple
REVISIONS: Multiple rounds
APPROVAL: David Bowie
INVOLVEMENT WITH FINAL PRINTING: None

'You would imagine with that much adulation in your life it could make him a difficult person to deal with, but with Bowie it was quite the contrary,' Barnbrook explains. 'It was an absolute joy. Having said that, I would practically kill myself getting to the design solution, of course. Several months before the artwork was due I would be contacted by David and from then on, I would think about trying my absolute best to do something worthy of the music. It would fill almost every waking moment.'

TITLE: John Foxx and the Maths, *Evidence*
CLIENT: John Foxx and the Maths
SIZE: 12 x 12 cm (4.7 x 4.7 in.)
PRINTING PROCESS: Offset
INKS: CMYK
COMPS PRESENTED: Multiple
REVISIONS: Multiple rounds
APPROVAL: John Foxx
INVOLVEMENT WITH FINAL PRINTING: None

Barnbrook's relationship with synth electropop pioneer John Foxx (Ultravox and his solo work) has created a special universe of bold graphics and Day-Glo colours. It says a great deal that Foxx trusts Barnbrook to help him bring his vision to life, as Foxx himself was a graphic designer of note in the 1990s.

TITLE: John Foxx and the Maths, *Rhapsody*
CLIENT: John Foxx and the Maths
SIZE: 12 x 12 cm (4.7 x 4.7 in.)
PRINTING PROCESS: Offset
INKS: CMYK
COMPS PRESENTED: Multiple
REVISIONS: Multiple rounds
APPROVAL: John Foxx
INVOLVEMENT WITH FINAL PRINTING: None

Barnbrook has designed all of the releases for John Foxx and the Maths. *Rhapsody* is one of Foxx's 'live in rehearsal' albums, in which he and the band record alternative arrangements of older songs, bringing about experimentation and reinvention, but holding on to the core skeleton of the songs.

TITLE: John Foxx, *Exponentialism*
CLIENT: John Foxx
SIZE: 12 x 12 cm (4.7 x 4.7 in.)
PRINTING PROCESS: Offset
INKS: CMYK
COMPS PRESENTED: Multiple
REVISIONS: Multiple rounds
APPROVAL: John Foxx
INVOLVEMENT WITH FINAL PRINTING: None

This EP of cover versions of John Foxx tracks by I Speak Machine and Gazelle Twin continues Foxx's desire to reinvent and push his music into ever-evolving pathways.

TITLE: John Foxx, *Underpass*
CLIENT: John Foxx
SIZE: 30.4 x 30.4 cm (12 x 12 in.)
PRINTING PROCESS: Offset
INKS: CMYK
COMPS PRESENTED: Multiple
REVISIONS: Multiple rounds
APPROVAL: John Foxx
INVOLVEMENT WITH FINAL PRINTING: None

Barnbrook created a hand-stamped artwork for a limited-edition vinyl release of this track. The song 'Underpass', from 1980, was Foxx's first-ever solo single, and many consider it to be one of the most iconic songs from the electronic new wave era. Here, he remakes the track, much in the way that he has continued to reimagine his earlier work.

TITLE: John Foxx and the Maths, *Interplay*
CLIENT: John Foxx and the Maths
SIZE: 12 x 12 cm (4.7 x 4.7 in.)
PRINTING PROCESS: Offset
INKS: CMYK
COMPS PRESENTED: Multiple
REVISIONS: Multiple rounds
APPROVAL: John Foxx
INVOLVEMENT WITH FINAL PRINTING: None

This was the first outing for John Foxx's new band, working in collaboration with musician/producer Benge, which would become quite active afterwards. Barnbrook establishes the look of the graphics and palette here that will serve as the jumping-off point for so much of his work with Foxx moving forward.

TITLE: John Foxx & Jori Hulkkonen, *European Splendour*
CLIENT: John Foxx & Jori Hulkkonen
SIZE: 30.4 x 30.4 cm (12 x 12 in.)
PRINTING PROCESS: Offset
INKS: CMYK
COMPS PRESENTED: Multiple
REVISIONS: Multiple rounds
APPROVAL: John Foxx & Jori Hulkkonen
INVOLVEMENT WITH FINAL PRINTING: None

'The vinyl edition of this EP uses an image of a stone sculpture created by John Foxx,' explains Barnbrook. 'The design features reappropriated 19th-century-style typography,' Foxx describes the songs on the EP as a 'Lynchian love story set against the background of a convulsed Europe … where dark forces insinuate the cafes, alleyways and penthouses.'

TITLE: Ghost Harmonic *Codex*
CLIENT: Ghost Harmonic
SIZE: 12 x 12 cm (4.7 x 4.7 in.)
PRINTING PROCESS: Offset
INKS: CMYK
COMPS PRESENTED: Multiple
REVISIONS: Multiple rounds
APPROVAL: Ghost Harmonic
INVOLVEMENT WITH FINAL PRINTING: None

'This CD packaging design is for a collaborative music band consisting of Benge, John Foxx and Diana Yukawa,' explains Barnbrook. 'The record serves as a bit of a departure with long song lengths and loose structures, playing off the improvised interplay of the musicians with Yukawa's classically trained violin.

TITLE: Tuxedomoon, *7707 Tm*
CLIENT: Tuxedomoon
SIZE: 30.4 x 30.4 cm (12 x 12 in.)
PRINTING PROCESS: Offset
INKS: CMYK
COMPS PRESENTED: Multiple
REVISIONS: Multiple rounds
APPROVAL: Tuxedomoon
INVOLVEMENT WITH FINAL PRINTING: None

To celebrate the band's thirtieth anniversary, they packaged their album *Vapour Trails* along with a wide assortment of extras, with demos, out-takes and live tracks stretching back to 1977, along with a fascinating DVD that showcases the live aspect of such a visual band. Barnbrook houses all of this in a brilliantly engaging box set.

ROBERT BEATTY

CELEBRATED WEIRDNESS

 In a turn of events that proves how great work will somehow find an audience, designer Robert Beatty has emerged from the experimental music underground – where he has released music as Hair Police and Three Legged Race, and created a slew of psychedelic artwork that has graced record sleeves, prints and small press publications – to see his services sought after by mainstream companies and big-time musical acts. No less than the *Washington Post* and the *Guardian* have run profiles on him, celebrating a wildly unique voice in the dense visual landscape. As one would hope, and those that know Beatty would expect, he has responded by delivering some of his wildest creations yet. When the *Post* described how his 'drawings and digital airbrush paintings mulch vintage counterculture – old sci-fi paperbacks, sixties zines – with a grotesque punk-inspired sensibility,' they were more on the mark than they realized.

This all puts Beatty in a unique position. 'For me, it's not so much how the packaging has changed, but how my position in relation to the music industry has changed,' he explains. 'I started out with no formal training in graphic design or art, doing things in a very DIY fashion for years. Early records that I worked on were silk-screened, paste-on photocopies and cassettes, and I slowly moved to doing releases that were more "legitimate". Now that I am working more in the traditional music industry, it often seems that attention is focused on creating an iconic image that looks good as a thumbnail and creating elaborate packages that people find collectable,' he says. 'I tend to just focus on what I think looks good and not worry too much about that stuff,' he adds with a smile.

Even though he may be asked to do different things these days, Beatty always looks to work in the same manner. 'Most of the time when people are contacting me it is to design a physical release, but there are often singles or alternate versions that are digital only, so I do end up making art that is never printed. But I always think of creating artwork in terms of it being printed eventually, so it doesn't affect my process much,' he explains.

THE NEW COLLECTORS

The 'collector' mentality can still leave him a little perplexed. 'I tend to err on the side of simpler is better and not get too involved in elaborate packaging or things made specifically for collectors,' he explains. More tellingly for a designer with an obvious love of the past, he adds that 'there is so much music being produced these days it's hard for me to see anything new as collectable.'

Having said that, Beatty does fully embrace the new ways in which the Internet and social media have changed how designers interact with artists and their fans and directly with consumers. 'I think that aspect of making record covers is my favourite part of it,' he explains. 'That these objects are out in the world and take on a life of their own that will last for a long time beyond the initial release. It pushes my work to the far corners of the world long after I'm done with it,' he says. 'I love going to record stores and seeing albums I've done covers for on the wall or flipping through and seeing something I've done, and people tell me all the time that they go to record stores all over the world and see several records I've done artwork for. I don't really have much direct involvement with merchandise other than creating the images, and I haven't sold any prints of my record covers. I usually just encourage people to buy a copy of the record,' he laughs.

For someone with such a wonderfully unique style, Beatty shows that he did not arrive at it without taking in a multitude of influences. He loves the album sleeves of Roger Dean, Stanisław Zagórski,

Mati Klarwein, Cal Schenkel, Carol Goss, Ralph Records' Porno Graphics, Barney Bubbles, Milton Glaser, Reid Miles at Blue Note, Ronald Clyne's work for Folkways, 'not to mention more current people like Julian House and the Designers Republic,' he adds. 'A lot of people who made my favourite record covers didn't do more than a couple, though.' Swirling that appreciation into a more direct influence forms the heart of Beatty's work. 'I'd say the biggest influence on my work is experimental animation and film,' he explains. 'Films by people like Rene Laloux and Roland Topor, Suzan Pitt, Lillian Schwartz, John and Faith Hubley, John and James Whitney, Steina and Woody Vasulka, Piotr Kamler, Yoji Kuri, Kenneth Anger, Robert Nelson, Jan Švankmajer, Shuji Terayama, Toshio Matsumoto, so many more. There is a ton of eastern European animation from Poland, the Czech Republic, Russia and Hungary that is totally unreal and endlessly inspiring to me.' Once he gets started, he can be a one-man treasure trove of visual resources. 'Also, a lot of pre-digital artists, illustrators and graphic designers from the sixties and seventies – Tadanori Yokoo, Keiichi Tanaami, Alan Aldridge, Eduardo Paolozzi, Aquirax Uno, Jan Lenica, Öyvind Fahlström, Mary Bauermeister,' he adds. 'I could go on for days,' he laughs. 'I love generic and kind-of-trashy ephemera and product packaging and advertising. Things that maybe aren't really held in high regard but have a unique and strange presence that a lot can be learnt from.' His watchful eyes are also 'always inspired by the natural world and its simulated recreation – Chladni patterns, video feedback, cellular automata. And the documentation of these phenomena by people like Ernst Haeckel and Karl Blossfeldt.'

When it's time to get down to work, Beatty's already in album mode. 'My default approach when I start anything new is to imagine it as a twelve-by-twelve-inch square, so it's often more of a challenge to do things for me that aren't record covers, I have to reformulate my brain to see things not in that format.' It also allows him to really and truly enjoy what he does, in every way. 'I love meeting people and the variety of work I get to do,' he explains. 'Working with one band or record label can be worlds apart from the next thing I do. I also can't imagine a better job. It's a dream come true and I'm happy this is what I get to do.' He also has 'a pretty balanced range of people that I work for – I'd say it's about fifty-fifty between artists and labels. A lot of times, even if there is a label involved, I still deal with the artists directly.'

When it comes to album design, Beatty thinks 'something that is iconic, unique and memorable that has the same presence and soul as the music is what makes a successful cover'. Few artists and designers working today fit those criteria as well as the work of Robert Beatty.

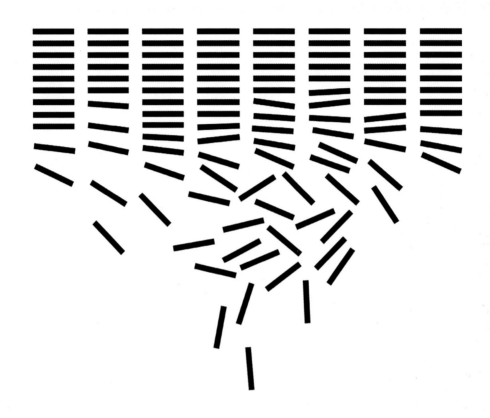

TITLE: Oneohtrix Point Never, *Commissions* (front)

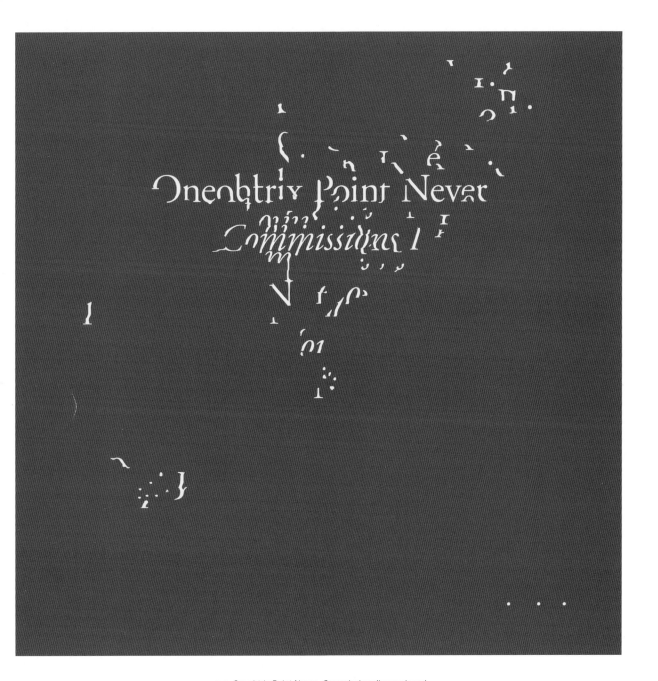

TITLE: Oneohtrix Point Never, *Commissions* (inner sleeve)

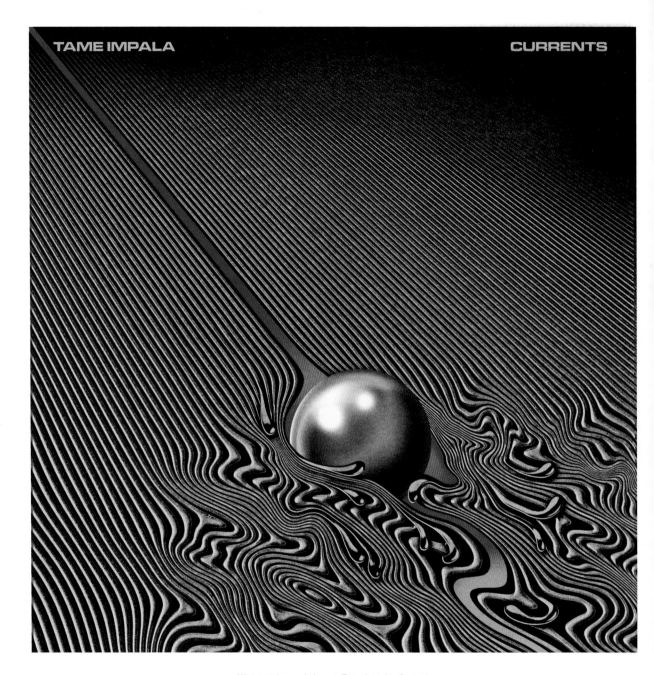

TAME IMPALA **CURRENTS**

(Above and opposite) **TITLE:** Tame Impala, *Currents*

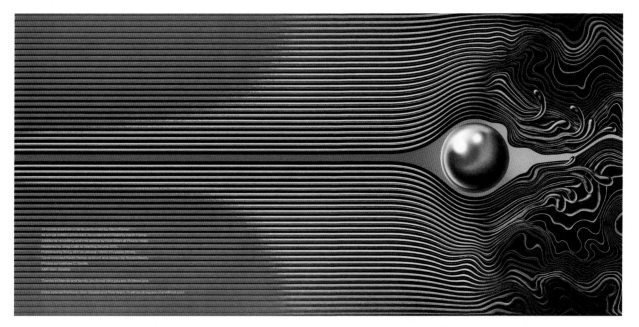

(Clockwise from top left) TITLE: Brad Laner, *Nearest Suns* (back and front)
TITLE: Oneohtrix Point Never, *R Plus Seven*; TITLE: Lord Raja, *A Constant Moth*

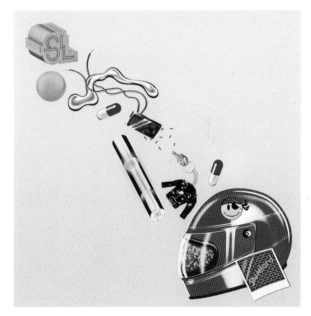

(Clockwise from top left) TITLE: Neon Indian *Annie*; TITLE: Acoustic Division, *s/t*
TITLE: Neon Indian, *Slumlord*; TITLE: Neon Indian, *The Glitzy Hive*

TITLE: Kesha, *Rainbow*

TITLE: Ariel Pink, *Dedicated To Bobby Jameson*

TITLE: Oneohtrix Point Never, *Commissions*
CLIENT: Warp
SIZE: 30.4 x 30.4 cm (12 x 12 in.)
PRINTING PROCESS: Offset + foil + diecut
INKS: Spot ink and spot foil
COMPS PRESENTED: 1
REVISIONS: 1 round
APPROVAL: Oneohtrix Point Never, Warp
INVOLVEMENT WITH FINAL PRINTING: Proof

'The artwork for this EP was actually presented when I was working on art for OPN's *R Plus Seven* album the year prior,' explains Beatty. 'I had created several simple sequences of collapsing geometric patterns that we ended up not using for the LP art. When we started to work on the art for this collection of commissioned pieces I revisited the glut of leftover artwork from *R Plus Seven* and found this piece that worked really well with the deconstructed music on this EP – music tumbling apart like dominoes.'

TITLE: Tame Impala, *Currents*
CLIENT: Interscope
SIZE: 30.4 x 30.4 cm (12 x 12 in.)
PRINTING PROCESS: Offset
INKS: CMYK
COMPS PRESENTED: 2
REVISIONS: 1 round
APPROVAL: Tame Impala
INVOLVEMENT WITH FINAL PRINTING: Proof

'Kevin Parker of Tame Impala wanted a cover that evoked scientific diagrams and images of fluid dynamics and vortex mechanics, playing on the title of the record, *Currents*. I wanted to convey this as directly as possible but also play up the psychedelic and op art characteristics of the parallel lines in the reference images I was presented with,' Beatty explains. 'At first, I ended up doing an overhead view of the liquid going around the sphere, which ended up being the gatefold artwork, before showing the second draft, which went through without revisions,' he adds.

TITLE: Brad Laner, *Nearest Suns*
CLIENT: Hometapes
SIZE: 30.4 x 30.4 cm (12 x 12 in.)
PRINTING PROCESS: Offset
INKS: CMYK
COMPS PRESENTED: 1
REVISIONS: 1 round
APPROVAL: Brad Laner, Hometapes
INVOLVEMENT WITH FINAL PRINTING: Proof

'For this cover for a solo album from Medicine's Brad Laner, I wanted to capture the spirit of sixties psychedelic pop with a darker, more damaged edge,' Beatty explains. 'The music on this record is very dense and angular but also has its moments of breezy acoustic arrangements and lush vocal harmonies. I tried to take the feeling of classic psychedelic artwork by Peter Max and Heinz Edelmann and crush it into an abstract mess – a sort of nightmarish landscape that was hard to make head or tails of. This still stands as one of my favourite covers I've ever done.'

TITLE: Oneohtrix Point Never, *R Plus Seven*
CLIENT: Warp
SIZE: 30.4 x 30.4 cm (12 x 12 in.)
PRINTING PROCESS: Offset
INKS: CMYK
COMPS PRESENTED: 3
REVISIONS: 3 rounds
APPROVAL: Oneohtrix Point Never, Warp
INVOLVEMENT WITH FINAL PRINTING: Proof

'I had worked with Daniel Lopatin of Oneohtrix Point Never for a few years and this project seemed more ambitious,' Beatty explains. 'The album was a bit of a change for him and that had to be represented with the artwork. We went through several months of passing ideas back and forth with countless drafts until we oddly settled on a recreation of a still from a film by the Swiss animator Georges Schwizgebel that I recreated from scratch (with permission), as no high-res images of the original artwork existed. Once the front cover was done, we realized when turned upside down the shapes looked like they spelled the title of the record – "r + 7". After that insane serendipity, we ended up making the back cover an abstracted upside-down version of the front cover.'

TITLE: Lord Raja, *A Constant Moth*
CLIENT: Ghostly International
SIZE: 30.4 x 30.4 cm (12 x 12 in.)
PRINTING PROCESS: Offset
INKS: CMYK
COMPS PRESENTED: 1
REVISIONS: 2 rounds
APPROVAL: Lord Raja, Ghostly International
INVOLVEMENT WITH FINAL PRINTING: Proof

'As inpiration for the artwork for the debut LP by Lord Raja I was sent a folder full of images of colourful cut-glass prism sculptures and images of the light installations of James Turrell,' Beatty explains. 'I tried to keep this one as simple as possible, but it felt too bare, so I worked to add a frame and logo that ended up being a reference to the production library music label Bruton Music,' he adds.

TITLE: Acoustic Division, *s/t*
CLIENT: Acoustic Division
SIZE: 30.4 x 30.4 cm (12 x 12 in.)
PRINTING PROCESS: Offset
INKS: CMYK
COMPS PRESENTED: 1
REVISIONS: None
APPROVAL: Acoustic Division
INVOLVEMENT WITH FINAL PRINTING: Proof

'Lexington, Kentucky – my hometown – electronic label Acoustic Division wanted me to make a disco-style sleeve for all of the twelve-inch singles they were releasing,' Beatty explains. 'Based loosely on a past release for the label, I took my old design and stripped back most of the elements to simplify it so that it would work as a more generic design for the label. The first twelve-inch to use this sleeve was a single the label released for my own electronic music project Three Legged Race,' he smiles.

TITLE: Neon Indian, *Annie*
CLIENT: Mom + Pop
SIZE: 30.4 x 30.4 cm (12 x 12 in.)
PRINTING PROCESS: Digital
INKS: Digital
COMPS PRESENTED: 1
REVISIONS: 2 rounds
APPROVAL: Neon Indian
INVOLVEMENT WITH FINAL PRINTING: N/A

TITLE: Neon Indian, *Slumlord*
CLIENT: Mom + Pop
SIZE: 30.4 x 30.4 cm (12 x 12 in.)
PRINTING PROCESS: Digital
INKS: Digital
COMPS PRESENTED: 1
REVISIONS: 2 rounds
APPROVAL: Neon Indian
INVOLVEMENT WITH FINAL PRINTING: N/A

TITLE: Neon Indian, *The Glitzy Hive*
CLIENT: Mom + Pop
SIZE: 30.4 x 30.4 cm (12 x 12 in.)
PRINTING PROCESS: Digital
INKS: Digital
COMPS PRESENTED: 1
REVISIONS: 2 rounds
APPROVAL: Neon Indian
INVOLVEMENT WITH FINAL PRINTING: N/A

Serving as an interesting window into how both Beatty and Neon Indian work visually, 'these three singles were created based on hundreds of references that Alan Palomo from the band sent me,' Beatty explains. 'The images he sent ranged from Italian clothing ads, stills from Japanese anime, postmodern furniture, CIA PSYOPs patches and tons of other seventies and eighties cultural detritus. I treated each cover almost as a kinetic sculpture frozen in anti-gravity. Each one was made up of objects that I recreated from the references or came up with on my own to echo the themes of the songs they were paired with.'

TITLE: Kesha, *Rainbow*
CLIENT: RCA Records
SIZE: 30.4 x 30.4 cm (12 x 12 in.)
PRINTING PROCESS: Offset
INKS: CMYK
COMPS PRESENTED: 1
REVISIONS: 2 rounds
APPROVAL: Kesha, Brian Roettinger
INVOLVEMENT WITH FINAL PRINTING: None

'I was expecting the process on this cover to be a whole different experience from anything that I had done before, as it's the highest-profile release I've ever done and it was the first time working with an art director for a record,' Beatty adds. 'But it ended up being pretty similar to how I normally design. I worked very closely with Brian Roettinger [see pages 230–240] to bring Kesha's ideas for the artwork to life. She wanted something that felt like a classic sixties/seventies album cover, something iconic and surreal but not retro. The cover photo was taken by Olivia Bee, and I worked with that and art direction from Brian to create the surrealistic aquatic outer space landscape that frames her.'

TITLE: Ariel Pink, *Dedicated To Bobby Jameson*
CLIENT: Mexican Summer
SIZE: 30.4 x 30.4 cm (12 x 12 in.)
PRINTING PROCESS: Offset
INKS: CMYK
COMPS PRESENTED: 2
REVISIONS: 3 rounds
APPROVAL: Ariel Pink
INVOLVEMENT WITH FINAL PRINTING: Proof

'I've been a long-time fan of Ariel Pink's music,' Beatty says, 'so when he told me he wanted something that felt like one of his earlier albums and not in my typical style, I was psyched to do something that was reverent to his earlier, more DIY covers. He specifically wanted to echo the vibe of his record *The Doldrums*, which features a grimy Polaroid of him standing next to a tree. I worked with a set of photos of Ariel lurking in a graveyard taken by Charlotte Ercoli. I worked to combine several photos into new scenes and treated everything almost in a cinematic way, while keeping it pretty raw and strange.' In an interesting flip, though not that unusual in Beatty's process, he insists that 'the front cover was what I had originally presented as the back cover, and we liked the way it looked with the song titles on there so much that we left it. This also worked as a reference to older LP covers, as the record is dedicated to obscure sixties singer-songwriter Bobby Jameson.'

CHRIS BIGG

THE STUDENT BECOMES THE TEACHER

Finishing his final project at university, Chris Bigg could hardly have expected his life was about to change forever. Writing a paper about the current wave of exciting British designers, he contacted everyone he could think of. Only one person replied: Vaughan Oliver. Coming to interview Oliver, Bigg would also meet 4AD label head Ivo Watts-Russell, and the rest would be design history. Bigg's work for 4AD, while a part of the v23 design studio with Oliver, would bring him quickly to international prominence. Creating an intoxicating mix of the raw and handmade, along with delicate typography, his wild calligraphic explorations have formed some of the most memorable record covers of the past thirty years. Bigg soon struck out on his own, continuing to refine that potent mix of sophistication and surprise that makes his work so incredible. Clients in fashion and exhibition came calling, but music was always the mainstay. His sensibilities, along with an openness to the creative process, made him a favourite of artists who approach their work in much the same way. Bringing things full circle, Bigg began giving lectures, pulling back the curtain on that creative process, and recently settled into teaching, feeling that 'it was time to share what I have learnt and experienced during my career. The strange thing is I really feel my work has improved during this teaching period,' he adds. 'Pushing myself more, having the confidence to believe in a simple mark, not to overcomplicate things. I spend more time working away from computers, especially in the early stages of a project and after many years I feel more in touch with my projects,' he marvels.

'When I graduated the computer was a distant dream of clever people,' Bigg explains, 'but I finally rolled over and embraced a long, painful relationship with technology. It was a such a change for me, I found it really hard to relearn a way of making work! Twenty years later, I am honoured to have lived through such a re-imaging of the art form I truly love.' That has also inspired him to 'feel with more passion that we have to make marks, sketch, build and construct things. Spending hours with a screen is not a way forward; you need to take an idea to technology, or is it an attitude?' he wonders. Since the industry pushed everything in a digital direction, Bigg loves it that 'people have responded with a desire for vinyl and cassettes, something physical,' but also worries about the overpriced limited-edition mania that can sometimes develop.

Adjusting to the digital workplace and the social media circus means that Bigg seems to slip under the radar when it comes to getting his work reviewed. 'I have always enjoyed the outside, I never wanted to join in, always been quietly confident in my abilities, not in a big show-off sort of way but in a way that I like what I do,' Bigg explains. 'I do remember thinking, "Do stuff and then wait for everybody else to catch up." Now that could come across as being a little cocky, but it's not … Maybe those people will never catch up, because they know it's rather poor to. I have never really cared about them, to be honest!'

WHAT COLOUR IS THAT SOUND?

'I tend to find inspiration outside of design,' Bigg admits, 'and then take that back into what I do. There are so many creative characters that have influenced me, such as Sigmar Polke, Antoni Tápies, Anselm Kiefer, Marcel Broodthaers, Andy Warhol, Joseph Beuys, Mark Rothko, Greta Stern, Christian Boltanski, Eugene Atget, J. John Priola and Lee Friedlander.' As for graphic designers, Bigg explains, 'my all-time favourite cover is an album by Duet Emmo designed by the Quay Brothers. I look at it again and again. It's always in my mind when I start any project. It's more about an attitude. I don't copy it, I just want to reflect its attitude.' He adds, 'Tomato, Irma Boom, Matt Willey, Piet Zwart, Karel Teige, László Moholy-Nagy and Shinro Ohtake, who is not technically a graphic designer, but very graphic, and I will never forget the early days of Neville Brody.'

That visual brew intact, Bigg tackles every project with the same attitude, 'refining later in the process what you need to do specifically for the client's industry'. Working in the music industry, Bigg relishes the entire process, 'and when you get it right and all parties are satisfied. I have always admired musicians. I have no idea how you write a song or make music. It's always been a mystery and I like it that way,' he admits. 'I like to have conversations …. Listening, understanding and suggesting – once you have mastered those

three points, you can start the journey of educating a client visually. That is tough, but when it works that is the satisfaction. I always think of the job as visualizing the sound with image and typography. I listen to the lyrics, if possible experience the live performance, join the artist in the pub for a few drinks to discuss moods, likes and dislikes. I like musicians that are constructive with their criticism. On occasions management and record-label bosses also have an opinion,' he adds. Once he is ready, at the beginning of the process, Bigg sends out various images that he feels create the correct mood, for everyone's consideration.

Bigg has concentrated on visualizing music for thirty years. 'Music and sound are my passion. I think sound and visuals are joined at the hip, one informs the other, and it's such a privilege to be in a position to digest a sound, make that into something that leaves the listener with a curious understanding of the project within, but also leaves it open for their own interpretation.' Realizing a successful final solution often means finding 'something that reflects the sound, obviously. There are far too many efforts out there that are great pieces of work, but are soulless in that they don't relate to the sonic adventures within. I set myself some questions, such as what typeface is that sound? What colour is that sound? What shape is that sound?' He continues to push the boundaries of his work, always questioning along the way.

'I am a maker and not a thinker; I do the thinking afterwards,' Bigg explains. 'I have to make stuff. Once you create something, you have something to react to, be it positive or negative. It exists, therefore it's something to push against. There are too many pages of boring long-winded research making for heavy reading that don't say anything about the individual. As the lovely David Byrne of Talking Heads said, "Stop making sense." I am a keen follower of all that is wabi-sabi, embracing the beautiful imperfections,' he adds. 'Almost every project I have completed involves elements of the accidental, if not directly, but in attitude and problem solving, what I have learnt over the years is to embrace this approach.'

'I think a lot of my work is very personal,' Bigg continues. 'There is no difference between my personal and paid work. I work hard to develop my typography skills, keeping my own self-initiated typographic experiments available for any number of projects.' He is constantly honing his skills and amassing visuals and inspirations. 'Mark making and taking photographs are a very important part of my routine – it has to be done!' he insists. 'Of course, the digital download has played havoc with the importance of album artwork,' he laments, 'but there must be a future between music and visuals as they can never be separated!'

TITLE: Kim Deal, *Biker Gone*

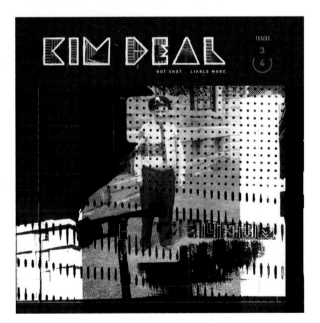

(Clockwise from top left) **TITLE:** Kim Deal, *Walking With A Killer* (front); **TITLE:** Kim Deal, *Walking With A Killer* (back); **TITLE:** Kim Deal, *Hot Shot* (back); **TITLE:** Kim Deal, *Hot Shot* (front)

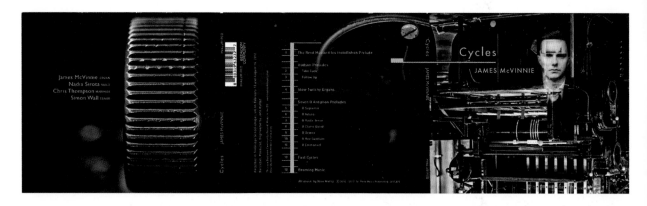

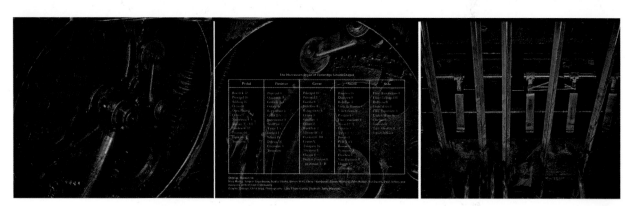

(Opposite, top and middle) **TITLE**: James McVinnie, *Cycles*
(Opposite, bottom) **TITLE**: Adrian Corker, *Start Merge Fade*
(Above) **TITLE**: Puzzle Muteson, *Theatrics*
(Left) **TITLE**: Red House Painters box set (box design)

David Sylvian

THE GOOD SON VS The Only Daughter

THE BLEMISH REMIXES

TITLE: David Sylvian, *The Good Son vs The Only Daughter – The Blemish Remixes*

(Clockwise from top left) TITLE: Lush, *Blind Spot* (front); TITLE: Lush, *Blind Spot* (back)
TITLE: My Home Sinking, *King Of Corns* (back); TITLE: My Home Sinking, *King Of Corns* (front)

TITLE: Kim Deal, *Biker Gone*
CLIENT: Kim Deal
SIZE: 17.7 x 17.7 cm (7 x 7 in.)
PRINTING PROCESS: Offset
INKS: CMYK
COMPS PRESENTED: 10
REVISIONS: 6 rounds
APPROVAL: Kim Deal
INVOLVEMENT WITH FINAL PRINTING: None

'This was the third in Kim Deal's seven-inch solo series,' explains Bigg, who worked with original tape type by Sarah Todd. 'As with all of my projects, it starts with the music: I worked in collaboration with Martin Andersen, who provided the photos, and after a number of conversations he suggested going to this place called the Ace Cafe in North London, which has been a gathering place for bike enthusiasts since the early 1960s.' The cover photo itself 'is a double exposure, so the accidental played a part in the outcome. We don't need to see a face/head!' he exclaims. 'It was a space motorcycle moment that gives us the crystal-meth vibe of a night-riding Hells Angel.'

TITLE: Kim Deal, *Walking With A Killer*
CLIENT: Kim Deal
SIZE: 17.7 x 17.7 cm (7 x 7 in.)
PRINTING PROCESS: Offset
INKS: CMYK
COMPS PRESENTED: 8
REVISIONS: 6 rounds
APPROVAL: Kim Deal
INVOLVEMENT WITH FINAL PRINTING: None

'This was the first in Kim Deal's seven-inch solo series, and Kim sent me a number of images from her family archive as a starting point,' Bigg says. 'I really liked them, but they were a little nostalgic. I felt they needed some processing, roughing up, as the music was recorded using analogue equipment. I decided to print out the images and overprint with textures from my archive, screen-print and break up the structures. The logo I made out of paper on a train on my way home, a restriction if you like – no computer at hand!'

TITLE: Kim Deal, *Hot Shot*
CLIENT: Kim Deal
SIZE: 17.7 x 17.7 cm (7 x 7 in.)
PRINTING PROCESS: Offset
INKS: CMYK
COMPS PRESENTED: 5
REVISIONS: 3 rounds
APPROVAL: Kim Deal
INVOLVEMENT WITH FINAL PRINTING: None

'This was the second in Kim Deal's seven-inch solo series, and these images from Ed Deal were processed in the same way as the previous sleeve, all completed at the same time, full of inspiring accidents. I really enjoy this way of working as it's hands-on and by its nature throws up many possibilities – a very satisfying working process.'

TITLE: James McVinnie, *Cycles*
CLIENT: Bedroom Community
SIZE: 12 x 12 cm (4.7 x 4.7 in.)
PRINTING PROCESS: Offset
INKS: CMYK
COMPS PRESENTED: 10
REVISIONS: 8 rounds
APPROVAL: James McVinnie, Valgeir Sigurdsson
INVOLVEMENT WITH FINAL PRINTING: None

'An album for a great little Icelandic label called Bedroom Community, the brief was machines,' explains Bigg. 'I had worked with photographer Luis Filipe Cunha on a number of occasions and used work that he had already taken. Luis took the brief and spent a day at an old printer in Portugal, and the amount of quality work he produced was excellent,' Bigg marvels. 'The typography was inspired by practical engineering manuals, and yellow and black is always a striking combination.' He does have second thoughts about the last-minute addition of the artist portrait now. 'In my mind it stops it being about cold machines.'

TITLE: Adrian Corker, *Start Merge Fade*
CLIENT: SNVariations
SIZE: 30.4 x 30.4 cm (12 x 12 in.)
PRINTING PROCESS: Offset
INKS: Black and metallic silver
COMPS PRESENTED: 7
REVISIONS: 20 rounds
APPROVAL: Adrian Corker, SNVariations
INVOLVEMENT WITH FINAL PRINTING: None

Working with Luis again, this EP followed an album, 'so visually we wanted it to relate to the previous album, as the music was recorded at the same time,' Bigg says. 'Cropping the images and turning to mono and then incorporating the metallic ink takes the image to a new area, but it's still familiar. There is no front and back – or is there no back or front!'

TITLE: Puzzle Muteson, *Theatrics*
CLIENT: Bedroom Community
SIZE: 30.4 x 30.4 cm (12 x 12 in.)
PRINTING PROCESS: Offset
INKS: CMYK
COMPS PRESENTED: 3
REVISIONS: 2 rounds
APPROVAL: Puzzle Muteson, Valgeir Sigurdsson
INVOLVEMENT WITH FINAL PRINTING: None

The wonderfully named Puzzle Muteson 'brought these beautiful images by photographer Costanza Gianquinto to the project,' Bigg explains. 'It was a pleasure cropping them and adding typography. I really enjoy how you discover the different moods within the CD digipak panels as you open them in order,' he adds.

TITLE: Red House Painters box set
CLIENT: 4AD/Beggars
SIZE: 30.4 x 30.4 cm (12 x 12 in.)
PRINTING PROCESS: Offset
INKS: CMYK
COMPS PRESENTED: 1
REVISIONS: 1 round
APPROVAL: 4AD
INVOLVEMENT WITH FINAL PRINTING: None

'This was an interesting project, as I had worked on all the four separate albums twenty years ago,' Bigg explains. 'I wanted something that hinted at the photographic language we had used on the collected albums, but without favouring any one individually. Many years ago I had spent time experimenting with a Land Polaroid camera and when you pull the two parts of the Polaroid apart the image is one side and the other is thrown away …. I kept them in a drawer. This is a simple scan of the rubbish. I like the fact that all the images for the Red House Painters albums were shot on Polaroid. It's a respectful appreciation of that process.'

TITLE: David Sylvian, *The Good Son vs The Only Daughter – The Blemish Remixes*
CLIENT: David Sylvian
SIZE: 12 x 12 cm (4.7 x 4.7 in.)
PRINTING PROCESS: Offset
INKS: CMYK
COMPS PRESENTED: 10
REVISIONS: 5 rounds
APPROVAL: David Sylvian
INVOLVEMENT WITH FINAL PRINTING: None

'My working relationship with David Sylvian is a special one,' explains Bigg. 'David brings the images to the projects, and I am left to work on the typography. He is very open to experimenting with layout and gives such clear and constructive feedback,' he adds. For this project Sylvian brought the work of Atsushi Fukui, 'which is always such a pleasure to work with,' Bigg says. 'It was indeed a challenge to work with such a long title,' he adds with a wry smile, 'but I feel the outcome has a delicate feel that relatesto the delicate details within the recordings.'

TITLE: Lush, *Blind Spot*
CLIENT: Lush
SIZE: 25.4 x 25.4 cm (10 x 10 in.)
PRINTING PROCESS: Offset
INKS: CMYK
COMPS PRESENTED: 30
REVISIONS: 8 rounds
APPROVAL: Lush
INVOLVEMENT WITH FINAL PRINTING: None

'Lush were back together after twenty-five years,' Bigg says, 'and we talked about colours, lights and space and what aspect of the previous work they thought they would like to focus on for a new collection of work. I was very happy with the new logo, which is simple and direct but also showing respect for what had gone previously. Photographer Martin Andersen had sourced some offcuts from a company that cut acrylic. These random shapes were then suspended, lit and photographed. Martin produced a vast amount of work, and with the process of layouts and client feedback narrowed us down to the chosen few.'

TITLE: My Home Sinking, *King Of Corns*
CLIENT: Infraction Records
SIZE: 30.4 x 30.4 cm (12 x 12 in.)
PRINTING PROCESS: Offset
INKS: CMYK
COMPS PRESENTED: 8
REVISIONS: 12 rounds
APPROVAL: Infraction Records, Enrico Coniglio
INVOLVEMENT WITH FINAL PRINTING: None

'This is my first project for Infraction Records, and I had been listening to the music and searching for a visual direction for the art, but nothing was really feeling right,' Bigg laments. 'Frustration was setting in. This corresponded with the students I teach at the University of Brighton hanging their graduation show. This young man, James Heginbottom, had always worked hard but had been rather distant in previous weeks. It became clear he had been busy working on this body of work. Straight away I knew it was perfect for this project.'

STEFAN SAGMEISTER

'LIKE MANY DESIGNERS MY AGE, I BECAME A DESIGNER BECAUSE I WANTED TO DESIGN ALBUM COVERS.'

 The brilliant career of Stefan Sagmeister has taken many twists and turns on its way to the current incarnation that is Sagmeister & Walsh. While the current studio is breaking down boundaries in the fashion world and exploring very personal concerns of the heart in very public ways, it all links back to a man with an intense love of rock and roll setting out to find a way to get involved in the music industry. His early career saw Sagmeister pushing and pulling the CD and LP in ways that had not been imagined previously and gaining worldwide recognition. It was here that he perfected his overlaid transparencies for H. P. Zinker, which would be put to work again on his groundbreaking monograph *Made You Look*. It was his work for Lou Reed that would bring about an entire movement of hand-lettering that continues to this day. He would drill through layers of paper for Skeleton Key, wrap an exhaustive mountain of music for Talking Heads in nude paintings, discuss nine-million-dollar paintings with The Rolling Stones and just reinvigorate the industry as a whole with his creative energy. As incredible as his design work is, it was his exploitation of the manufacturing process that really changed the game. 'Considering I had no education in industrial design, this often involves a lot of trial and error, many dummies and a lot of help from my friends.'

Where do you see differences in how designers today approach designing for the music industry versus when you started out?
Because of the need for the image to work very small on various online platforms, the need to design something simple and powerful obliterated any love of detail and storytelling. I myself was always interested in creating an emotional connection to an audience. I have always been jealous of the musicians themselves, who can often achieve this much deeper, quicker and more immediately.

What are your feelings on the current vinyl boom and resurgence of large-format music packaging?
I am very much in favour of it. There is something deeply satisfying (and human!) about listening to a technology that goes back directly to Thomas Edison, and that has been continuously improved over the years to such a degree that listening to new vinyl in 2017 is utterly astounding: it's incredible that such rich and full sounds can come out of a plastic groove touched by a needle. Numerous bands sound remarkably better listened to on my green sofa than live in concert (I've tried it out).

The fact that I have to get up, go to the closet, select an album sleeve, take the inner sleeve out, take the record out of the inner sleeve, put it on the player and place the needle on the record also makes sure that I select carefully. I now and again listen to music exclusively, i.e. I don't do anything else while sitting on the sofa. It is VERY enjoyable.

How important is it to present music with a physical representation?
Right now I am mostly listening to music I bought because of their great physical covers. This would include: SBTRKT, FKA Twigs, Beach House, Darkside, Sufjan Stevens, Karen O, Washed Out, Gabriel Garzón Montano.

But most bands who truly created a strong graphic presence come from a pre-download time: I have not seen any visual band identity who could match the Rolling Stones' tongue logo, the singular iconographic status of Pink Floyd's *Dark Side of the Moon* cover or the impact on visual culture of the Sex Pistols' *Never Mind the Bollocks*. While Arcade Fire and Jamie XX are doing a pretty good job, maybe they have simply not been around long enough.

How has selling music changed for you?
Bands are truly in a difficult situation as many listeners are not even aware of the name or the look of the band that they liked quite a lot listening to at work from some playlist on Spotify. So not only do musicians not get paid for the majority of the music they produce, but their name on the poster also might not be recognized when they play in someone's neighbourhood. I have seen a number of media proposals that would change this and have not seen one that truly became effective.

Which designers are really exciting you currently in music packaging?
Very surprising to me is that some of my favourite recent vinyl covers have been designed by the musicians themselves: Sufjan Stevens, Beach House, Grimes and Karen O created some of my favourite covers. There are always stand-out designers who form long visual relationships with artists, like M/M Paris for Björk.

It's also a great time in album art as I also think that contemporary album covers right now are higher in quality (and significantly cheaper) than much art exhibited in the galleries of Chelsea or the Upper East Side. For proof of this bold claim, check out my Instagram @StefanSagmeister.

DEAN BLACKWOOD & SUSAN ARCHIE

MONUMENTAL TASK

In working on the Paramount Records box set, Susan Archie found out how valuable a team of inspired creatives can be. 'Jack White had done a review in a magazine wherein he gave *Screamin' and Hollerin' The Blues*, Revenant's Grammy-winning box set, the "Nobel Prize" of design back in 2004 or so,' she explains. 'In 2011, a friend of Dean Blackwood's from Nashville, Paul Burch, was playing in a band WPA Ball Club, occasionally with Fats Kaplin, and Fats was also playing in the studio with Jack. Somehow a connection was made and Dean had a meeting with Jack at Third Man Nashville in Fall 2012. Dean had developed his own timeline of the Paramount releases for a potential Revenant project. He shared the timeline with Jack at that meeting and, before you know, the project was off to the races,' she adds.

In doing these kinds of projects, there is a balancing act between staying true to the subject matter, and using modern techniques. 'We used traditional lithographic CMYK and web presses to reproduce the inserts, and spot metallic inks and opaque white on foil (reflective) or vellum (an acrylic translucent sheet) to achieve special effects,' Archie explains. 'Volume one reflected what Paramount would have done if they gave a damn. The techniques and forms we used were from that era and typical of the gramophone furniture and portables. Paramount was at first the Wisconsin Chair Co. They got into the record business to move gramophone-enabled furniture,' she adds. 'Volume two represents what we would have done if they had hired us. Jack has an inherent love of machines of all kinds, and as a designer, Dean loves the Deco era – shiny and highly crafted. Another designer designed an Airstream-type portable for the player. And the USB drive became similar to his hood ornament.'

While Susan makes it sound like a smooth process, a job of this magnitude is sure to have lots of challenges. 'Replicating vintage processes and finishes. Vendor management. Work with vendors on the other side of the globe at opposite ends of the work day, who have different holidays than you, who can produce anything – you just have to learn how to communicate with them. The pressing of the Airstream-type case came to be hard to find vendors for. Vendors see what we want to do and they question until they make the model. Then they appreciate it. So many challenges!' she laughs.

To complete everything needed 'we had around forty people,' she explains. 'I live in Atlanta and had some friends on the graphics team. I hired freelance kids from India, Philippines and South Carolina to do photo/line-art restoration. Dean hired a coding team in NYC to build an app that worked with existing platforms. There were about twelve to fifteen writers, editors, indexers and fact-checkers. Song selection committee. The illustrators comprised another team. We had designer Tony Mostrom in LA, Katy Deedy Robison in NYC, and Bryce McCloud's Isle of Printing team in Nashville, with Elizabeth and the guy who developed the embossed gold labels. Jack's legal team in LA. Also in Nashville was the vinyl team, which was Dean, Jack, Ben Blackwell and the engineers at United Record Pressing. Ben Swank and the TMR marketing team, the folks who hand-applied labels to the LPs. The people who stuffed sleeves: 6 x 5,000. The project management team, the brokers. It was a massive undertaking,' Archie details.

'The great part about something like this is that Dean's mission is to go where no designer has gone before, which is a good creed,' Archie says. 'It's the Revenant aesthetic. We made a solid plank of wood into a bound book cover. We inked foils with white flood. We made negative-positive image setups for ink screens on vellum. We used cloth, emboss, deboss, opaque foil, aluminum foil as fly sheets, and after all of that, Jack made sure that people could afford to own these, keeping the price for a massive depository of musical history at $450, thinking that was a reasonable expense for this object.'

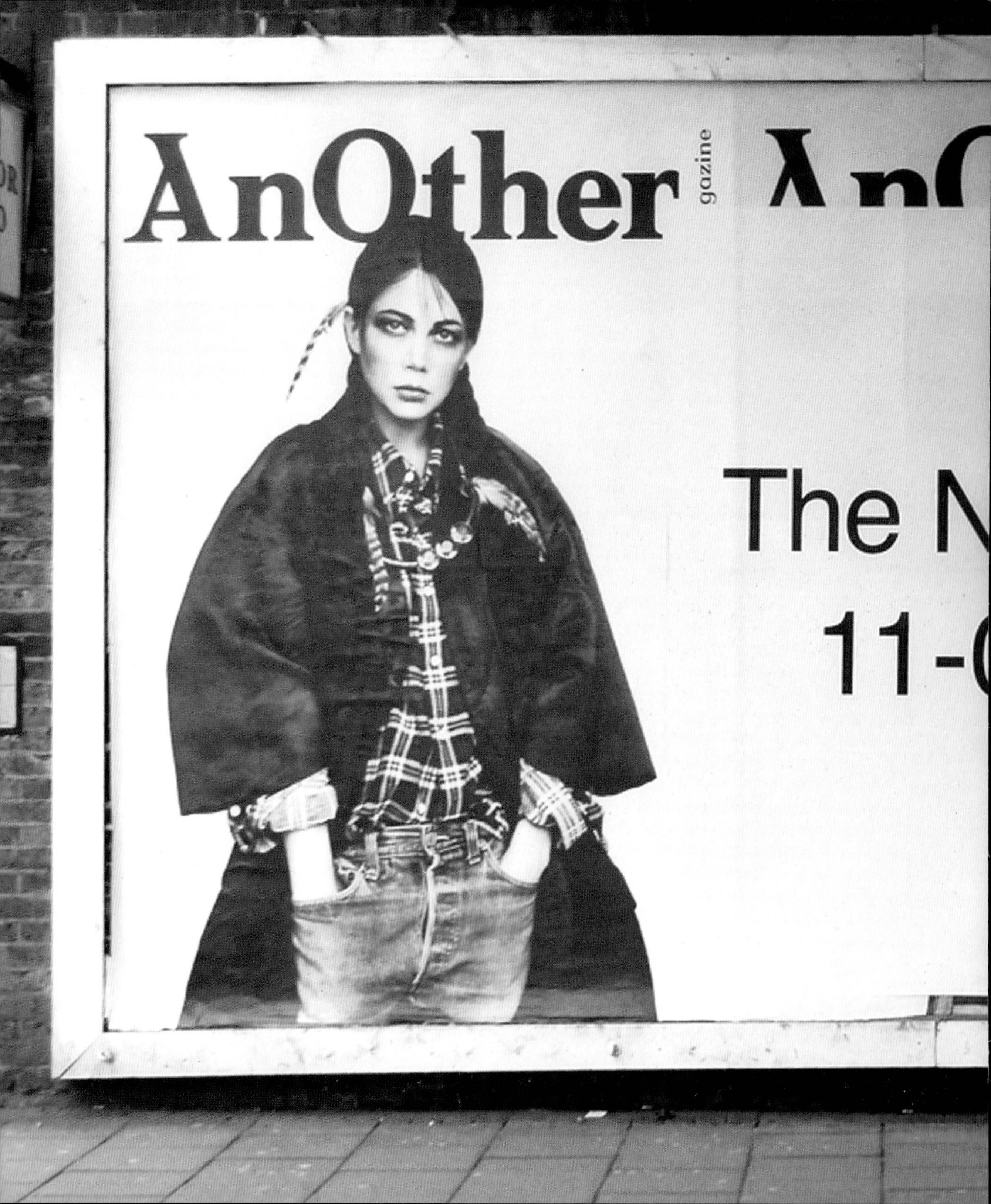
AnOther
gazine
The N
11-

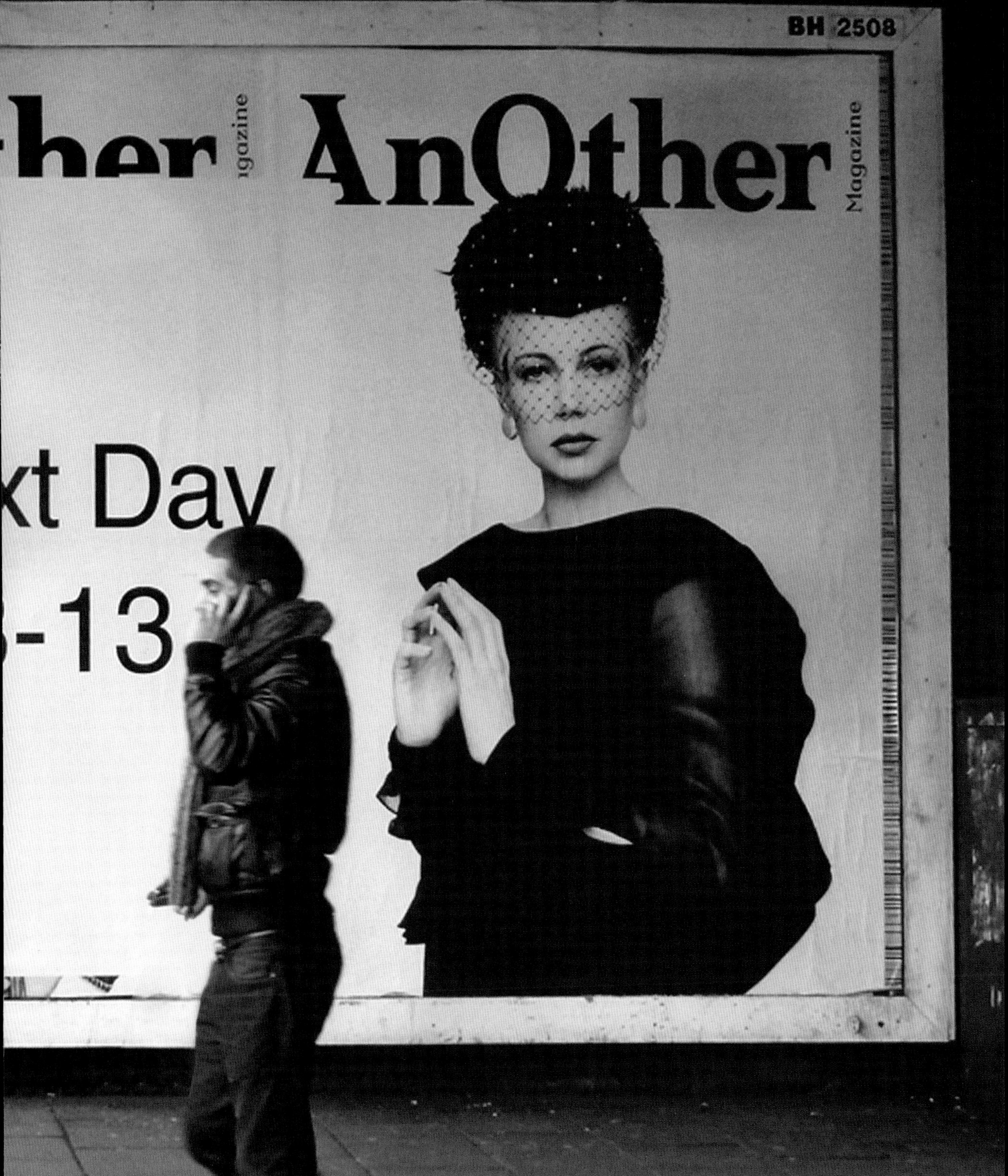
BH 2508
ther
agazine
AnOther
Magazine
xt Day
-13

DANIEL CASTREJON

WE ARE NOT ACCEPTING DEMOS

 Daniel Castrejon has a major advantage over most of the other designers in this collection. Not only is he one of the best designers walking the planet, but he is also the owner of one of the coolest record labels in the world. Having his label, Umor Rex, was certainly one of the biggest factors in accelerating his work to its current heights. Working on cassette and vinyl releases and limited editions allowed him to fine-tune his aesthetics with minimal risk. He also learned to turn small budgets into maximum impact. Soon, his talents were bringing other artists and labels down to Mexico City, looking for the man behind these incredible pieces. Working on his own label gives Castrejon an intimate knowledge of both manufacturing and distribution, and also allows him to take advantage of both where possible. He was also able to build his skills around music that he is passionate about, so he was always striving to wrap records that he loved in the best possible visual solutions. He also tapped in to musical artists from all over the world, creating an unlikely centre for experimental music in Mexico City – a centre that both looks and sounds incredible.

'I think the principal change in package design has been the fanciness in some products – not anything new regarding the process,' says Castrejon. 'I think the era that overlapped the nineties and early 2000s was the digital boom, and the design was relegated to a simple cover image. It was easy. With the "revival" of physical media, the labels have been putting more enthusiasm into each piece, but in the end we're back to what we had in the seventies or eighties – letterpress, varnish, special colours, and stock paper. I think it's fantastic. We came out of the dark age at the end of the nineties.'

Fortunately, he's only had a few requests in recent years for just the digital component, and in those cases he's passed on the project because, as he says, 'I like to think in terms of designing a tangible object. I like to play with spot colours that are not available in RGB [digital] or textures. All these things are integral to design, at least for me. I'm an editorial designer, so I think in terms of paper, inks and bindings.' He also loves clean aesthetics created with simple materials and limited colours, but adds, 'It would be a lazy solution if done on the desktop.'

In fact, he relishes the opportunities that good design can bring to music packaging. 'The physical album is a love relationship between the object and the content. At the end the important thing is the music, but the presentation should be what the music deserves,' Castrejon notes, adding, 'It's a little bit sad when you listen to a fantastic record, but the album aesthetic isn't up to par. It's not fair for the musicians, and savvy record buyers are attuned to this as well – the look of the album is a big reason why they fork over their hard-earned cash in the first place.'

'I like to follow the reactions to my design work. Fortunately, there are people that have something to say from time to time, and I'm glad to sometimes be recognized only by the style,' he says. 'But at the end, the design is a service to the music, so I feel honoured when an album is recognized for the music itself. And speaking of that, I'm lucky in that so far I've only worked for artists I really like. Many of my works are for my own label, Umor Rex, but I have designed for several other labels, mostly in the US, Germany and UK.' He admits that he tends to work in specific genres because of his style. 'I'm not a versatile designer. I find it difficult to play with different styles of design. That's why I believe I'm always working for musicians within the electronic and experimental genre, those making sophisticated pop music.'

MEXICO REMIXED

It's no surprise that he's heavily influenced by classic album designers such as Peter Saville and Vaughan Oliver, whose work in the discography of 4AD Castrejon describes as 'pure art'. 'He inspired me to dedicate my life to this, and I recently had the honour to work with 4AD', he says proudly, adding other influences such as, 'the Designers Republic and their work in the construction of the aesthetic of WARP, and artists like Aphex Twin or Autechre. I believe it is the perfect match between music and design. Not only music, a music genre perhaps.'

Outside music, Castrejon's design influences are varied. 'I like the modernist architecture and graphic design from the forties and sixties, the aesthetic of the statements from Weimar, the principles of Walter Gropius. Much of my visual influence comes from old German, Swiss and Russian traditions. And there was a time I really enjoyed American paintings by 20th-century artists like Robert Rauschenberg. I feel that was reflected in my previous collage works, but not today. Today I'm more into the geometric research, I like to be inspired by Josef Albers, László Moholy-Nagy, or Kandinsky. Mexico City is very close to these practices: structuralism, but also the mix with the old colonial architecture and coloured mixes from the antique civilizations – Mexico is a remix per se. Mexico City has a rich tradition in the visual arts. I like the natural disorder of things.'

His tight, geometric designs definitely have an architectural quality about them, and the connection between the music and visual components is quite striking. Contrasting colours and shapes are what Castrejon uses to describe the feeling of the music. 'When I'm contacted by a label, I study their catalogue, music and design. I start with the music, and then I work in the possible connections to the label, the artist and the work that I can do. I like to achieve something coherent for all the parts,' he says. And when he achieves that, he says the packaging is a success, 'when the listener recognizes that the work of art and the music are things that coexist alone but are inseparable by nature'.

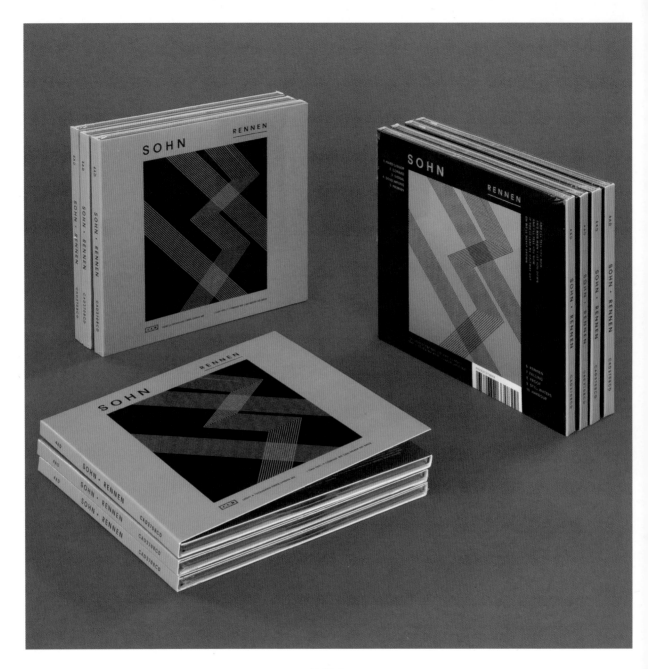

TITLE: SOHN, *Rennen*

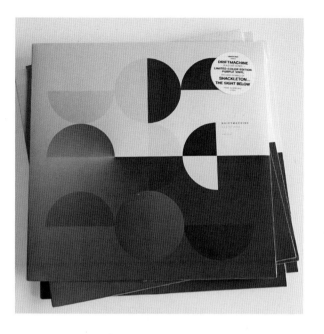

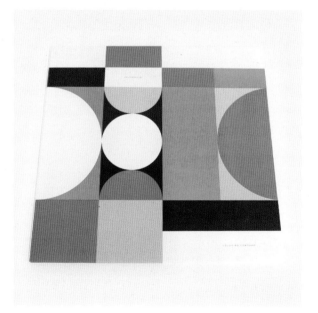

(Top) **TITLE:** Driftmachine, *Radiations*
(Bottom) **TITLE:** Driftmachine, *Colliding Contours*

(Top) **TITLE:** Alex Menzies, *Order & Disorder*
(Bottom) **TITLE:** Dino Spiluttini and Nils Quak, *Modular Anxiety*

TITLE: James Place, *Voices Bloom*

TITLE: Koen Holtkamp, *Voice Model*

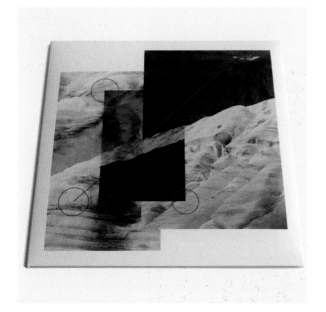
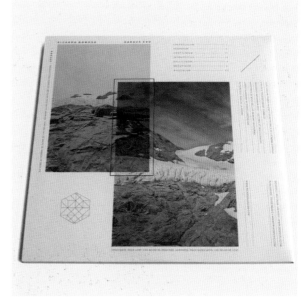

(Top) **TITLE:** Lorelle Meets The Obsolete, *Balance*
(Bottom) **TITLE:** Ricardo Donoso, *Sarava Exu*

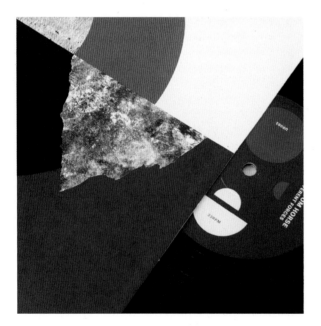

TITLE: Phantom Horse, *Different Forces*

TITLE: Ricardo Donoso, *Symmetry*

TITLE: SOHN, *Rennen*
CLIENT: 4AD
SIZE: 30.4 x 30.4 cm (12 x 12 in.)
PRINTING PROCESS: Offset
INKS: CMYK + 1 spot ink
COMPS PRESENTED: 1
REVISIONS: 4 rounds
APPROVAL: 4AD, SOHN
INVOLVEMENT WITH FINAL PRINTING: Proof

For Castrejon, a designer who has patterned a lot of his efforts around the early years of the 4AD label and its legendary creative director, Vaughan Oliver, the chance to work for the label 'was very special. That catalogue is a massive influence on me,' he explains.

TITLE: Driftmachine, *Radiations*
CLIENT: Umor Rex
SIZE: 30.4 x 30.4 cm (12 x 12 in.)
PRINTING PROCESS: Offset
INKS: 1 spot ink
COMPS PRESENTED: 1
REVISIONS: 1 round
APPROVAL: Driftmachine, Umor Rex
INVOLVEMENT WITH FINAL PRINTING: Proof

'This record was fun to design, as it is a kind of EP/rarities around the previous album from Driftmachine [*Colliding Contours*, see below], and I tried to make a visual reference to that record, while simplifying, like an abstraction,' Castrejon explains.

TITLE: Driftmachine, *Colliding Contours*
CLIENT: Umor Rex
SIZE: 30.4 x 30.4 cm (12 x 12 in.)
PRINTING PROCESS: Offset
INKS: 3 spot inks
COMPS PRESENTED: 1
REVISIONS: 1 round
APPROVAL: Driftmachine, Umor Rex
INVOLVEMENT WITH FINAL PRINTING: Proof

Working with artists and people very close to you can sometimes make the task at hand even more difficult. Driftmachine's album was 'a very hard challenge', admits Castrejon. 'This was the second LP for the band on my label. They are a mainstay for Umor Rex and also excellent friends.' With all of that in the back of his mind, he 'wanted to do something very special, something that reflects the complex music with modular synths that they make,' he adds. He finally had a breakthrough in creating this simple graphic diagram harking back to the modular synths he so wanted to capture.

TITLE: Alex Menzies, *Order & Disorder*
CLIENT: Kathexis Records
SIZE: 30.4 x 30.4 cm (12 x 12 in.)
PRINTING PROCESS: Offset
INKS: 2 spot inks
COMPS PRESENTED: 1
REVISIONS: 1 round
APPROVAL: Alex Menzies, Kathexis Records
INVOLVEMENT WITH FINAL PRINTING: Proof

'This really is a fantastic record,' raves Castrejon. He was brought in to design the sleeve for 'the score of a BBC documentary on high-level physics, with music by Alex Menzies, resulting in one of my favourite records from Kathexis Records.' The tracks, a mix of electro and acoustic instruments, are a unique departure for Menzies and create a work of intricate beauty.

TITLE: Dino Spiluttini and Nils Quak, *Modular Anxiety*
CLIENT: Umor Rex
SIZE: 30.4 x 30.4 cm (12 x 12 in.)
PRINTING PROCESS: Offset
INKS: CMYK
COMPS PRESENTED: 1
REVISIONS: 1 round
APPROVAL: Dino Spiluttini, Nils Quak, Umor Rex
INVOLVEMENT WITH FINAL PRINTING: Proof

'I love architecture, and I love Germany,' smiles Castrejon. 'The photos by Matthias Heiderich that are used here are just amazing, and I love the clean and elegant aesthetic of this album,' he raves.

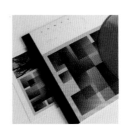

TITLE: James Place, *Voices Bloom*
CLIENT: Umor Rex
SIZE: 30.4 x 30.4 cm (12 x 12 in.)
PRINTING PROCESS: Offset
INKS: 1 spot ink
COMPS PRESENTED: 1
REVISIONS: 1 round
APPROVAL: James Place, Umor Rex
INVOLVEMENT WITH FINAL PRINTING: Proof

'With this album I began a kind of new visual stage for Umor Rex,' Castrejon explains. 'We kept the same international focus, but I began looking at older printing process aesthetics.' This would bring about an onset of one- and two-colour jobs and a proliferation of spot inks covering sophisticated, but clean, design work. This is also a fine example of Daniel's photographic talents, incorporating his images into the design.

TITLE: Koen Holtkamp, *Voice Model*
CLIENT: Umor Rex
SIZE: 30.4 x 30.4 cm (12 x 12 in.)
PRINTING PROCESS: Offset
INKS: CMYK + 1 spot ink
COMPS PRESENTED: 1
REVISIONS: 1 round
APPROVAL: Koen Holtkamp, Umor Rex
INVOLVEMENT WITH FINAL PRINTING: Proof

For Koen Holtkamp's album, Castrejon pulled out 'one of my Giorgio de Chirico modest tributes,' he smiles. Using simple colour blocks for perspective, he plays with the field with a surrealist's bent, but luckily doesn't go so far as to paint himself into the image like de Chirico.

TITLE: Lorelle Meets The Obsolete, *Balance*
CLIENT: Captcha/Sonic Cathedral
SIZE: 30.4 x 30.4 cm (12 x 12 in.)
PRINTING PROCESS: Offset
INKS: 2 spot inks
COMPS PRESENTED: 1
REVISIONS: 1 round
APPROVAL: Lorelle Meets The Obsolete
INVOLVEMENT WITH FINAL PRINTING: Proof

'I love the way this sleeve turned out,' admits Castrejon, 'especially as I was a little nervous while working on it. I knew that I wanted something with my personal aesthetic but I also knew that I wanted to layer in some psychedelic forms as well,' he adds. The aspect of including his own touch was secured with the use of his photographs, and the typography began a more distorted and twisted viewpoint. 'This band is my favourite music project of Mexico City,' he adds.

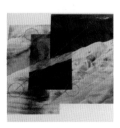

TITLE: Ricardo Donoso, *Sarava Exu*
CLIENT: Denovali Records
SIZE: 30.4 x 30.4 cm (12 x 12 in.)
PRINTING PROCESS: Offset
INKS: CMYK + spot varnish
COMPS PRESENTED: 1
REVISIONS: 1 round
APPROVAL: Ricardo Donoso, Denovali Records
INVOLVEMENT WITH FINAL PRINTING: Proof

For the *Sarava Exu* album, 'Ricardo wanted something subliminal, which I really took to heart, and we did some words that appear only in the spot varnish on top, so that you can only see them as they turn in the light.'

TITLE: Phantom Horse, *Different Forces*
CLIENT: Umor Rex
SIZE: 30.4 x 30.4 cm (12 x 12 in.)
PRINTING PROCESS: Offset
INKS: 3 spot inks
COMPS PRESENTED: 1
REVISIONS: 1 round
APPROVAL: Phantom Horse, Umor Rex
INVOLVEMENT WITH FINAL PRINTING: Proof

Incorporating his own photographs into the saturated overprinting of this three-colour design, Castrejon compares the use of spheres as a metaphor for so much more: 'The circles are about the process of life, constantly going around and around,' he adds.

TITLE: Ricardo Donoso, *Symmetry*
CLIENT: Denovali Records
SIZE: 30.4 x 30.4 cm (12 x 12 in.)
PRINTING PROCESS: Offset
INKS: 1 spot ink + 1 spot varnish
COMPS PRESENTED: 1
REVISIONS: 1 round
APPROVAL: Ricardo Donoso, Denovali Records
INVOLVEMENT WITH FINAL PRINTING: Proof

'Ricardo Donoso is a big musical influence on me,' Castrejon explains. 'It was a real pleasure to do this box set, which compiles his early albums, creating a massive collection of amazing music.' The Brazilian electronic composer sees his much-sought-after trilogy of records finally assembled with mountains of love and care and wrapped in the sophistication that they deserve.

MICHAEL CINA

INTENSE SERENITY

 The number of creative lives that Michael Cina has already lived is staggering. Heading to Minneapolis in the mid-nineties after college, craving the Midwestern ad agency battlegrounds, Cina quickly emerged as a powerhouse in the world of commercial design. Helping form the studio WeWorkForThem, Cina would tackle massive corporate assignments for many of the biggest brands in the world. Soon after, the launch of YouWorkForThem brought design tools and cutting-edge typography into the hands of designers all over the world. It is impossible to quantify the influence that Cina has had on design over the last twenty years from that alone. All through those years there was still a yearning to reconnect with the kid blasting dance records from his youth, sitting there poring over the sleeves and packaging. That opportunity arrived when he began working closely with the record label Ghostly International. Soon Cina was painting as much as he was designing. Reinvigorated with a sense of experimentation, his work, already world-class, did the unthinkable – it took a step up. After a few years going down this path, he knew he needed to keep pushing in this direction. He left the studio in 2010 and formed his own setup under his own name, and got down to the business of reinventing both himself and the record sleeve.

Photographer, John Klukas

'When I was a younger designer, there were so many amazing people out there doing phenomenal work, it was overwhelming,' Cina explains. 'It seemed like all of the best designers would gravitate to music packaging because the creative freedom was high, but the budget was also there.' Dreaming of that same scenario Cina found that 'around ten years ago, the budgets dried up and you saw a mass exodus away from top creatives working in music packaging'. This was the landscape he surveyed as he started working with Ghostly International. 'When I dove back in, I felt like overall it was a creative wasteland,' he laments. But that also served as an inspiration, both personally and professionally. 'My passion is music and creative freedom and that is what has kept me in the game,' Cina adds. Soon, his breathtaking work would be joined by a new wave as part of the vinyl resurgence. 'There has been a renaissance in cover design,' he smiles. 'Now that vinyl is chic and there are so many designers, the overall quality has really gone through the roof.'

That vinyl push has also left him wondering where it all sits in the marketplace, far removed from his former days of massive corporate projects. 'If you put out a record and it doesn't get pressed to vinyl, it makes me wonder: why?' he asks. 'I think it is very important to have a physical element if you are creating timeless music. If it is a dance single, I don't see it as having the same level of importance necessarily, but I still buy singles.' He is conflicted between his desire for these releases to be physically in people's hands and his understanding that this can fly in the face of conventional retail wisdom.

That means that he will avoid music jobs with only a digital presence. 'Digital-only normally means hardly any budget, and I stay away from those jobs,' he explains. 'Every project I work on, I acknowledge that there is a strong digital presence and I do consider that aspect, but in the end my gut says to do what is right for the project. That is the most important part to me,' Cina underlines.

Working in the dance field means being part of a tuned-in culture that is instantly reactive. That makes it all the more heartwarming that Cina often interacts with the audience for his work in charmingly low-tech ways. 'I think the biggest compliment, and my ultimate goal, is when people buy/collect the album based on the artwork,' he admits with a smile. 'Whenever I get emails or tweets saying they bought it for the cover, it always makes me feel like I did a great job on the package.' Cina also shops 'at all of the record stores in town, and they recognize my face, if they don't know me by name,' he adds. 'Occasionally someone in the shop will compliment me on a new cover or say they saw something they really liked and went to see who it was and were surprised to see my name, as they know me as a customer and not as a designer. Most of the reactions are probably felt by the band

or artist, because people will let them know what they think. I don't really have time to Google my name or read people's reactions, but I do feel like I get a sense as to how good the cover is by the amount of direct feedback through friends and fans,' he laughs.

EVERYTHING OLD IS NEW AGAIN

Launching his design career with the work of Barbara Wojirsch, Peter Saville, Hipgnosis, Reid Miles and TDR firmly imprinted on his creative psyche, Cina quickly fashioned his own forms of exploration, though in time that would be turned upside down. 'Lately, seeing the world through my kids' eyes has been a big influence on my work,' he admits. 'I have no desire for nostalgia or looking into the past, but enjoying the world through a kid's eye is amazing. When I was younger, I had my favourite designers and artists, etc .... Now, I am not really influenced by visual things as much as ideas, thoughts, processes. My main influence is being in the studio and learning new things, making mistakes, being in that state of creativity and exploring.'

That thirst for exploration fuels all of his work. 'A huge thing to me is working with different people with different interests, while trying to make the project work within the set of limitations they provide,' he explains. 'I love it when clients are working in an area, or wanting to explore a topic that I don't know a lot about, because I can explore that world with fresh eyes. I am a curious person and I love to learn,' he adds. Perhaps seeing the world through the eyes of his children is not so different for Cina after all.

'I have been working on music packaging so much that I have lost some perspective in funny ways,' Cina explains. 'Every project, I try and ask what it could be ... more than "what is it?" Budget is a real thing, though, and that always brings me down to earth fast,' he adds. 'I approach every project differently. I use my experience and instinct to lead the way because no job is the same, even if it is a logo, etc ....' And that is even more the case when applied to a creative output like music. 'When someone messes with that process of creating, that is the real challenge that can derail the whole thing. There are many ways people do this but the perfect client is someone who has an idea of what they want but not in a visually specific manner. When it works I really love to collaborate,' he adds. That has made him very selective. 'Most of my music packaging comes from Ghostly International, and I do things with bands I like or friends. I turn down almost all of the job offers for music packaging because establishing a working relationship takes time and I don't have that kind of time. Working with musicians can be very rewarding but a lot of times it is frustrating.'

'The process of creating – that is what brings me the most joy.'

(Above and opposite) TITLE: Matthew Dear, *Beams* (and related singles and EPs)

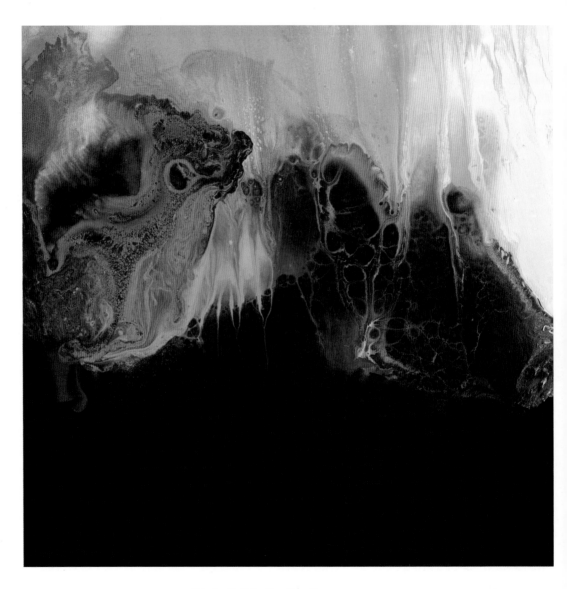

TITLE: Shigeto, *No Better Time Than Now*

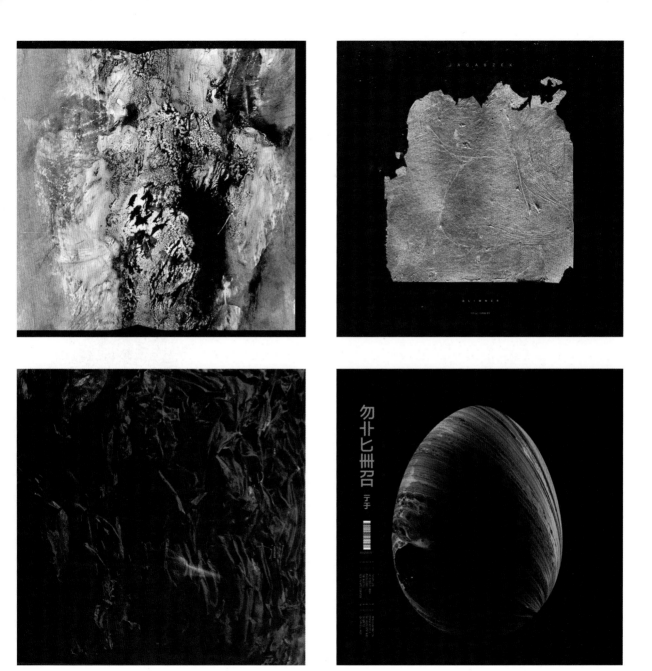

(Clockwise from top left) **TITLE:** The Sight Below, *Glider*; **TITLE:** Jacaszek, *Glimmer*
TITLE: Michna, *Thousand Thursday* (back); **TITLE:** Various Artists, *SMM: Context*

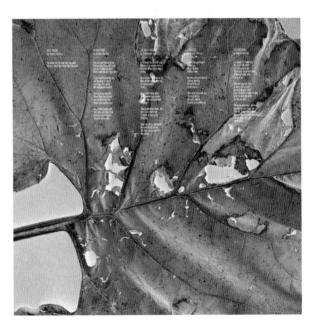

TITLE: Jacaszek, *KWIATY*

勿卝匕卝召 丁于

MICHNA
THOUSAND
THURSDAY

米希納
千星期四
警告
這張光碟含有可能
損害您聽力的內容

G/-733

TITLE: Michna, *Thousand Thursday*

TITLE: Matthew Dear, *Beam*
CLIENT: Ghostly International
SIZE: 30.4 x 30.4 cm (12 x 12 in.)
PRINTING PROCESS: Offset
INKS: CMYK
COMPS PRESENTED: 1
REVISIONS: 1 round
APPROVAL: Matthew Dear, Sam Valenti
INVOLVEMENT WITH FINAL PRINTING: None

'First time I spoke with Matthew on the phone, we came up with the entire concept in fifteen or so minutes,' Cina explains. 'I was on a plane within weeks, it was before Christmas. We drove a massive six-foot [1.8-metre] canvas to an unused floor of an advertising agency, and I painted all day while dancers came in, poets, musicians played live, etc... while Matthew sat in a chair all day. I finished the original painting in fifteen minutes but I had to try another painting, which was used for the final.'

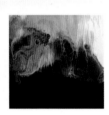

TITLE: Shigeto, *No Better Time Than Now*
CLIENT: Ghostly International
SIZE: 30.4 x 30.4 cm (12 x 12 in.)
PRINTING PROCESS: Offset
INKS: CMYK
COMPS PRESENTED: Almost
REVISIONS: None
APPROVAL: Zach, Molly Smith
INVOLVEMENT WITH FINAL PRINTING: None

'A lot of times with Zach [Saginaw, Shigeto], I try different things and see what sticks,' Cina adds. 'It's normally a long process, but enjoyable still, as we are all searching for the right cover. I presented this idea and everyone was really into it,' he explains. But Cina is not one to be easily satisfied. 'I kept trying other ideas and none of them could beat this one,' he adds.

TITLE: The Sight Below, *Glider*
CLIENT: Ghostly International
SIZE: 30.4 x 30.4 cm (12 x 12 in.)
PRINTING PROCESS: Offset
INKS: CMYK
COMPS PRESENTED: 1
REVISIONS: None
APPROVAL: RAF, Sam Valenti
INVOLVEMENT WITH FINAL PRINTING: None

'I had worked on Jacaszek's EP before this, so I had a good idea of where we were going,' Cina explains. The solution was quickly before him. 'I could see it,' he adds. 'I took three paintings that I had done and combined them to make this cover. When RAF [Rafael Anton Irisarr, The Sight Below] saw the cover, he said, "This is exactly what I see when I make music." The layout is what took most of the time. I really wanted it to feel like a piece of art.'

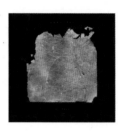

TITLE: Jacaszek, *Glimmer*
CLIENT: Ghostly International
SIZE: 30.4 x 30.4 cm (12 x 12 in.)
PRINTING PROCESS: Offset
INKS: CMYK
COMPS PRESENTED: Many
REVISIONS: Many
APPROVAL: Jeff Owens, Sam Valenti
INVOLVEMENT WITH FINAL PRINTING: None

Even after working with an artist numerous times, the process can still be filled with twists and turns and surprises. 'Jacaszek had already designed a cover with bokeh dots that he wanted to use,' Cina explains. 'I had other plans,' he adds. 'One day while working on a logo, I got up and did this cover art in fifteen minutes or less. It just came to me.' That doesn't mean the adventure was over, though. 'I don't believe he liked anything I did, and Ghostly had to come to an agreement to use it in the US and he could use his cover in Europe,' he explains. 'The inside cover was a painting I did with gold leaf shot during the daytime, and at night the painting looked like burnt embers.'

TITLE: Various Artists, *SMM: Context*
CLIENT: Ghostly International
SIZE: 30.4 x 30.4 cm (12 x 12 in.)
PRINTING PROCESS: Offset
INKS: CMYK
COMPS PRESENTED: 1
REVISIONS: None
APPROVAL: Jeff Owens
INVOLVEMENT WITH FINAL PRINTING: None

'Jeff Owens put together this compilation and I had thought about it a lot,' Cina explains. 'I knew that I was going to burn a book for this, so I got out my encyclopaedia and lit it on fire and took photos.' The desired effect achieved, he didn't need to do too much more. 'Nothing from this series was Photoshopped, I just adjusted some levels. I really try to make the final piece "as is" without relying on tricks,' he adds.

TITLE: Jacaszek, *KWIATY*
CLIENT: Ghostly International
SIZE: 30.4 x 30.4 cm (12 x 12 in.)
PRINTING PROCESS: Offset
INKS: CMYK
COMPS PRESENTED: 3
REVISIONS: 1 round
APPROVAL: Molly Smith
INVOLVEMENT WITH FINAL PRINTING: None

TITLE: Jacaszek, *KWIATY*
CLIENT: Ghostly International
SIZE: 30.4 x 30.4 cm (12 x 12 in.)
PRINTING PROCESS: Offset
INKS: CMYK
COMPS PRESENTED: 3
REVISIONS: 1 round
APPROVAL: Molly Smith
INVOLVEMENT WITH FINAL PRINTING: None

Strong creative minds come together once again as Cina works with a starting point of Jacaszek's concepts. 'Jacaszek asked me to do his second release on Ghostly, and I did a little creative dancing around his ideas,' he smiles. 'The record was about death under the guise of flowers, and I had a strong concept in my head,' he explains, before leaving an air of mystery behind. 'There is a ton to talk about, but I will just say that the cover is not a photograph. I was very happy with the outcome and I believe he was, too!'

TITLE: Michna, *Thousand Thursday*
CLIENT: Ghostly International
SIZE: 30.4 x 30.4 cm (12 x 12 in.)
PRINTING PROCESS: Offset
INKS: CMYK
COMPS PRESENTED: Many
REVISIONS: Many
APPROVAL: Adrian Michna, Molly Smith
INVOLVEMENT WITH FINAL PRINTING: None

'I worked with Michna very closely on this. We were going for a science-fiction cover. I did hundreds of ideas and would show him them as I was working. Nothing was really hitting, but we had a collective mood that we were trying to hit. I kept making it more simple as we went on and on, and we used a rock and an egg for the front and back covers. Thanks to Corey Holms for the rendering of the egg.'

JACOB ESCOBEDO

A LITTLE BOY AND HIS PARENTS' RECORDS

 The little boy growing up out in Nevada, in a home crammed to the ceiling with books, comics, art, thrift-store finds and items others might charitably refer to as trash, saw a creative future, fuelled in large part by his outsider artist father's encouragement. That creative journey was a little bumpy, with menial jobs to pay the bills as he did illustration assignments at night, but those illustrations eventually led him to Cartoon Network, where he rose into a dream job as VP/Head of Design at Cartoon Network and Adult Swim's Creative Group. Working with a variety of amazing properties, and surrounded by some of the most talented people in the world, Jacob Escobedo has emerged as perhaps the most exciting in-house creative of the past twenty years. It made for an incredibly fulfilling career, with only one tiny piece missing: a place to put his most personal explorations – the weird stuff that could never merge with the needs of the network. Thus, he began targeting little projects during his evenings and weekends, which soon grew to encompass his love of music and equal the acclaim he enjoyed on a day-to-day basis. 'I feel like I geared my life to do this work,' he explains. 'In a way, as a kid, I surrounded myself with my parents' albums and was really intensely interested in the artwork. I needed this so much that I almost feel like I willed it to happen.'

'I feel that the side work that I do really balances me creatively. I'm able to express myself through those projects more on a personal basis than having to be forced to work with set rules or set things laid out in front of me,' Escobedo details. 'It's much more of a personal endeavour. To me, those projects are more fulfilling, or they just become necessary for me.' With the music projects, he never loses perspective on what he needs from his day job, either. 'I truly love my job at Cartoon Network and Adult Swim. Without all of that I wouldn't be anywhere,' he says. 'What's great about those jobs is that they've allowed me to create my own worlds in a way. They've allowed me to build my teams the way I want and to give life to those brands. I really feel like I have a lot of ownership there, and I am so invested, and it gives back in the same way.'

CONNECT TO THE CHANGE

'The music industry has evolved a lot in interesting ways,' Escobedo says. 'I think that we lost touch with album packaging. There was a gap where everybody was going digital and nobody really cared about the physical package of a release. This return to vinyl has been amazing because I feel that that's an expression of album art. I feel like the future is about collecting and about figuring interesting ways to package album art,' he adds, like the avid collector that he is. 'I also hope that my job is around forever because I don't really want to do anything else,' he is quick to underline.

Working with acts who have a dedicated fanbase in the new digital marketplace has allowed Escobedo to experience things in real time with fans. 'It's almost live as things are released,' he marvels. 'I also enjoy seeing the interaction between people who like the work and like the music.' He has found himself using the new tools in interesting ways, whether 'checking in behind the scenes, or showing drawings or rough sketches or whatever on Instagram. It seems pretty great that we have that connection with the fans of the work.' He also worries about the impact all of this moving so fast will have. 'At the same time I feel like these movements and the art you put out moves much faster and is forgotten much faster. When we were kids you were able to sit with an album and listen to the music and enjoy the artwork all together as one experience. It's completely changed now. It's almost looked at as two different things. It's not a whole experience any more.'

SIMPLE, BUT NOT SO SIMPLE

As much as Escobedo studied record sleeves as a kid, he didn't 'necessarily follow artists who created album packaging in the past. For my own work I've come at all of this stuff from such a different angle. Not having an art education and just arriving here. The influences that I draw from are from things like the massive collection of paperback science fiction novels that I have. I also have a lot of art history books, Japanese art. My house is just full of books [not unlike his childhood

home] so I refer to those constantly,' he admits. 'With my older records I am really drawn to simple packaging of albums,' he explains. 'One of my favourite album covers of all time is Wire's *Pink Flag*. Just the simplicity of it. The same goes for the Saville Factory Records sleeves.'

The *Pink Flag* reference serves as a great bridge to Escobedo's own work. In many ways it is what it says it is, an image of a flagpole with a pink flag atop it, but it works on so many levels, and is more like a literary cover than a record sleeve. Though obvious, it is far from being a commercial solution. This is a huge strength in Esobedo's work. He is not trying to fool the audience or the viewer. He is willing to just let one big object or one obvious pose tell the story. It's how you interpret that, that raises it up to a completely different level. It's a woman with a space helmet, but is it? He elevates it to something much larger.

Escobedo is quick to explain that working on these music projects is a completely different process for him. 'I take much more of a personal approach with everything. A lot of the references or the work that goes into it is in my home or out of my selection of things. A lot of the imagery that you'll see on album covers is deeply personal because a lot of it is just surrounding me in my own personal life,' he adds. 'In my day job I build these worlds there that feed me differently. I'm surrounded by illustrators and animators and designers, who are all very talented and we are reacting to incredible content. I built those teams and the creative spaces there to reflect an environment to transport yourself, into thinking differently and finding new solutions,' he adds. 'The music projects are directing me inward.' The one commonality, though, is that he tries to sit with anything he is working on for as long as is possible, letting it seep into his mind as he sketches and sketches until the ideas flow.

He also knows how lucky he is, even if his talent and ambition opened these doors. 'I feel it's incredibly fulfilling to be working with bands that I respect and music that I love,' he explains. Working directly with James Mercer from the Shins or Danger Mouse allows him access to their 'interesting perspectives, where they want things to go, finding a better outcome.' He is well aware that 'trying to nail an image for a creative person that's coming to you with their music is incredibly difficult. They have a certain vision of where they want things to go. There's a lot of time spent, experimenting and trying out things. Awkward conversations or interaction with the band. That stuff can get really challenging because you have to have a lot of endurance to make it through that and not take everything so personally.' In both jobs, might Escobedo's skills in that area be just as important as his visual skills? 'I think that I've gotten to a point where people come to me for a certain thing, for my perspective. I think that I'm able to get to those points much quicker or more easily now because I have a lot of work that I can ... fall back on.'

(Above and opposite) TITLE: The Shins, *Heartworms*

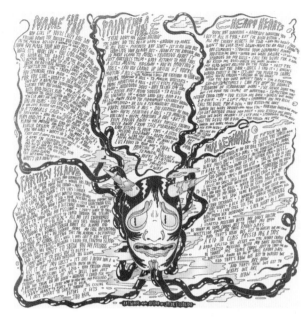

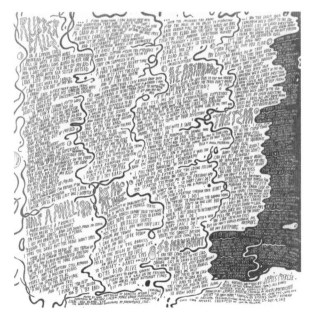

TITLE: Broken Bells, *s/t* (LP and singles)

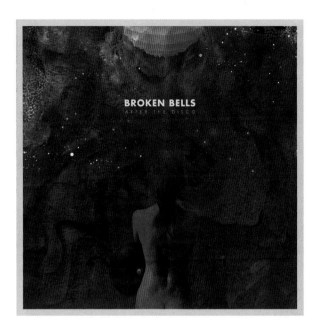

TITLE: Broken Bells, *After The Disco* (LP and singles)

TITLE: Run The Jewels, *36" Chain*

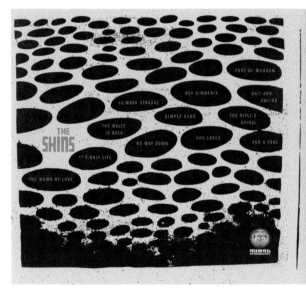

(Top left) TITLE: Matt Costa, *Sacred Hills EP*; (Top right) TITLE: Matt Costa, *s/t*
(Bottom) TITLE: The Shins, *Port Of Morrow*

TITLE: The Shins, *Port Of Morrow* (materials)

THE
SHINS
SIMPLE SONG

TITLE: The Shins, *Simple Song*

TITLE: The Shins, *Heartworms*
CLIENT: Columbia
SIZE: 30.4 x 30.4 cm (12 x 12 in.)
PRINTING PROCESS: Offset
INKS: CMYK
COMPS PRESENTED: 30
REVISIONS: 1 round
APPROVAL: James Mercer, Columbia
INVOLVEMENT WITH FINAL PRINTING: Proof

'*Heartworms* was a really difficult cover to come to,' Escobedo admits. Even though he had worked well with main man, James Mercer, for a long time, he knew they 'had a completely different type of art that they were looking to use on this cover. I don't think I was even in the running for doing the cover for a while,' he adds. Once on board, Escobedo 'went through rounds and rounds and then it went quiet for a while.' He found himself just doing patterns for Mercer to look through. 'It was all of these different drawings, I kept sending them in and nothing was working for months,' he laments. Once he got to hear the album, things took a quick turn. 'They finally sent me the album and I was able to sit with it, and the album was so fun and psychedelic and it was dark and lovely,' he explains. 'I immediately started drawing just a skeleton. It was a very obvious thing to have worms all over the place. It kind of captured the music in a way. I felt really strong about that. I spent an entire two days working on that cover and made sure that it was totally finished before sending it to him.' Having that gut feeling meant that he was also willing to risk wasting that time if it fell on the scrap heap with the earlier ideas, but he knew it needed to be completely fleshed out to get the proper effect. 'When James saw it, he was like, "That's it!" and we both breathed a sigh of relief,' Escobedo says with a wry smile.

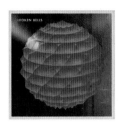

TITLE: Broken Bells, *s/t*
CLIENT: Columbia
SIZE: 30.4 x 30.4 cm (12 x 12 in.)
PRINTING PROCESS: Offset
INKS: CMYK
COMPS PRESENTED: 30
REVISIONS: 10 rounds
APPROVAL: Broken Bells, Columbia
INVOLVEMENT WITH FINAL PRINTING: Proof

'Getting to the pink orb was a really difficult process, because I was approaching it from all the wrong angles,' Escobedo explains. 'They didn't really like any of the directions that I was sending. I think I was taken off that project midstream,' he says with a rueful shake of the head. 'Then it was very similar to the Shins' *Heartworms* in that right before the artwork was due, they reached out to me and gave me the album. I sat with it for a couple of weeks. It was like giving birth to that image. It was very ... I keep using the word "personal", but it was .... I was surrounded by all of the science-fiction books that I have and also these bold architectural drawings from this book that I have. That imagery poured out from that,' he explains. 'Danger Mouse [who forms Broken Bells with James Mercer] was really looking for something iconic to represent that album. Something really simple and memorable. When that orb happened they saw it and immediately knew that was it. Arriving at that moment was almost like this sweet victory for me. It was such a difficult process to arrive at such a simple solution.'

TITLE: Broken Bells, *After The Disco*
CLIENT: Columbia
SIZE: 30.4 x 30.4 cm (12 x 12 in.)
PRINTING PROCESS: Offset
INKS: CMYK
COMPS PRESENTED: 10
REVISIONS: 30 rounds
APPROVAL: Broken Bells, Columbia
INVOLVEMENT WITH FINAL PRINTING: Proof

For the *After The Disco* album, the duo came to Escobedo and said they wanted a girl on the cover. 'I could make that jump easily as I always saw the pink orb as inhabited by a human from the beginning – that was the light from within,' he explains. 'It was then just a matter of trying to figure out what she looked like. What would be her relationship to the pink orb? It was like trying to hold some narrative or story together.' It seemed like this project might find a quick resolution. 'The process was fairly quick in that I did a drawing of a woman curled up, sleeping on the edge of a cliff. I had imagined that she was in a landscape lost and alone. They really reacted to that and so I did quite a few versions of that.' However, Escobedo found that he struggled to nail the style that they wanted. 'All of the solutions that I sent them just weren't what they were looking for. They were too illustrated and they wanted it more realistic.' That brought about a prolonged back and forth before they began sending science-fiction covers featuring photographic figures. 'It was women that were depicted more realistically, and I could easily connect to the science-fiction aspect. After that, I started working with photographs and manipulating them into that world,' he explains.

TITLE: Run The Jewels, *36" Chain*
CLIENT: Adult Swim
SIZE: 30.4 x 30.4 cm (12 x 12 in.)
PRINTING PROCESS: Digital
INKS: Digital
COMPS PRESENTED: 1
REVISIONS: 1 round
APPROVAL: Adult Swim
INVOLVEMENT WITH FINAL PRINTING: N/A

Combining his two worlds, 'the whole Adult Swim single series came about really organically,' explains Escobedo. 'Jason DeMarco, who is VP/Creative Director for on-air for Adult Swim, was really involved in the music movement of Adult Swim and built that whole business up. He collaborated with me from the beginning on projects, starting with that *Danger Doom* album. That was one of the first projects that I had worked on with him.' These covers can be a big team effort. 'In some instances I've had help from the internal designers at Adult Swim and Cartoon Network. In other instances I've done it all myself,' he explains. 'It just depends on how heavy the lifting is. For this one it was an installation that I pulled together. That whole project was all photographs. It wasn't digital at all. I had to pull in a prop person, and it was a big thing to do for a smaller project because it was only a digital release and one of many covers. Having those resources is the plus side of working in a place like that because you can pull off much larger and more ambitious ideas.'

TITLE: Matt Costa, *s/t* and *Sacred Hills EP*
CLIENT: Matt Costa
SIZE: 30.4 x 30.4 cm (12 x 12 in.)
PRINTING PROCESS: Offset
INKS: CMYK
COMPS PRESENTED: 1
REVISIONS: 1 round
APPROVAL: Matt Costa
INVOLVEMENT WITH FINAL PRINTING: Proof

'When Matt Costa contacted me, I actually didn't understand why they wanted me because the artwork they were describing that they were looking for was absolutely not what I was working with,' he laughs. 'It was a lot of collage, a lot of handwork stuff. Oddly enough I did have a lot of that kind of thing lying around, but I had never shown it,' he adds. 'I ended up sending them some artwork that I had done years ago that was hanging on my wall. It was a collage, it was radial collage, and they reacted to that. Matt really liked it, the label really liked it, so I started riffing on that and ended up arriving at that cover pretty quickly. Somehow they just knew that I had what they needed. Amazing.'

TITLE: The Shins, *Port Of Marrow*
CLIENT: Columbia
SIZE: 30.4 x 30.4 cm (12 x 12 in.)
PRINTING PROCESS: Offset
INKS: CMYK
COMPS PRESENTED: 10
REVISIONS: 10 rounds
APPROVAL: James Mercer, Columbia
INVOLVEMENT WITH FINAL PRINTING: Proof

'This album cover was a very personal project for me because I had driven across the United States and was camping out at the town that I grew up in, in Nevada. When they reached out to me, I was sitting there staring at the mountains in Nevada and James Mercer from The Shins said that he wanted to it be influenced by Hopi kachina dolls,' explains Escobedo. 'That whole experience helped jump-start that artwork. The process to get to where we needed to go from that beginning was very quick because I had all of those influences around me already and it was geared to push that one out,' he says. 'I started basically building the mountain, and then I would get feedback from James and I would go and add another layer to the artwork, with this going for about ten rounds until we got to a place where we both knew the mountain was perfect.' For the supporting singles and marketing materials, Escobedo continued on that theme to amazing results, with the mountain turning more ominous, and the doll connection being made more obvious.

JAD FAIR

ROBOTS AND MONSTERS AND LOVERS, OH MY!

 As a couple of rock and roll-loving kids, brothers David and Jad Fair turned their enthusiasm and fearlessness, and lack of traditional instrumental skill, into Half Japanese, one of the greatest underground bands of all time. Right from the very beginning there was a strong artistic element to the group: raw, cartoonish drawings, tribal paintings with Day-Glo colours, quirky patterns and, soon afterwards, a more painterly approach from David's brush. Jad would develop a unique mode of drawing that began to adorn releases he had worked on, or those of friends or sympathetic artists. With his reputation as a celebrated outsider artist fully intact, both musically and visually, he decided to further refine the graphic sense in his work and turn to paper cuttings. Working in this manner, and in only black and white, took his work to stratospheric levels. Stripping everything down to the very basics revealed not only his keen sense of humour and happily skewed worldview, but also his strong sense of graphic elements and white space, along with a keen visual balance and attention to detail. Collectors and galleries around the world were soon clamouring for his work, but Jad continued to make it available for the low price of a single LP.

Jad has seen a lot change over the years of working on album sleeves. 'Having a computer has made it a lot easier,' he laughs. 'I first started working on cover art in 1977. Back then I needed to lay it out using a T-square and wax gun to get things in place. Some of the lettering was done using press-down type.' He is also thrilled at the return of his favourite canvas. 'I'm glad that LPs are popular now. When I do a cover for a CD I feel the need to keep it as simple as I can. Art which looks great at twelve inches square can look too busy when it is at a much smaller size.'

That is not to say that he can't work small. 'I have done art for digital-only releases and try to keep the image as simple as I can,' he explains. 'Digital covers are often two inches square, or less. At that size it needs to be easy to read, and easy to recognize what the image is.'

The return of the LP is not just down to the physical wrapping, though that plays a big part. 'The popularity of LPs is partly for the sound,' he explains, 'and in part for the packaging. People like the look and feel of a record album.' Jad loves to take that further where possible, and make a limited-edition version or unique printing of a release. 'I've done several limited-edition releases with silk-screened and letterpress covers. It makes it more of an art piece.' It also celebrates his love of the small press in all formats – both in printing and in music. He has even gone as far as to work on a laser-die-cut cover for a lathe-cut release.

ONE HELPS THE OTHER

One of the most interesting aspects of Jad's move into paper cutting, as well as his extensive work on record sleeves, is the knock-on effect on his fine-art work. They often dovetail in surprising ways. 'Doing album covers has been helpful in getting offers from galleries,' he explains. 'I've had exhibitions in many countries. I'm so glad to have work in both music and art. One complements the other,' he adds. This is often made even more intertwined by Jad performing concerts at his gallery openings, making for a one-of-a-kind event to coincide with the unique work on display.

Jad is not the first desinger to take this kind of graphic approach. 'I've always loved the covers of Jim Flora,' he explains. 'His art was very playful, uplifting and colourful. I'm a big fan of his work!' he says. Jad takes a nod to Flora in his simple shapes and almost cartoonish characters and then allows for the paper-cutting process to require even further simplification and creativity in the use of space and shape, so it creates something that in the end could have come from no one other than Jad himself. He also immerses himself in the work of like-minded artists and illustrators. 'My brother David

has been a huge influence,' he says. 'We have different styles, but I think we have some things in common. Other artists I'm very fond of are Gary Panter, Arrington de Dionyso, Flavio Morais, Gary Taxali, Cal Schenkel, Aggi Wright and Nikki McClure.'

Jad also finds himself doing other design work, but music packaging affords him a platform that others cannot. 'For most of the cover art I've done, I've had a bit more freedom in what I do,' he explains. 'When I've done logos, the person I do it for usually has something in mind and I try to get as close to what they want as I can. I'm also mindful that logos are often printed very small. It needs to look good if it is printed one inch [2.5 cm] in size,' he laughs.

He also loves the fact that these are instant artisitic artefacts. 'I like making something which will have some longevity,' he explains. 'Covers I've worked on thirty or forty years ago are still around today.'

That's not to say that he doesn't encounter the usual challenges. 'If I do a cover for a band, it can often mean that the people in the band have differing opinions on what the cover should look like,' he says. 'I don't just need to please one person, which can make for additional work trying to have a cover everyone is happy with. I often prefer the first design I propose, but I'm willing to make changes. It's to be expected.' He also knows his way around the label process, both as a designer and as an artist, lending a unique perspective. 'I'm usually contacted first by the artist, but it's the label that makes the payment. Labels will often have someone in charge of packaging that I will work with for the final layout.'

For Jad, the record packaging 'needs to make a fast impression. At a record store people will thumb through records and CDs, and may see the cover for less than a second. If it can stand out from the hundreds of other covers, it's a success.' Trust me when I say that Jad's record covers always stand out.

TITLE: Screen-printed custom box set containing all of the albums on the opposite page.

(Clockwise from top left) TITLE: Jad Fair & Norman Blake, *Yes*; TITLE: Jad Fair & Danielson, *Solid Gold Heart*
TITLE: Jad Fair & Strobe Talbot, *Let's Born To Rock!*; TITLE: Jad Fair & R. Stevie Moore, *The Great American Songbook Volume 1*

(Clockwise from top left) TITLE: Jad Fair + Hifiklub + kptmichigan, *Bird House*; TITLE: Jad Fair + Hifiklub + kptmichigan, *Don't Give Up*
TITLE: Half Japanese, *Overjoyed*; TITLE: Half Japanese, *Perfect*

TITLE: Jad Fair & Jason Willett, *The Greatest Power*

TITLE: Jad Fair & Norman Blake, *Yes*
CLIENT: Joyful Noise
SIZE: 30.4 x 30.4 cm (12 x 12 in.)
PRINTING PROCESS: Letterpress
INKS: 1 spot ink
COMPS PRESENTED: 12
REVISIONS: None
APPROVAL: Jad Fair
INVOLVEMENT WITH FINAL PRINTING: Proof

As part of Joyful Noise's Artist In Residence series, four albums from Jad Fair and collaborators were compiled together in a screen-printed wooden box, and numbered and signed by Jad himself, with each sleeve letterpress-printed, using a colour to match the coloured vinyl inside and with in-house art director David Woodruff lending a hand where needed. For the record with frequent collaborator Norman Blake, best known as one of the main songwriters in Teenage Fanclub, Jad 'wanted an image with two figures, and something musical going on – hence the two musicans sitting on a guitar'.

TITLE: Jad Fair & Danielson, *Solid Gold Heart*
CLIENT: Joyful Noise
SIZE: 30.4 x 30.4 cm (12 x 12 in.)
PRINTING PROCESS: Letterpress
INKS: 1 spot ink
COMPS PRESENTED: 14
REVISIONS: None
APPROVAL: Jad Fair
INVOLVEMENT WITH FINAL PRINTING: Proof

'Working with Daniel Smith of Danielson, Daniel and Kramer worked on the music and then I came in to record vocals, as well as Gilles Rieder on drums,' Jad explains. 'A lot of these songs started as tape loops, with Daniel bringing the loops in and out during the songs.' For the image, Jad showed a number of different paper cuttings that he thought might be a good fit. 'Daniel really loved the image of the two people drinking wine together, tying in the romantic image with the *Solid Gold Heart* title.'

TITLE: Jad Fair & Strobe Talbot,
Let's Born To Rock
CLIENT: Joyful Noise
SIZE: 30.4 x 30.4 cm (12 x 12 in.)
PRINTING PROCESS: Letterpress
INKS: 1 spot ink
COMPS PRESENTED: 30
REVISIONS: None
APPROVAL: Jad Fair
INVOLVEMENT WITH FINAL PRINTING: Proof

'This cover definitely has an outer space theme going on,' Fair explains. 'Out of the thirty options we looked over, this one was everyone's quick favourite.' In contrast with the other cover illustrations in this series, Jad has lots of details stretching right to the edge, making the paper cutting much more difficult to complete. 'Adding in the arrows and planets really helped me fill in the spaces and balance out the image,' he adds.

TITLE: Jad Fair & R. Stevie Moore,
The Great American Songbook Volume 1
CLIENT: Joyful Noise
SIZE: 30.4 x 30.4 cm (12 x 12 in.)
PRINTING PROCESS: Letterpress
INKS: 1 spot ink
COMPS PRESENTED: 10
REVISIONS: None
APPROVAL: Jad Fair
INVOLVEMENT WITH FINAL PRINTING: Proof

This illustration has practically all of Jad's favourite subjects in it, while also using the space well by altering the size relationship with each of the figures, with the horse and bird larger than the person in the car and the monster. Put together by recording with Conrad Choucroun and trading tracks with Stevie, the end result is a merging of masters of skewed poptastic rock and roll. Moore and Fair go back to the very beginning of Jad's musical adventures. 'We started corresponding with each other probably back in 1979. Stevie was actually one of the first people to buy the first Half Japanese single, so working with him is always special,' Jad says.

TITLE: Jad Fair + Hifiklub + kptmichigan, *Bird House*
CLIENT: Joyful Noise
SIZE: 30.4 x 30.4 cm (12 x 12 in.)
PRINTING PROCESS: Offset
INKS: CMYK
COMPS PRESENTED: 15
REVISIONS: None
APPROVAL: Jad Fair
INVOLVEMENT WITH FINAL PRINTING: Proof

'I don't know what came first – the title "Bird House" – or the image,' Jad explains. 'I feel like we saw this image first and then went with the title,' he adds. 'Hifiklub is a band in France that we were lucky enough to have open for us for a show and we really hit it off and they suggested doing some recording together and that sounded good to me.'

TITLE: Jad Fair + Hifiklub + kptmichigan, *Don't Give Up*
CLIENT: Joyful Noise
SIZE: 30.4 x 30.4 cm (12 x 12 in.)
PRINTING PROCESS: Screen-print
INKS: 1 spot ink
COMPS PRESENTED: 20
REVISIONS: None
APPROVAL: Jad Fair
INVOLVEMENT WITH FINAL PRINTING: Proof

Printed with silver ink on black cardstock, 'we settled on the title first, and the band wanted an image that had some contrast to the image,' Fair explains. 'So having something spooky, and having the juxtaposition of a band of skeletons that can still rock and roll is funny.'

TITLE: Half Japanese, *Overjoyed*
CLIENT: Joyful Noise
SIZE: 30.4 x 30.4 cm (12 x 12 in.)
PRINTING PROCESS: Offset
INKS: CMYK
COMPS PRESENTED: 30
REVISIONS: None
APPROVAL: Jad Fair
INVOLVEMENT WITH FINAL PRINTING: Proof

Jad does so many paper cuttings that he is always doing subtle things to challenge himself or tweak the process. At one point he started taking a square sheet of paper and folding it in half, before creating an image where the top half is one image and the bottom is completely different. Once they are unfolded, they combine so that the two halves make a whole. Jad is also quick to add that 'getting the band to choose an image can be a bit of a challenge at times, but I do know that any image with a monster in it will be a favourite for Gilles [Rieder].'

TITLE: Half Japanese, *Perfect*
CLIENT: Joyful Noise
SIZE: 30.4 x 30.4 cm (12 x 12 in.)
PRINTING PROCESS: Offset
INKS: CMYK
COMPS PRESENTED: 30
REVISIONS: None
APPROVAL: Jad Fair
INVOLVEMENT WITH FINAL PRINTING: Proof

Keeping in the theme of navigating the process of Half Japanese choosing artwork, any image that has a monster, Gilles will go for, 'so that helps narrow the choices,' Jad adds. 'For this one, you have a happy couple sitting together, with a monster standing on the table separating them – perfect!'

TITLE: Jad Fair & Jason Willett, *The Greatest Power*
CLIENT: Dymaxion Groove Records
SIZE: 30.4 x 30.4 cm (12 x 12 in.)
PRINTING PROCESS: Offset, die-cut
INKS: CMYK
COMPS PRESENTED: 20
REVISIONS: 3 rounds
APPROVAL: Jad Fair
INVOLVEMENT WITH FINAL PRINTING: Proof

Fair's artwork lends itself to the die-cut process, as he has already worked out a lot of the interconnected parts in doing the paper cutting. Here, he makes the most of the bright inner sleeve by cutting circles and triangles to form a flurry of shapes shimmering around the main image. 'Figuring out the laser die-cut meant that I had to work out the image to not have things be too close together and to avoid thin lines,' he explains. 'As Jason and I looked at possible paper-cutting images, we worked with the label to sort through which ones had the best chance of being successful with the die-cut process.' Working with designer Krissy Madrid, Jad altered the original image to accommodate the die-cutting process and to make sure that the structural integrity of the sleeve would hold up. They then took care to colour-match the inner sleeve with a blend to mimic the two-colour vinyl inside.

FELD

THE BEST WAY TO CALM ME DOWN

 FELD was founded by a group of Berlin-based designers who share a common mode of thinking and working. Few studios in the world combine the conceptual as both an artistic sensibility and a technical application. The studio creates massive installations, builds one-of-a-kind technological products and delivers intensive digital communications projects. So what are they doing in a book about record sleeve design? It is in that design work that they remain most grounded, applying their problem-solving skills on smaller projects without the massive financial risks involved. It is also a place where they shine far too bright to be ignored. The studio is helmed by Torsten Posselt and Frederic Gmeiner, with the music industry work primarily Posselt's domain. Growing from a chance meeting with musician Nils Frahm that led to a decade-long close friendship, Posselt began helping various artists, playing music and housing musicians when they came to Berlin. The projects soon morphed into a neccessary part of his mental health. 'I have always found that doing packaging design kind of calms me down,' he admits. 'You also can have a slight tendency to become quite nerdy in this, which is of course a nice thing. I find it's good to work on several projects at a time with different projects that involve different methods and different material and also a different approach. For me, all of our work is connected because an aesthetic visual manifestation can be on paper, but it can also be in a sculpture.' That desire to build beautiful and interesting things rings true for FELD, whether it is a massive three-storey-tall installation or a wonderful little twelve-inch sleeve.

'I'm not sure if I should say this, but I tell this to every artist I work with,' Posselt cautions. 'With most of the artists I design for I tell them that I have an idea who you are. I have an idea what kind of music you do. I also think you know me and so that's why you came to me. I then design around that, as opposed to listening to the music. That leaves this little element of surprise and also kind of this fascinating element for me as a person to wait until everything is together. I also have the sensation of unwrapping it, like everybody else who buys the record,' he adds. 'The only thing consumers see before buying a record is some digital squares on iTunes or on the label site or wherever. Then if they like it, they buy it. Then they have the sensation of holding the actual object in their hand, and I also want to have this. I also want to experience the same things.'

He then unpacks the record and puts it on the player, listening to it for the first time, just like everyone else. 'I'm always surprised at how well the visuals fit or at least how much space it has for people to throw their own ideas and draw the lines in between the artwork and the music.' In keeping that element of surprise, he doesn't dismiss all of his advantages on the creative side. 'I'm in this lucky position. I can talk to the artist before, and I have this nice moment where they explain to me in their own words what they want to do, what they want to achieve, and what kind of sound they are aiming for,' he explains. 'At some point while sorting out my working process, I decided, OK, maybe that's a good constraint. Maybe that's a good thing for me as well because then I closely rely on the things the artist tells me and not so much on my inner feelings when I listen to something, because music is also about taste.' He knows this will sound odd to most sleeve designers but Posselt embraces it. 'I have to force myself to be disciplined, but keeping that surprise means that I am so excited when the postman brings the finished album to my door. I still have that kid-in-the-candy-store feeling inside me working on these projects.'

BRING ON THE CHALLENGES

The firm embraces challenging work, as well as occasional mind-melting problem solving on their installation projects. 'When it comes to design, the biggest challenge I face with the artist or the labels is really just the way packaging for music is done these days,' he explains. 'As soon as you reach a certain quantity, everything will be manufactured at a pressing plant. And that brings scheduling issues and also the concern where the printing portion is just something the plant does to also get the record pressing work,' he laments. 'On my side, I care a lot about these details so I have to build up a network of open communication and trust so that we can all get the most out of our resources.'

Living in such a digital world with their other work, Posselt treasures the physical product aspect of his music work. 'I basically have this single dream,' he admits. 'It's quite romantic in a way, but I still kind of like it. In ten or twenty years, or when I'm older and I'm visiting friends or visiting people in their houses, and I see they have a record collection, and I can go through the collection, same as I go through a bookshelf. You take out books. You open it up, you check the cover, check the paper, and you actually see how they age. My wish is just that I can, in twenty or fifty years from now, have the same moment. I will go through somebody else's record collection and see copies of the things I have done but also other people have done, and I can just enjoy the way they have aged over time, hopefully for the better and not for the worse,' he says with a smile. 'In the end, that's what everybody who does this always aims for, to make something that survives the times and is not just something that gets thrown into the trash.'

He also enjoys the personal connection this work affords him. 'Every sleeve I work on is connected to people I know, so it's not an email and some blurry, ghostly face on some Skype channel. It's always a real person. I sit next to them. We have a glass of wine. We talk,' he says. 'I'm in this lucky position from starting this quite early with musicians and artists; they were also smaller at that time. Before anything else, we became friends. Now we speak a common artistic language, we have the same goals in mind and we know each other. Sometimes we don't even have to talk so much about it, and it just falls into place so naturally that it's even kind of weird that it just happens like this. I consider myself incredibly lucky.'

Deep into his graphic design studies Posselt began to worry that everything he was seeing in books was looking the same. He knew he needed outside influences, and this was when he began experimenting with electronics. He fell in love with the poster work of Otto Baumberger, following how his work evolved as it became more commercial, while staying true to his typographic sensibilities. At the same time, he became fascinated with the work of Carsten Nicolai, who bridges design and art and technology in fascinating ways. 'His work is pretty German, which I also somehow like,' he adds. 'Maybe I'm more German than I think sometimes,' he laughs. Somewhere in that broad and sophisticated mix is the perspective with which Posselt approaches his work on record sleeves.

Sometimes the music industry can make all of us crazy, but Posselt admits that he likes it all. 'I also like to argue about things,' he says. 'I like to argue about the big things. I like to argue about the little things. The paper I picked or the typeface I picked. I like to work with artists and labels that will argue about these things, because we all care so much. With music, the most important thing is to care.'

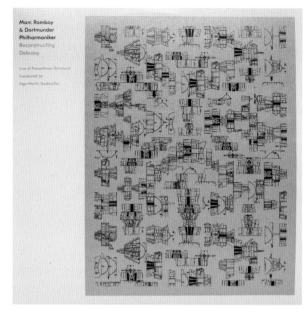

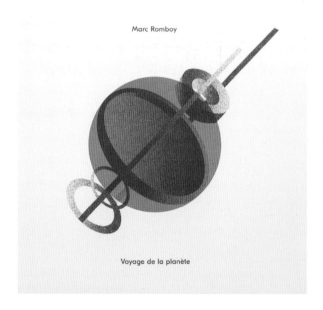

(Clockwise from top left) **TITLE:** Ben Lukas Boysen, *Spells*; **TITLE:** Marc Romboy, *Reconstructing Debussy*
TITLE: Marc Romboy, *Voyage De La Planète*; **TITLE:** Woodkid and Nils Frahm, *Ellis*

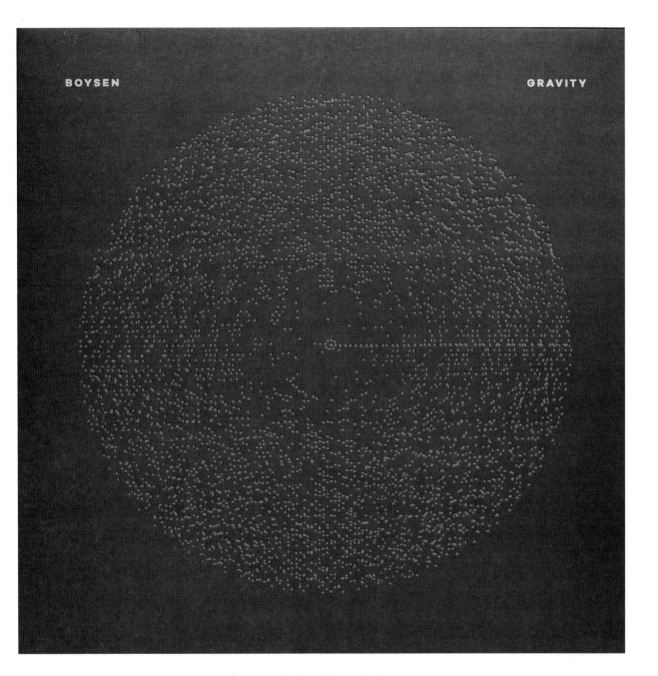

TITLE: Ben Lukas Boysen, *Gravity*

(Top) TITLE: Ólafur Arnalds and Nils Frahm, *Life Story Love And Glory*; (Middle) TITLE: Ólafur Arnalds and Nils Frahm, *Loon*
(Bottom) TITLE: Ólafur Arnalds and Nils Frahm, *Stare*

(Top) TITLE: Kiasmos, *s/t*; (Middle) TITLE: Kiasmos, *Thrown*
(Bottom) TITLE: Kiasmos, *Swept*

(Above and opposite) **TITLE:** Nonkeen, *Oddments Of The Gamble*

»So second chance became a band m
A brief introduction to the oddments of th

en shaped by the mysterious convergence of coincidence
n of as yet unheard sounds. After all, ever since Frederic
wald discovered, in their childhood days, a shared passion
e refused to shy away from letting their music respond
process. What started as a playground radio show in
and Frahm experimented with their cassette players
soon developed into a long-lasting friendship, and
s. So those in possession of their debut album
the band's most loyal member, Chance Others.

Sebastian Singwald spent two weeks at
nge with the DDR Staat Athletics team
ling around his neck, and intrigued by
ded with Singwald as they drew

their tape machi
nostalgically, add
grown organically

The Gamble's song
even more primitive
take with a bad one b
record multiple takes
acceptable. These fur
chance became a band
Studio for playback, whe
down to compute, wha

TITLE: Ben Lukas Boysen, *Spells*
CLIENT: Erased Tapes
SIZE: 30.4 x 30.4 cm (12 x 12 in.)
PRINTING PROCESS: Offset
INKS: Black
COMPS PRESENTED: 1
REVISIONS: 3 rounds
APPROVAL: Erased Tapes
INVOLVEMENT WITH FINAL PRINTING: Proof

Continuing the work he started on *Gravity*, Ben Lukas Boysen created a more soothing set of sound collages, creating a lighter and more energetic listen. Posselt responded with a more nocturnal setting of flat black broken up by the darting intersections of white lines, which create dimensional contructions that then seem to disappear before your eyes.

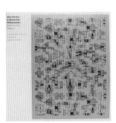

TITLE: Marc Romboy, *Reconstructing Debussy*
CLIENT: Hyperharmonic
SIZE: 30.4 x 30.4 cm (12 x 12 in.)
PRINTING PROCESS: Offset
INKS: CMYK
COMPS PRESENTED: 1
REVISIONS: 1 round
APPROVAL: Hyperharmonic
INVOLVEMENT WITH FINAL PRINTING: Proof

Composer Marc Romboy tackles the task of editing, remixing and reconstructing several pieces by his favourite French composer, performed with the Dortmund Philharmonic Orchestra. Posselt delivers an ode to the orchestral sleeves of the past.

TITLE: Woodkid and Nils Frahm, *Ellis*
CLIENT: Erased Tapes
SIZE: 30.4 x 30.4 cm (12 x 12 in.)
PRINTING PROCESS: Offset
INKS: CMYK
COMPS PRESENTED: 1
REVISIONS: 1 round
APPROVAL: Erased Tapes
INVOLVEMENT WITH FINAL PRINTING: Proof

Ellis is a movie directed by artist JR, starring Robert De Niro, which makes its way through the crumbling hallways of the abandoned Ellis Island hospital complex, where new immigrants to the United States were processed, and which now houses JR's *Unframed* art installation. The score is composed by Woodkid and performed and co-written by Nils Frahm. 'Robert says it all in seventeen minutes. We are not facing a refugee crisis. We are facing a crisis because we do not embrace, we do not sympathize and we cannot give up fear. Art can encourage, so I hope this project will help fight the fear in all of us,' explains Frahm.

TITLE: Marc Romboy, *Voyage De La Planète*
CLIENT: Hyperharmonic
SIZE: 30.4 x 30.4 cm (12 x 12 in.)
PRINTING PROCESS: Offset
INKS: CMYK
COMPS PRESENTED: 2
REVISIONS: 2 rounds
APPROVAL: Hyperharmonic
INVOLVEMENT WITH FINAL PRINTING: Proof

Marc Romboy emerges with an album of what he refers to as 'down-tempo-tronica with a fizzing melodic structure' and Posselt responds with a wonderful collection of images that could double for science textbook illustrations from the fifties.

TITLE: Ben Lukas Boysen, *Gravity*
CLIENT: Erased Tapes
SIZE: 30.4 x 30.4 cm (12 x 12 in.)
PRINTING PROCESS: Offset, emboss
INKS: 2 spot inks
COMPS PRESENTED: 2
REVISIONS: 1 round
APPROVAL: Erased Tapes
INVOLVEMENT WITH FINAL PRINTING: Proof

Using an illustration by Prokop Bartonicek, Posselt beautifully executes a design that plays on the merging of programmed piano pieces with live instruments, combining the controllable technical world and the often unpredictable aspects of live improvisation.

TITLE: Ólafur Arnalds and Nils Frahm, *Life Story Love And Glory*
CLIENT: Erased Tapes
SIZE: 30.4 x 30.4 cm (12 x 12 in.)
PRINTING PROCESS: Offset
INKS: CMYK
COMPS PRESENTED: 1
REVISIONS: 1 round
APPROVAL: Erased Tapes
INVOLVEMENT WITH FINAL PRINTING: Proof

'You can hear in the beginning of *Life Story* how I have already started playing the piano while Nils is still moving microphones around and preparing everything. It was all kept in!' exclaims Ólafur Arnalds. The record documents two long pieces of improvisation from the two musicians. 'We would meet in Reykjavik or Berlin with the intention to share some days off work, hiking, swimming or eating pizza. That is great for a couple days, but after a while we would always end up back in the studio, fiddling with synths or pianos,' adds Nils Frahm.

TITLE: Ólafur Arnalds and Nils Frahm, *Loon*
CLIENT: Erased Tapes
SIZE: 30.4 x 30.4 cm (12 x 12 in.)
PRINTING PROCESS: Offset
INKS: CMYK
COMPS PRESENTED: 2
REVISIONS: 2 rounds
APPROVAL: Erased Tapes
INVOLVEMENT WITH FINAL PRINTING: Proof

'When I was young I was smuggled into Goa parties by my brother. The music played there in the late nineties had a somewhat deep effect on me. *Loon* is almost a blurry memory of these times. In other words, it is what I'd like to remember that music sounded like back then. In fact it sounded probably really cheesy,' explains Nils Frahm. Posselt gives it all a weird effect with the tight black and white pattern that swirls the longer that you look at it.

TITLE: Ólafur Arnalds and Nils Frahm, *Stare*
CLIENT: Erased Tapes
SIZE: 30.4 x 30.4 cm (12 x 12 in.)
PRINTING PROCESS: Offset
INKS: CMYK
COMPS PRESENTED: 1
REVISIONS: 1 round
APPROVAL: Erased Tapes
INVOLVEMENT WITH FINAL PRINTING: Proof

Posselt took the title to heart as he developed a simple yet stunning solution, with the black dot at the heart slowly fading out in a gradient that seems to pulse as you look at it, both mimicking an eye and rewarding the viewer for literally doing as the title asks.

TITLE: Kiasmos, *s/t*
CLIENT: Erased Tapes
SIZE: 30.4 x 30.4 cm (12 x 12 in.)
PRINTING PROCESS: Offset, spot varnish
INKS: CMYK
COMPS PRESENTED: 2
REVISIONS: 2 rounds
APPROVAL: Erased Tapes
INVOLVEMENT WITH FINAL PRINTING: Proof

The combination of Ólafur Arnalds and Janus Rasmussen creates a textured ambient sound that keeps feet on the dance floor. Posselt's treatment of smoky backgrounds mixes with a devotion to icons in his graphic system that is highlighted via simple, gorgeous printing techniques.

TITLE: Kiasmos, *Thrown*
CLIENT: Erased Tapes
SIZE: 30.4 x 30.4 cm (12 x 12 in.)
PRINTING PROCESS: Offset, spot varnish
INKS: CMYK
COMPS PRESENTED: 2
REVISIONS: 2 rounds
APPROVAL: Erased Tapes
INVOLVEMENT WITH FINAL PRINTING: Proof

Thrown highlights the title track, along with the B-side *Wrecked*, after which the duo allow others to then go wild with remixes of both tracks.

TITLE: Kiasmos, *Swept*
CLIENT: Erased Tapes
SIZE: 30.4 x 30.4 cm (12 x 12 in.)
PRINTING PROCESS: Offset, spot varnish
INKS: CMYK
COMPS PRESENTED: 1
REVISIONS: 2 rounds
APPROVAL: Erased Tapes
INVOLVEMENT WITH FINAL PRINTING: Proof

For *Swept*, Kiasmos take their sound into darker regions, while also pushing the percussion in dramatic ways. Posselt highlights that drama with the isolated icon and the drifting dry-ice-like smoke trails catching the flickers of light.

TITLE: Nonkeen, *Oddments Of The Gamble*
CLIENT: R & S Records
SIZE: 30.4 x 30.4 cm (12 x 12 in.)
PRINTING PROCESS: Offset
INKS: CMYK
COMPS PRESENTED: 5
REVISIONS: 3 rounds
APPROVAL: R & S Records
INVOLVEMENT WITH FINAL PRINTING: Proof

Featuring artwork from Frederic Gmeiner, who both works at FELD and performs in Nonkeen, the record packaging has a wild, brightly coloured drunken vibe packaging that quickly sobers up with the images of home life on the interior. The wild juxtaposition of space-age paintings and children idly playing makes sense of the jazzy-rock-improv sound collage clash inside.

ART CHANTRY

50,000,000 GARAGE ROCK SLEEVES CAN'T BE WRONG

Art Chantry quite literally changed the way that many of us think about design. It is as simple as that. He was able to reimagine what many would have dismissed as trash art. The tiny clip art in the ads that lined the back pages of pulp magazines, the throwaway matchbooks, the beat-up old painted signs, comic books, fifties hot-rod artists, and the in-your-face commercial nature of fifties and sixties roadsides were all married with wildly expressive typography and a wicked sense of humour to create many of the most exciting pieces of graphic design of the last forty years. Despite the efforts of a mountain of aesthetic admirers to mimic it, Chantry's work today still looks fresh and cutting-edge. Forever linked with the late eighties/early nineties grunge and garage rock scenes in Seattle, Chantry defined the look with his work at the *Rocket* newspaper and his ever-present gig posters. When he worked with Sub Pop Records during their vital launch period, and designed a barrage of record sleeves and merch for Estrus Records, every music lover worth a damn had a shelf full of his work next to their record player. Not only was his work rock and roll, but Chantry himself was rock and roll – always pushing and pulling and questioning and challenging. He is also a huge proponent of design for the people, unafraid to shine a light on our rougher edges and never putting on some fancy designer airs. Art Chantry was rock and roll. Art Chantry is rock and roll. Art Chantry will always be rock and roll.

Photographer, Rasmus Rasmusen

Where do you see differences in how designers today approach designing for the music industry versus when you started out?
Things have changed dramatically. For starters, in today's market, you don't need a record cover to steal a download, ya know? And even further out there: why hire an expensive professional designer when you can make your own record cover and it looks perfectly fine? Basically, the era of the freelance professional designer (like me) is coming to a close. It's being replaced by either in-house computer programme designers working for a low wage, or you simply design your own record cover. The punk world proved you can DIY. And now the digital internet world has removed all the roadblocks to total DIY. It's the modern world now.

What are your feelings on the current vinyl boom and resurgence of large-format music packaging?
The modern vinyl boom I really believe is a temporary retro fashion fad. Seriously. I wonder if people actually listen to the vinyl records for the music they buy. I do admire the fancy package design being created by the small vinyl indie record companies. But they are all speciality small-run collector's items by intent. I've lived through four or five rebirths of vinyl. They all end as soon as the pressing plants back up and deadlines get seriously missed, killing release schedules and killing cash flow.

How important is it to present music with a physical representation?
I used to think it was essential. Now? I'm not so sure. Record covers have only been around since World War Two. They're a post-war phenomenon. They went away in the late nineties. So, what is that? Fifty years total? Recorded music has been around for over a hundred. So, LP covers have been around a small portion of the record's existence. Now, with absolutely no essential necessity for them as point-of-sale advertising, the whole effort has no point. Today, we sell music with videos, TV commercials, web ads, and a variety of low-budget efforts. The best way to sell records has always been to tour the music. It's always been that way. It will always be that

way. At least now, they all have access to actual products online with downloads. Even the biggest acts in the biz make more money selling tickets than selling records. It's always been that way, except for brief moments in music history.

How has selling music changed for you?
Well, no one hires me any more, for one thing. That's a big change. All the small labels I was associated with have disappeared or become huge corporations with a vast infrastructure. Again, no need to hire an expensive professional. For the money they'd pay me, they could buy an entire computer and all the programmes they need. There's always a line at the door of hipster record companies of people who want to design record covers. Grab one, pay him as little as possible and let him (or her) rip. Done. Cheap. It feels like most of the great record cover designers I knew have stopped entirely. They all do other work that allows them to pay rent and eat. The only record cover work I get now is when an old friend is putting out a 45 for their bar band and wants a cool cover. Granted, these are GREAT bar bands, with famous musicians, but these are only intended to be sold in very small quantities.

Which designers are really exciting you currently in music packaging?
Well, I really love the crazy work Tom Hazelmyer of Amphetamine Reptile has been doing. Tom makes the lino-cut cover art himself (yup, he's a good artist) and then prints them on a letterpress. He presses incredibly wild colour vinyl and everything is custom and unique. Plus, he has access to classic bands, amazing music, old friends, the works. He releases this stuff as inexpensively as possible, sells them for very high collector prices, sells them all (everybody wants those cool Melvins discs) and makes enough to pay for the next project. And it's one of the most incredible series of record covers I've ever seen. Absolutely beautiful stuff. Dumbfounding. Someday, this stuff will be in museums. I'm waiting for somebody to make a book out of the series.

ERIC CARLSON

THE ART OF SURPRISE

Justin Vernon (Bon Iver) was holed up in an Eau Claire, Wisconsin studio when he reached out to designer Eric Timothy Carlson about working together on his upcoming project. Carlson had always been entrenched in music, deep in the Minneapolis scene. He interned with Aesthetic Apparatus, printing gig posters, before working with Michael Cina (featured on pages 84–93). Eventually, having then moved to Brooklyn, he found the Midwest was calling him back. More specifically, an indie rock star, fresh from collaborating with Kanye West, was calling him out to April Base, a studio in rural Wisconsin. Carlson would make several visits, staying for a week or more at a time, as the two worked closely, experimenting and just feeding off each other's creative energy. The result would be one of the most unexpected record designs of 2016.

'Bon Iver and I wanted to work together on something, and this felt like the appropriate project to pursue together,' Eric Carlson explains. 'The vision from the very beginning was that we would create a robust visual system, a tomb of material,' he continues. 'It also provided an opportunity to play with the assumptions of Bon Iver's audience – in the context of a band who has established an aesthetic,' he adds.

Carlson enveloped himself in the way the record was being assembled in the studio, finding easy inspiration in 'the music and its process; the individual/the everybody; secret knowledge; new language,' as he set about developing an intense system of symbols around the material and attaching them to each individual song. 'So much listening, work and time,' he says.

A project like this that differs so much from a traditional packaging assignment and record release brings with it certain complications. 'Releasing complex and idiosyncratic designs through printers and distributors internationally in multiple formats brings about a wide array of challenges,' Carlson laments. 'Things you wouldn't normally worry about, like the print template variations, the distribution limitations and a multitude of just day-to-day basic factors.'

Carlson was brought in not just to do the record sleeve, but to be a member of the larger creative team. 'The album art and design in every format is my work,' he explains, 'as well as the majority of the peripherals (murals, newsprint, print ads, web banners, social skins, tour posters, etc.). I worked with a designer from the label on production and pre-press, collaborated with the print shop on show posters and merch items, and art-directed the website redesign,' he adds. 'Of course, the whole thing is an inherent collaboration with the band. It's all organized through management and the record label, and their work makes the vast endeavour all possible. I collaborated with Aaron Anderson on all the videos. Cameron Wittig and Crystal Quinn did all of the photographs.'

Working on the project, Carlson really loved what he describes as 'the first stages of concept art, discovering what the cover would be, and all of the lyric videos.' The project would take three years from start to completion. He also found that, as he puts it, 'Bon Iver has a wide audience that hosts aesthetic assumptions,' which provided both Carlson and the artist with 'a unique opportunity to do something unexpected.' The full campaign also allowed for the design concept to become more realized and communicated in different ways. 'I think the lyric videos proved to be an important component,' he adds. 'While pushing the print and physical stuff is a focus, the videos were an opportunity to show the work in a contemporary vocabulary.' He also found that the development of so many visuals actually lent itself to the prolific campaign around the album, which he comfirms was part of the intent. 'Each variant format was an opportunity to expand upon the body of work. Very little was template output. We took great care to maximize every opportunity, whether it was a tiny online banner ad or painting the album cover on the side of a building.'

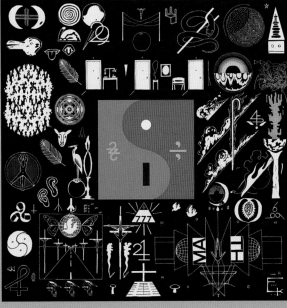

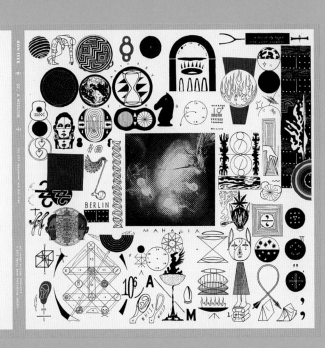

JACOB GRØNBECH JENSEN

DELICATELY BOLD

 Perhaps it is not a surprise to find that designer Jacob Grønbech Jensen creates work that feels sophisticated beyond his years when you learn that he was born in Kathmandu, Nepal, raised in Sweden, schooled at Konstfack University of Arts & Crafts in Stockholm and left soon after to head to France, where he worked for legendary studio M/M, before finding himself based in Copenhagen, Denmark, running his own studio, where his love of printed material shines. It is there that he has developed a tight relationship with the record label Smalltown Supersound, as well as co-publishers Drucksache, putting out gorgeous art books (a recent volume was a poem that consisted solely of the lines of a tennis court, net included, at full scale). It is that willingness to adapt to found graphics, illustrations or photographs, while always maintaining a discerning eye and light touch, that ties his work together, whether it might be bold lines, rough xeroxes, or lovely, delicate, hazy portraits.

Working in the world of experimental electronic music, Jacob has seen the music business shift rapidly at times. 'Things have changed in many, many different ways,' he explains. 'The easy answer is that it has gone more digital, but I think it is more than that. It's mostly a question of new ways of distribution. When I was younger I helped friends with designing 7-inch [18 cm] covers for their hardcore bands, but also covers for CD releases. So in that case it's about economy. But now I find myself listening to music on YouTube because a lot of people share rare records by posting a video with the album art,' he observes. 'Luckily, for me, the designs I do have mostly been for vinyl covers, which I then send in a digital version.' Knowing that a lot of consumers may not experience the full packaging if they are streaming the music does gnaw at him, even if he makes sure that the cover is impactful and works at a small digital scale. 'It is a bit of a shame if I have made something where I think the back is as nice as the front cover,' he laments. 'Or it might be the label on the record that is really lovely. I still prefer vinyl because it is a bigger format, a bigger canvas to work on. And if you're lucky you get more than two sides to work on,' he observes. Still, he knows that it could be worse: 'I really don't like "alternative" formats like USB sticks and those kinds of things – that's just annoying and stupid. Thank God that never really caught on!'

'I do prefer the physical packaging of a record myself and am more than willing to pay more for it,' Jacob adds. He knows that he is not alone. He also finds that even when listening digitally he wants a strong visual to go with the music. 'I just have a visual preference,' he says. 'I guess I browse more easily after images than text. Not that I judge the album by the cover, more that I recognize it faster visually,' he explains.

When asked how he interacts with the marketplace via social media, Jacob shyly confides that he mostly keeps it to comments from friends if occasionally posting something on Instagram. 'Otherwise I really have no idea what people think about my work.' He then rises up and adds, 'I'm just happy to get asked to do it once in a while. I suppose that is really the best reaction, when you get asked for more.'

He also likes that he is not the only one doing work for the label, and has a huge admiration for Kim Hiorthøy. 'I love all of the work for Rune Grammofon and Smalltown Supersound, creating a very impressive body of work.' While pushing himself against his contemporaries, he also finds himself picking up inspiration everywhere he goes. 'When it comes to influences and inspiration, I tend to find random things when googling/researching for something completely different,' he explains. 'The same goes for stuff I find at thrift stores or flea markets. Old books, tourist guides, art books, erotic novels and pretty much anything that catches my eye. But, of course, browsing for records gives a lot of influences and ideas as well.' Jacob also finds that he is constantly sketching, always having ideas at the ready. 'It is surprising to me how many times I will start a project and then see that I already have a strong idea for it sketched out and lying around the office,' he says. Jensen's mind is so active that it is solving problems he has yet to encounter.

JUST A MAN TRYING TO STAY SANE

When working on music packaging, he loves that 'it is much more free. I do what I like and usually just avoid getting stuck – even if that happens, I quickly work out of it,' he explains. It also fills up his record collection. 'It is mostly the freedom in the work, but it is also nice getting free albums,' he acknowledges, before adding, 'and it's nice that a lot of people see my work!' That can be offset by small budgets, which he encounters across most of his culture-based clients, so the balance of the other rewards is needed to keep a level of sanity and feed the other parts of the studio. He has also developed strong client relationships, forming a bond that exists above and beyond the normal freelance project system. 'Lately I have been working a lot with the Norwegian record label Smalltown Supersound,' he explains, 'and they mostly deal with the artists themselves, and that's nice since they also see a bigger picture of the release than I do.' Surprisingly, though, Jacob rarely talks directly with the artists if it's not friends asking.

When it all comes together, he finds a potent mix landing on his desk. 'A great album solves a lot of problems,' he explains. 'You also need timing – just the right record at the right time.' Once he has something wonderful on the musical side he pushes the visual side. 'I really feel like doing the opposite of what is expected is a huge aspect of how I work, as well as always pushing to try new things. Not to mention having fun! Don't get caught thinking in genres too much – create something unique and special! Don't do what everyone is already thinking.'

That push defines his work more than anything: the unexpected.

TITLE: Prins Thomas, *Principe del Norte*

(Clockwise from top left) **TITLE:** Prins Thomas, *Principe del Norte* (back); **TITLE:** Prins Thomas, *Principe del Norte Remixed*
TITLE: Mungolian Jet Set, *A City So Convenient* (back); **TITLE:** Mungolian Jet Set, *A City So Convenient* (front)

(Clockwise from top left) TITLE: Carmen Villain, *Planetarium* (cover); TITLE: Carmen Villain, *Planetarium* (back)
TITLE: Kelly Lee Owens, *Oleic*; TITLE: Biosphere, *Departed Glories*

(Clockwise from top left) TITLE: Lindstrøm, *Windings* (front); TITLE: Lindstrøm, *Windings* (back)
TITLE: Testbild!, *Barrikad* (back); TITLE: Testbild!, *Barrikad* (front)

TITLE: Prins Thomas, *Principe del Norte*
CLIENT: Smalltown Supersound
SIZE: 30.4 x 30.4 cm (12 x 12 in.)
PRINTING PROCESS: Offset
INKS: CMYK
COMPS PRESENTED: 1
REVISIONS: 3 rounds
APPROVAL: Smalltown Supersound
INVOLVEMENT WITH FINAL PRINTING: None

For Thomas's record of relaxed and loose ambient jams, Jensen provided an exceptionally cool sleeve, which fits the cool vibe of the album. The rough execution adds to the little rough edges in the long tracks.

TITLE: Prins Thomas, *Principe del Norte Remix*
CLIENT: Smalltown Supersound
SIZE: 30.4 x 30.4 cm (12 x 12 in.)
PRINTING PROCESS: Offset
INKS: CMYK
COMPS PRESENTED: 1
REVISIONS: 3 rounds
APPROVAL: Smalltown Supersound
INVOLVEMENT WITH FINAL PRINTING: None

'For the remix version of *Principe del Norte*, Thomas made over one-hundred minutes of music, so this was a series of twelve-inch records,' Jensen explains. Referencing the earlier album, with the repeated use of the panther, this time it is subduing a stallion. Jensen inverted the colours to both call to mind and differentiate from the original recordings. The resulting disc manages to stretch the loose tracks further into cool spaciness and a never-ending vibe.

TITLE: Mungolian Jet Set, *A City So Convenient*
CLIENT: Smalltown Supersound
SIZE: 30.4 x 30.4 cm (12 x 12 in.)
PRINTING PROCESS: Offset
INKS: CMYK
COMPS PRESENTED: 5
REVISIONS: 3 rounds
APPROVAL: Smalltown Supersound
INVOLVEMENT WITH FINAL PRINTING: None

For the first EP of fairly straightforward Nordic disco from Knut Sævik and Pål Nyhus, the duo known as Mungolian Jet Set, Jensen roughs up a quirky line drawing of a fragmented and jumbled urban landscape, with everything at opposing angles, creating a funky density and unexpected relationships.

TITLE: Carmen Villain, *Planetarium*
CLIENT: Smalltown Supersound, Su Tissue Records
SIZE: 30.4 x 30.4 cm (12 x 12 in.)
PRINTING PROCESS: Offset
INKS: CMYK
COMPS PRESENTED: 3
REVISIONS: 3 rounds
APPROVAL: Smalltown Supersound
INVOLVEMENT WITH FINAL PRINTING: None

The beautiful hazy photos of flowers are 'the work of photographer Frode Fjerdingstad,' Jensen states. They serve as the wrapping for the EP from half-Norwegian, half-Mexican former fashion model Carmen Maria Hillestad, who records under the name Carmen Villain. The tracks within continue that melancholy haze as Hillestad's celestial vocals glide over icy piano.

TITLE: Kelly Lee Owens, *Oleic*
CLIENT: Smalltown Supersound
SIZE: 30.4 x 30.4 cm (12 x 12 in.)
PRINTING PROCESS: Digital
INKS: Digital
COMPS PRESENTED: 6
REVISIONS: 2 rounds
APPROVAL: Smalltown Supersound
INVOLVEMENT WITH FINAL PRINTING: None

'To launch the Kelly Lee Owens EP we decided on this image,' Jensen explains. The perfect mix of haze and beauty and ethereal strangeness, it would be one of the most striking images in underground music all year.

TITLE: Biosphere, *Departed Glories*
CLIENT: Smalltown Supersound
SIZE: 30.4 x 30.4 cm (12 x 12 in.)
PRINTING PROCESS: Offset
INKS: CMYK
COMPS PRESENTED: 2
REVISIONS: 1 round
APPROVAL: Smalltown Supersound
INVOLVEMENT WITH FINAL PRINTING: None

Geir Jenssen decided to create a concept album around the tale of a medieval queen who had once hidden from her enemies in the forests outside Krakow, Poland. Those forests are beautiful, yet eerie, and certainly full of ghosts. The image used for the cover, by early 20th-century photographer Sergey Prokudin-Gorsky, perfectly captures that feeling.

TITLE: Lindstrøm, *Windings*
CLIENT: Smalltown Supersound
SIZE: 30.4 x 30.4 cm (12 x 12 in.)
PRINTING PROCESS: Offset
INKS: CMYK
COMPS PRESENTED: 5
REVISIONS: 3 rounds
APPROVAL: Smalltown Supersound
INVOLVEMENT WITH FINAL PRINTING: None

One of the leading lights in space disco, Lindstrøm creates music that is constantly reaching skyward. As he was making this record he imparted that 'I wanted to go back to the fun part of making music,' and Lindstrøm certainly succeeded. Jensen's design keeps the vibe going with his playful intermingling shapes and textures.

TITLE: Testbild!, *Barrikad*
CLIENT: Kalligrammofon
SIZE: 30.4 x 30.4 cm (12 x 12 in.)
PRINTING PROCESS: Offset
INKS: CMYK
COMPS PRESENTED: 2
REVISIONS: 4 rounds
APPROVAL: Kalligrammofon
INVOLVEMENT WITH FINAL PRINTING: None

'I was working in collaboration with Rikard Heberling for this project,' Jensen says. The duo also enlisted Cecilia Hultman to create a poster for the packaging. This record for the Swedish group was built primarily around acoustic instruments, resulting in a dreamy feel, as if sitting under the clouds as they part, which the design perfectly captures.

OLIVER HIBERT

DON'T LOOK STRAIGHT INTO THE SUN

 Residing in the land of grizzled retirees, under an unrelenting sun, seems an odd place for someone like Oliver Hibert. His work is so bold and magical, as well as having a sly sophistication behind the simple shapes, that you might find yourself struggling to reconcile a mental picture of him working through the night in some rusted-out urban loft. But that sunshine seeps into his work in the intensity of his colour choices, and the open terrain seems better suited to the mind-altering acid dreams that he is so adept at getting down on canvas. When you hear Oliver describe his home as a place where he is surrounded by cacti and a thousand peacocks, it all starts to make a little more sense. The working-through-the-night scenario is on the nose, though, as Hibert has been very busy throughout his young career. Showing his paintings in galleries at just sixteen, his work was soon across TV via music videos by eighteen. Museums across the world embraced him at the same time as Corporate America, and his psychedelic vision spread like wildfire. In a funny way, Hibert arrived at the music industry in the opposite manner to most designers. He didn't work his way up on small releases, using them as a springboard to bigger artists and eventually opportunities for large paydays outside the industry. He was already established by the time artists came asking for his special brand of pixie dust to be sprinkled on their projects, so that afforded him the ability to work with artists he both enjoys and admires. As you will see, Oliver and music are the perfect pairing.

'I personally haven't been in the album cover industry for too long,' Hibert explains, 'but it seems nowadays that packaging, especially vinyl releases, is a more special or nostalgic artform – it's a physical copy of something in a world full of digital puffy clouds that exist in invisible dimensions, and I think people really have been starting to miss holding things in their hands and smelling the yummy toxic plastic packaging fumes when opening something physical and brand new.' Considering this everything-old-is-new mindset, he is quick to add that 'new technologies allow us to explore old things in new ways, so really I think everything can come back in its own way, while still evolving into newer, cooler things.' It is an interesting parallel to Hibert's own fresh take on sixties psychedelia and its mix of sexual liberation and mind-altering drug use.

While having a distinctive affinity for physical products, he does get asked to work strictly digital at times. 'I have done some digital-only work, and from my experience the approach changes in the way that there is obviously much less to think about and/or do,' he explains. 'I like doing physical designing more because of all the nooks and crannies to think about: the spine, the record sticker, the inside cover, booklets, etc. As far as the actual art, it doesn't change anything with my approach but the physical presentation is quite different. Usually digital isn't more than just a square static single image. And that's it. Done. Kinda funny how even digital releases' covers are still square artworks, but I guess that is music's shape now forever thanks to the power of vinyl records. Good old square, and I'm cool with that,' he laughs.

That packaging is something Hibert cherishes and sees massive value in. 'I think there should be museums just full of physical album covers and packaging,' he exclaims. 'There probably already is such a place somewhere in the world. And you or I can walk into a record store and buy that twelve-inch [30 cm] piece of art and hang it on the wall or hold it in our hands and stare at it while we listen to the music it represents. That's a neat thing.' The wide-eyed enthusiasm he has for getting his hands on a record sleeve is the same enthusiasm that saturates the work he does for others. It is in every corner of his images and in every bend of his type.

GOTTA LOOK SHARP

One of the major differences between Hibert and psychedelic artists of the past is social media. His videos of his paintings, combined with posting-up sketches, reveal a lot about his work process, and you see a surprisingly old-school approach built upon his graphic drawing style. Interacting with his audience can be a rush while in the middle of a project, but once it is finished, there is always the next task waiting. 'It's always nice to hear when someone discovers that you did a certain album cover, or when you randomly see it online or in real life or at stores, but I really don't follow up with them intentionally on threads or anything. I pretty much have moved on to many other things by the time the art is finished and released. Gotta keep going!' he adds.

Hibert is not shy in detailing his album art heroes. 'Hands down, Martin Sharp,' he says. 'Sharp is the album art cover god in my world.' It is no surprise that detailed illustrations wrapped around Cream records inspired him, along with Sharp's ability to create little worlds for the figures in his artwork. You can trace a straight line from Sharp to Hibert and have a huge smile on your face the entire way. He also is keen to let life experience colour his work. There is definitely a personal viewpoint to Hibert's work, which is a mix of, in no particular order; art, music, life, sex, death, the female form, colour, magic, mystery, chaos, simplicity, beauty, drugs, psychedelia, time, fear and ugliness.

EYEHOLES AND EARHOLES

One of the main things Hibert loves about album design, in comparison to his flat art, is the dimensional aspect. 'What differs normally would be that it's a 3D object,' he says. 'So that entails thinking of how something looks at a glance, or from the side, or when opened up versus just something totally flat and static with no sides or crevices. So there's a lot more that goes into it, which I like.' He loves it even more when he is doing it for a band that he really loves. 'You can't beat that!' he says.

Working directly with those artists can be the key to a project going as well as it could. 'That is how I really prefer it, straight from the source, ya know?' he adds. 'I think that helps me get a quicker and more precise feel of what really might need to happen.' Once he has that connection, he is always striving to create 'something that represents the music or band well. It can be simple or loud, pretty or ugly. To me that doesn't matter as much as what and how the art can relate to the sounds or work with the sounds; or complement the sound as you look at the art with your eyeholes whilst hearing the sounds inside of your earholes.'

TITLE: The Flaming Lips, *With A Little Help From My Fwends*

(Clockwise from top left) **TITLE:** The Flaming Lips, *With A Little Help From My Fwends*; **TITLE:** The Flaming Lips, *Good Vibrations*
TITLE: House Ghosts, *s/t*; **TITLE:** The Flaming Lips and Tame Impala, *Peace And Paranoia Tour*

TITLE: Morgan Delt, *Phase Zero*

(Top) TITLE: Wooden Shjips, *Back To Land*
(Bottom, left) TITLE: Temples/Jagwar Ma, *Shelter Song/Man I Need*; (Bottom, right) TITLE: King Gizzard & The Lizard Wizard, *Head On/Pill*

TITLE: The Flaming Lips, *With A Little Help From My Fwends*
CLIENT: The Flaming Lips
SIZE: 30.4 x 30.4 cm (12 x 12 in.)
PRINTING PROCESS: Offset
INKS: CMYK
COMPS PRESENTED: 1
REVISIONS: 1 round
APPROVAL: Wayne Coyne
INVOLVEMENT WITH FINAL PRINTING: None

'This cover is one of my favourites,' explains Hibert. 'It was a little last-minute, but that can often have the best results, and that is life in the Flaming Lips universe,' he smiles. 'Wayne Coyne, of the Lips, knew that he liked one of the illustrations I had done for my tarot card deck, so I got to work redrawing it to fit the album.' The album is, in fact, an all-star cast of musicians covering track-by-track The Beatles' *Sgt. Pepper's Lonely Hearts Club Band*, to benefit the Bella Foundation.

TITLE: The Flaming Lips, *Good Vibrations*
CLIENT: The Flaming Lips
SIZE: 30.4 x 30.4 cm (12 x 12 in.)
PRINTING PROCESS: Offset
INKS: CMYK
COMPS PRESENTED: 1
REVISIONS: 1 round
APPROVAL: Wayne Coyne
INVOLVEMENT WITH FINAL PRINTING: None

Building off the artwork he had made for The Flaming Lips' Austin PsychFest appearance, Hibert says he 'rebuilt everything to work in this weird half-cover in a clear sleeve. That was vital to show people what the disc looked like.' The release itself was a limited edition at the festival and Hibert loved seeing the reaction to it. 'The record itself is really cool,' he adds, 'because it is hard plastic and not vinyl. It was hand-cut using this wild machine. See all of those circles and holes?' he asks. 'That is because it has three separate songs with three separate grooves. It literally is the weirdest and coolest release ever.'

TITLE: The Flaming Lips/Tame Impala, *Peace And Paranoia Tour*
CLIENT: The Flaming Lips
SIZE: 30.4 x 30.4 cm (12 x 12 in.)
PRINTING PROCESS: Offset
INKS: CMYK
COMPS PRESENTED: 1
REVISIONS: 1 round
APPROVAL: Wayne Coyne
INVOLVEMENT WITH FINAL PRINTING: None

'Wayne Coyne had his eye on a painting I had done for quite some time, always looking for a chance to fit it into one of the Flaming Lips projects,' Hibert explains. With this split single for their tour with Tame Impala, he finally had the perfect opportunity. 'The original image had a lot of drips, and then George Salisbury at Delo Creative, another member of the Lips creative team, added in even more before we were all happy with the results.'

TITLE: House Ghosts, *s/t*
CLIENT: House Ghosts
SIZE: 30.4 x 30.4 cm (12 x 12 in.)
PRINTING PROCESS: Digital
INKS: Digital
COMPS PRESENTED: 1
REVISIONS: 1 round
APPROVAL: House Ghosts
INVOLVEMENT WITH FINAL PRINTING: N/A

Sometimes the best thing to do is just to let Hibert completely loose. 'This project was a blast,' he explains, 'because I had total free rein to come up with whatever I wanted. After blasting the music, this was what instantly fell out of my head and onto the page,' he says.

TITLE: Morgan Delt, *Phase Zero*
CLIENT: Sub Pop Records
SIZE: 30.4 x 30.4 cm (12 x 12 in.)
PRINTING PROCESS: Offset
INKS: CMYK
COMPS PRESENTED: 3
REVISIONS: 2 rounds
APPROVAL: Morgan Delt, Sub Pop Records
INVOLVEMENT WITH FINAL PRINTING: None

'For this cover, Morgan was actually really specific about the feel and imagery he wanted, and we spent a lot of time working on the colours,' explains Hibert. 'I really enjoyed the back and forth and collaboration on that end, and the final vibe with the gold texture in the background turned out really amazing.'

TITLE: Wooden Shjips, *Back To Land*
CLIENT: Thrill Jockey
SIZE: 30.4 x 30.4 cm (12 x 12 in.)
PRINTING PROCESS: Offset
INKS: CMYK
COMPS PRESENTED: 1
REVISIONS: 3 rounds
APPROVAL: Ripley Johnson, Thrill Jockey
INVOLVEMENT WITH FINAL PRINTING: None

'This is far and away the most involved record sleeve I have ever worked on,' Hibert admits. 'I had a lot of fun with the kind of overloaded look of everything, designing into every little corner with tons of busy action,' he adds. 'We then had to figure out how to work everything into the die-cut slip case and make sure that all of the holes lined up as needed.'

TITLE: King Gizzard & The Lizard Wizard, *Head On/Pill*
CLIENT: Heavenly Recordings
SIZE: 30.4 x 30.4 cm (12 x 12 in.)
PRINTING PROCESS: Offset
INKS: CMYK
COMPS PRESENTED: 3
REVISIONS: 2 rounds
APPROVAL: Heavenly Recordings
INVOLVEMENT WITH FINAL PRINTING: None

TITLE: Temples/Jagwar Ma, *Shelter Song/Man I Need*
CLIENT: Heavenly Recordings
SIZE: 30.4 x 30.4 cm (12 x 12 in.)
PRINTING PROCESS: Offset
INKS: CMYK
COMPS PRESENTED: 3
REVISIONS: 2 rounds
APPROVAL: Heavenly Recordings
INVOLVEMENT WITH FINAL PRINTING: None

'This was a pretty crazy job, as there is no cover,' says Hibert with a smile. For the two Record Store Day exclusive releases featuring Temples, Jagwar Ma and King Gizzard & The Lizard Wizard, Heavenly had Hibert design the picture discs. 'I had created an entire series of swirl paintings that they had seen,' he explains. 'That was how they wanted the disc art, so I redesigned them for more clarity and as more of a graphic, with the end result being this really trippy and hypnotic experience once you put it on a turntable and get it spinning,' he adds.

MARIO HUGO

ALWAYS THE ARTIST

 Few people manage to straddle the roles of artist, designer, creative director, curator and typographer quite like Mario Hugo. He leaves a unique imprint on everything that he touches, whether it is detailed little drawings, or wild type explorations, or complicated constructions mixed with beauty and elegance. He is unafraid to follow his inspirations, whether that means having to hand-stitch type into fabric, collect seemingly unrelated objects and bring them together with subtle ease and a coat of white paint, cover Rihanna in quickly scrawled letterforms or go completely minimal for the launching of Lorde's debut. When you see his turning of classic shapes and structures on their sides for Chance The Rapper, you know it can only come from Hugo. The eldest child of Argentine parents, he soon had the art world in mind, bringing him to shorten his name from Mario Hugo Gonzàlez to just Mario Hugo, so as to avoid confusion with the painter of the same name. His fine art studies at Boston College would lead to a defining trip to Sydney, Australia. Upon returning, he moved to New York's Pratt Instititue to study art direction, and has quickly established Hugo & Marie, the studio he shares with his wife, as a haven for creative clients in both music and high fashion.

More than most, over the years Hugo has tackled packaging design assignments from wildly different clients. 'I've worked with acts of really varying sizes,' he explains, 'and, thankfully, the musicians I work with tend to love vinyl. If anything, my packaging work has now grown into longer engagements and a more holistic creative strategy with those artists.'

When he is starting a new project Hugo just listens to the music on repeat, almost as a mantra, and starts 'hammering away', as he puts it. He then starts to circle what that music looks like to him. 'Really, the image and expression is more important to me than the physical packaging,' he admits. Once he has that captured, he can then see how it plays out across the physical wrapping for the record.

That's not to say that the packaging is not important to him. Far from it! It's just the next step in the process. 'The only thing I can tell you is I'm a romantic.' Hugo smiles. 'I really love the physicality of vinyl. I think there is something just beautifully humanistic about the last sixty, seventy years of artists translating how music looks into the same square, naive, paper format.' Still, he adds that 'the vast majority of the music I consume is digital, and I am just as excited about stumbling on an amazingly talented musician with a hundred Soundcloud followers, or an old Garage Band site. The archaeology of music discovery is what has the most value for me.'

SAVILLE & HOBBES

Being a part of that history he outlined means nestling next to the past masters he admires. 'Too many people to name!' he laughs. 'I wouldn't do what I do without having been exposed to Peter Saville, Trevor Jackson, Barney Bubbles, Non-Format, and many, many others.' Hugo also finds that his work is 'influenced by so much – film in particular. Ferdinand Hodler is my favourite painter. Calvin and Hobbes changed my life as a kid. An aunt I was very close to died when I was eleven or twelve – she left three kids behind, and that event really left its mark on my life. Everything is some form of influence.'

Hugo also remains an inquisitive, as well as a tactile searcher. He is still very much the man who was profiled in *Print* magazine in his early days rummaging through the used bookstores of New York City for weathered blank end pages that he would use as the base of his illustrations. At the time he was quoted as saying, 'I'm inspired by a lot of cultural references, but none of them are recent.' That net has widened in the years that followed, but the sentiment remains very much the same.

It is that particular blend of influences that finds Hugo wondering. 'I don't know that a traditional design problem really needs to be solved,' he proposes. 'I think of the process more like a writer's adaptation or interpretation.' Especially when he is tackling a music project. 'Music work is completely subjective,' he explains. 'I really take pride in developing a rapport with my clients and cracking an emotional code. I also have some kind of love of psychotic deadlines and moving targets,' he laughs.

THE PUREST IDEAS

That emotional connection can leave the designer more exposed than they might be when working for a different kind of client. 'It can be painful to watch beautiful ideas get brushed aside, and it definitely happens,' he laments. 'I have also worked with a few acts that are too worried about trends, or worrying too much about the visual language of the day,' he adds. As the stakes get higher, breaking through that mindset can be both more difficult and more rewarding. 'I usually work with the artist alongside the label, sometimes the other way around. That process doesn't influence my work much, though it's best to have direct access to the musician,' he adds.

The constant struggle is not to get caught up in all of the trends but to break through with an image that 'has to be a pitch-perfect representation of the music – it should communicate with the perfect tone, inflection and vernacular,' he adds. 'The best sleeves aren't really aesthetic – they aren't works of fashion. They are about stumbling on an idea nobody's had, and stripping away aesthetic layers until there is nothing left to remove. The purest ideas make the most perfect sleeves. These are the rarest examples.'

TITLE: Rihanna, *Unapologetic*

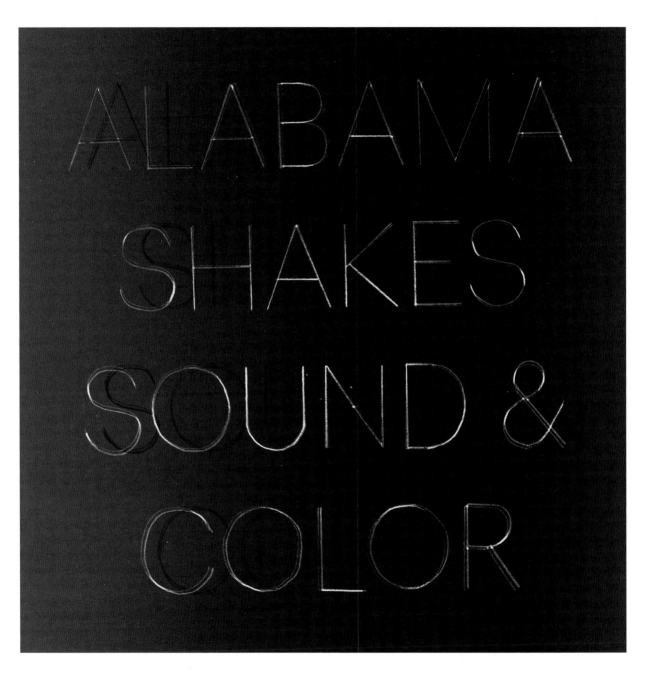

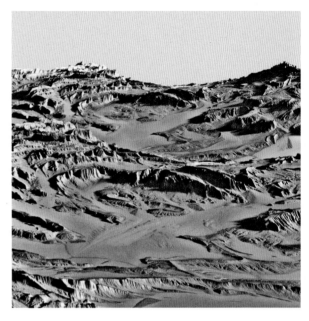
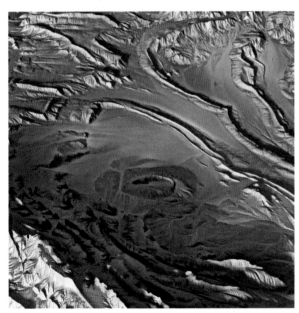

TITLE: Bartellow, *Panokorama* (front, back and inner sleeve)

(Clockwise from top left) TITLE: Shocks, *I-!V*; TITLE: Philopoemen, *s/t*
TITLE: 33.10.3402, *Mecanica*; TITLE: Lorde, *Pure Heroine*

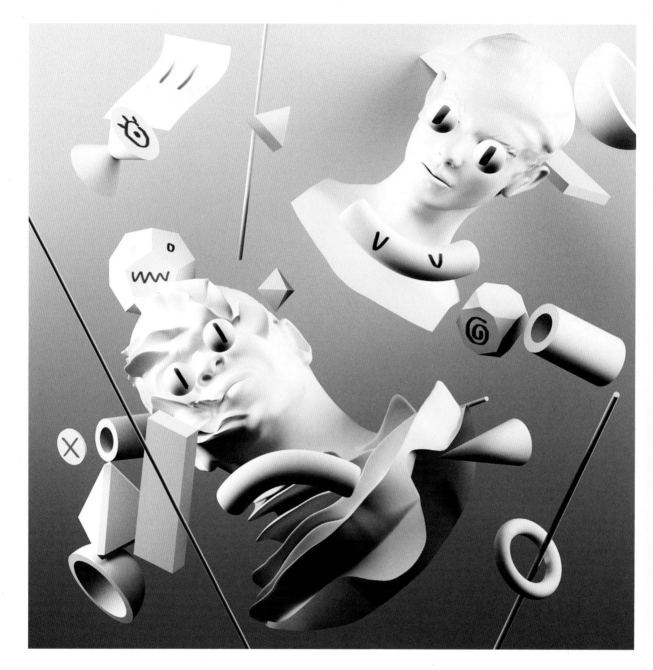

TITLE: Chance The Rapper x Nosaj Thing, *Paranoia*

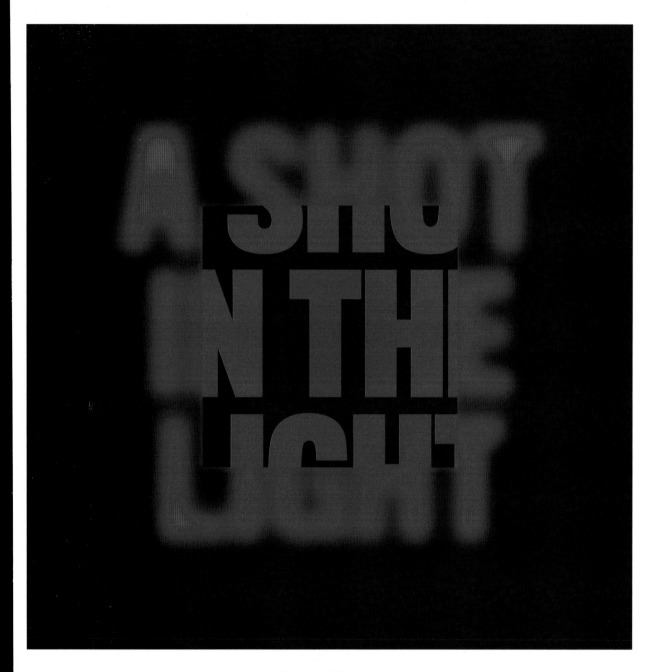

TITLE: Moscoman, *A Shot In The Light*

TITLE: Rihanna, *Unapologetic*
CLIENT: Def Jam
SIZE: 30.4 x 30.4 cm (12 x 12 in.)
PRINTING PROCESS: Offset
INKS: CMYK
COMPS PRESENTED: 30
REVISIONS: 10 rounds
APPROVAL: Def Jam
INVOLVEMENT WITH FINAL PRINTING: None

'This final Rihanna sleeve for her *Unapologetic* release isn't my favourite of the many we presented,' Hugo admits. 'That said, I do love all the development work and sketches for this record. I received thousands of photographs and ended up mixing chemical treatments with transfer drawings to make all the diverse photographs congeal, and the handwriting is my wife's. It was an insane, but rewarding, process,' he adds. 'We also had amazing photography by Michael Muller and Melissa Forde.'

TITLE: Alabama Shakes, *Sound & Color*
CLIENT: ATO Records
SIZE: 30.4 x 30.4 cm (12 x 12 in.)
PRINTING PROCESS: Offset
INKS: CMYK
COMPS PRESENTED: 7
REVISIONS: 3 rounds
APPROVAL: ATO Records
INVOLVEMENT WITH FINAL PRINTING: None

'*Sound & Color* is an amazing record, so the inspiration for this sleeve came quickly,' Hugo explains. 'The band sent the music well in advance of the release, so I got to live with it for a while.' He found that he wanted to make a candy box, 'austere and enigmatic on the outside – warm though, not cold – and rich and inviting on the inside.' The final sleeve has 'something celestial about it, and though we went a couple rounds, I think this concept was among the first batch,' he adds. 'I also had assistance by Dan Hennessy, an intern at Hugo & Marie.'

TITLE: Bartellow, *Panokorama*
CLIENT: ESP Institute
SIZE: 30.4 x 30.4 cm (12 x 12 in.)
PRINTING PROCESS: Offset
INKS: CMYK
COMPS PRESENTED: 5
REVISIONS: 3 rounds
APPROVAL: ESP Institute
INVOLVEMENT WITH FINAL PRINTING: None

Hugo provides 'art and direction for an esoteric indie electronica label called ESP Institute,' he explains. 'The label was started by Andrew Hogge back in 2008 or so, and this sleeve was created in collaboration with my friend and frequent creative partner, Sam Mason. Psychedelic landscapes and a lack of gravity fill the entire package.'

TITLE: Shocks, *I-!V*
CLIENT: ESP Institute
SIZE: 30.4 x 30.4 cm (12 x 12 in.)
PRINTING PROCESS: Offset
INKS: CMYK
COMPS PRESENTED: 1
REVISIONS: 2 rounds
APPROVAL: ESP Institute
INVOLVEMENT WITH FINAL PRINTING: None

'I've always been really interested in playing with light and shadow,' Hugo confesses. 'I love surface relief, and I like to give covers a bit of volume and dimension. Supported by Fie Lindholm, a former design intern at Hugo & Marie, we built a cover that plays with your eyes a little if you look at it long enough.'

TITLE: Philopoemen, *s/t*
CLIENT: ESP Institute
SIZE: 30.4 x 30.4 cm (12 x 12 in.)
PRINTING PROCESS: Offset
INKS: CMYK
COMPS PRESENTED: 1
REVISIONS: None
APPROVAL: ESP Institute
INVOLVEMENT WITH FINAL PRINTING: None

'This was an early stab at record packaging for me,' Hugo explains. 'Though this typography is the more reduced side, the entire package has a weird mix of elements that I think feels somewhere between baroque and psychedelic.'

TITLE: 33.10.3402, *Mecanica*
CLIENT: ESP Institute
SIZE: 30.4 x 30.4 cm (12 x 12 in.)
PRINTING PROCESS: Offset
INKS: CMYK
COMPS PRESENTED: 5
REVISIONS: 2 rounds
APPROVAL: ESP Institute
INVOLVEMENT WITH FINAL PRINTING: None

'This album is a bit darker and has a grit,' adds Hugo. Underscoring that feeling, 'the sleeve treats typography as an image, and as kind of a visualization or musical code.'

TITLE: Lorde, *Pure Heroine*
CLIENT: Universal
SIZE: 30.4 x 30.4 cm (12 x 12 in.)
PRINTING PROCESS: Offset
INKS: CMYK
COMPS PRESENTED: 17
REVISIONS: 10 rounds
APPROVAL: Lorde
INVOLVEMENT WITH FINAL PRINTING: None

'I was approached about Lorde's debut album, and upon first listen it was clear the record would be everywhere,' Hugo explains. Aware of the weight involved in working on what was sure to be a massive album, Hugo was happy to find that 'Lorde was amazing to work with and really involved in the process. We wanted to abandon photography, set some type with gravitas, and photocopy everything. It ended up being among my most reduced and enigmatic sleeves, and the excellent title does the lifting.'

TITLE: Chance The Rapper x Nosaj Thing, *Paranoia*
CLIENT: ESP Institute
SIZE: 30.4 x 30.4 cm (12 x 12 in.)
PRINTING PROCESS: Offset
INKS: CMYK
COMPS PRESENTED: 1
REVISIONS: None
APPROVAL: ESP Institute
INVOLVEMENT WITH FINAL PRINTING: None

'I wasn't familiar with Chance the Rapper or Nosaj Thing before Yours Truly got in touch about me creating art for this single, and now they are staple listens around the office,' Hugo is happy to add. 'I was intrigued by the title. I wanted to carve representations of the collaborating musicians, and then I wanted to hide threatening, naive, cartoon faces throughout. It's a weird one, but I kind of love it,' he admits.

TITLE: Moscoman, *A Shot In The Light*
CLIENT: ESP Institute
SIZE: 30.4 x 30.4 cm (12 x 12 in.)
PRINTING PROCESS: Offset
INKS: CMYK
COMPS PRESENTED: 8
REVISIONS: 5 rounds
APPROVAL: ESP Institute
INVOLVEMENT WITH FINAL PRINTING: None

'This was a record with fantastic song titles,' Hugo explains, the anticipation clear in his voice. 'They each build such a rich visual world without much additional work, and I wanted to celebrate them – my contribution was setting some type and building these frosted suggestions of geometry, panelling, rooms, all placed atop titles.'

HVASS&HANNIBAL

PAIRED TO PERFECTION

 There is a unique magic that is formed when two distinct, yet sympathetic voices intertwine, raising the combined effort to something far more than the sum of its parts. The final result can be something so beautiful that it brings a tear to your eye. Such is the wonderful partnership between designers and illustrators Nan Na Hvass and Sofie Hannibal. Their collaborative mode of working has brought a fresh sensibility as to the use of imagery and colour, all of it with a playful nature and the inherent joy of exploration. The two met while studying at the Royal Academy of Fine Arts in Copenhagen, finding that they shared many interests and influences. A quick bond would blossom into the 2006 formation of their studio, and the design and illustration world, and an international collection of clients, would soon be the better for it. Over more than a decade the dynamic duo have applied their skills to everything from woodworking to painting to digital solutions, always bringing a unique voice that could only come from both Hvass&Hannibal.

Nan Na and Sofie delight in somewhat surreal imagery, infusing everything they touch with that quality. For a twosome that started out working by handing a project back and forth until completion (they have since learnt to work alone when needed, as the studio and their lives have become busier) it is stunning how consistently that comes across, and how they manage to apply it differently to so many different clients. The area where this is most apparent is in their incredible music packaging. That industry continues to change and keep them on their toes. 'Packaging probably doesn't have quite the same importance for an album as when we started, when the CD was still around,' ponders Hvass. 'The physical packaging really has to work as a thumbnail now, which is such a different format from a vinyl cover, and this has certainly affected the design process for the physical packaging for us.' Now, when they have a concept that involves a big photoshoot and construction of objects and sets, they have to be certain that it will play out equally well in tiny digital applications, as well as in the hands of the consumer in a retail environment. It is a huge complication for a firm that loves to linger over the details, but they are clearly up to the challenge.

'I think the packaging defintely adds value to the product, even if most people consume music digitally,' adds Hvass. 'It becomes a part of the story about the album as a whole, and people who are interested in these things find out, either through the packaging, or other ways that we are able to tell the story. There are dedicated fans who collect vinyl and love to see the little details, as well as people who find an artist based on the feeling they get from our artwork, and we love creating these for both audiences.'

In a funny way, they are often too caught up in current work to even know how the earlier projects are doing with fans and the marketplace. 'Generally, we are just on to new projects and too busy to really follow up in that sense,' Hvass laments. 'However, sometimes, being on tour with some of the bands we've worked with, it is very nice to hear direct feedback on the artwork from people buying merchandise at the performances.'

SURE AND REAL

While the pair have clearly created a voice that is all their own, a debt to those who brought a surrealistic vantage point to photographic album covers can be seen throughout their work. Everyone drinking from that fountain acknowledges Hipgnosis, and Hvass&Hannibal are no different. Possibly even closer to home is a love of French master Jean-Paul Goude and his more playful way of working. They combine that with combing through fine art and Danish folklore to form

something new and exciting. It is that mindset that they bring to the 'absurd amount of times that we will listen to an album on repeat when we are working with an artist,' laughs Hvass.

Hvass&Hannibal take that intense listening experience and often see it inspire the creation of something new that needs to be created – objects that are grounded in some fragment of reality, but also in their own way from another world. Once they have these concepts, they are both willing, and talented enough, to find a way to bring them to life. It may be a detailed collection of graphic patterns, or whimsical illustrations dotted with layer upon layer of revelations. It can also be a photoshoot where they physically build and manipulate the props. This can be in their studio or it may require a journey deep into the Danish woodland, or to a deserted area deep in the city. The sole constant is their willingness to do whatever it takes to see their concept through and deliver it with maximum impact and artistic flair.

Compared to their more commercial assignments, working with musical artists affords them something special that they will always loop back to. 'Working for other artists,' Hvass explains, 'rather than, say, for a commercial or corporate client, is just something special. The conversations about where to take the project are often so very different, and so much more magical and free.'

That process of working directly with the artist means that they can have a very close relationship and an intense process. Hvass also feels 'the pressure it puts on you to know that this piece of artwork is going to stick to that album forever!' Success can come with 'giving it all the love and time that you can, and collaborating closely with the musicians … I think if the musician feels that the artwork is in touch with the music and who they want to be, and what they want to tell the world, then the artwork will always be a successful extension of the music/musician. It is something that can be so subjective as to what imagery would work with what music, and you can't really measure its success or accuracy in that sense, but I feel if the artist is pleased then it's a success,' she says. 'It's actually super hard to "dress" a product that is so personal to someone else,' she adds. 'Normally, we are designing to add identity, but when the subject is music and already has its own clear artistic voice, we have to support that and make it clear, and adding too much identity would seem calculating. It's a fine balance,' she admits.

'Ah, wait,' Hvass adds, 'a much more fun answer as to what makes a project a success is when we've heard people say to us: I only bought this album for the cover!'

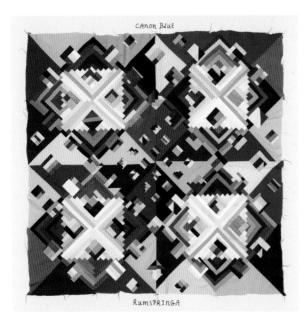

TITLE: Canon Blue, *Rumspringa*

(Clockwise from top left) TITLE: Efterklang, *Magic Chairs* (front); TITLE: Efterklang, *Magic Chairs* (back)
TITLE: Turboweekend, *Shadow Sounds*; TITLE: Turboweekend, *Ghost Of A Chance*

TITLE: Turboweekend, *Bound*

(Top) **TITLE**: Clogs, *The Creatures In The Garden Of Lady Walton*
(Bottom) **TITLE**: Clogs, *Veil Waltz*

TITLE: Efterklang, *Parades* (cover and artwork)

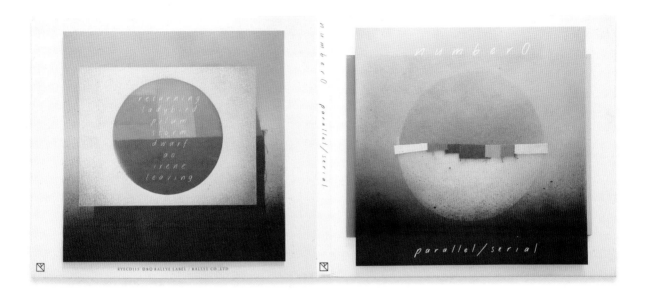

(Above) **TITLE:** Number0, *Parallel/Serial*
(Left) **TITLE:** Efterklang/Fundal, *Leaves: The Colour Of Falling*

TITLE: Canon Blue, *Rumspringa*
CLIENT: Rumraket/Temporary Residence
SIZE: 30.4 x 30.4 cm (12 x 12 in.)
PRINTING PROCESS: Offset
INKS: CMYK
COMPS PRESENTED: 12
REVISIONS: 5 rounds
APPROVAL: Canon Blue
INVOLVEMENT WITH FINAL PRINTING: None

One of the things that set Hvass&Hannibal apart is the ends they will go to in creating their designs, even if it means breaking out a sewing machine. 'Because of the [Amish reference in the] album title, we chose to find inspiration in Amish quilting,' Hvass explains, 'and so we sewed a tapestry made out of scraps of fabric, some of which were hand-dyed and others found.' They still had more to do. 'We then collaged it digitally,' she adds. 'We did this to create an ambiguity in the material, where it's partly very handmade but then also has a digital finish, as we like when it's a little hard to tell how the work is actually done. We feel that this gives the imagery more depth, and you can keep returning to it.'

TITLE: Efterklang, *Magic Chairs*
CLIENT: Rumraket/4AD
SIZE: 30.4 x 30.4 cm (12 x 12 in.)
PRINTING PROCESS: Offset
INKS: CMYK
COMPS PRESENTED: 1
REVISIONS: None
APPROVAL: Efterklang
INVOLVEMENT WITH FINAL PRINTING: None

After spending an immense amount of time discussing concepts and planning out the details, the duo still found that 'this project was so intense for us in terms of surprises, setbacks and bad weather, but turned out to become one of our all-time favourite projects. We hand-dyed and sewed all the ribbons, and from the beginning we wanted to create some kind of a happening and photograph it, a sort of live illustration process. What you can't see in the final artwork is that we actually assembled a team of twenty-five teenage ribbon dancers for the photoshoot, but while doing the shoot, we realized together with the photographer Brian Buchard that it would look much more magical if you didn't see them, so we ended up having them come in one by one and throw their ribbon in the air, and then all the photos were merged and the dancers were erased. The photoshoot took one day, but the preparations leading up to it took much longer and we prepared for several months.'

TITLE: Turboweekend, *Shadow Sounds*
CLIENT: EMI
SIZE: 30.4 x 30.4 cm (12 x 12 in.)
PRINTING PROCESS: Offset
INKS: CMYK
COMPS PRESENTED: 2
REVISIONS: 1 round
APPROVAL: Turboweekend
INVOLVEMENT WITH FINAL PRINTING: None

'Sometimes,' Hvass explains, 'you just really want to do some lettering by hand, and luckily, we had the perfect project for it.'

TITLE: Turboweekend, *Ghost Of A Chance*
CLIENT: Mermaid Records
SIZE: 30.4 x 30.4 cm (12 x 12 in.)
PRINTING PROCESS: Offset
INKS: CMYK
COMPS PRESENTED: 1
REVISIONS: 1 round
APPROVAL: Turboweekend
INVOLVEMENT WITH FINAL PRINTING: None

'The floating ball is made up of hundreds of little pieces of paper that we printed on our super-slow inkjet printer in different shades,' Hvass says with a smile. 'We then folded and assembled them to make this origami ball, which we had found a recipe for online. It took several days of meticulous work to do this, and we then took the ball to the woods with our favourite photographer, Brian Buchard, and took a photo of it hanging among the trees. In the end, most people can't tell that the ball is actually a physical and handmade object, so you could call it a waste of time. But we feel that it gives the picture a lot of depth (and meaning, to us) that we have crafted it ourselves.'

TITLE: Turboweekend, *Bound*
CLIENT: Turboweekend
SIZE: 30.4 x 30.4 cm (12 x 12 in.)
PRINTING PROCESS: Offset
INKS: CMYK
COMPS PRESENTED: 1
REVISIONS: 1 round
APPROVAL: Turboweekend
INVOLVEMENT WITH FINAL PRINTING: None

Photographer Emil Rønn Andersen created an image of the three band members, 'entangled to become one strange entity,' Hvass explains. Entralled with the image, the pair then brought Jody Barton on board to add the final touches with her fantastic hand lettering.

TITLE: Clogs, *The Creatures In The Garden Of Lady Walton*
CLIENT: Brassland
SIZE: 30.4 x 30.4 cm (12 x 12 in.)
PRINTING PROCESS: Offset
INKS: CMYK
COMPS PRESENTED: 15
REVISIONS: 20 rounds
APPROVAL: Clogs
INVOLVEMENT WITH FINAL PRINTING: None

'The album includes a collection of beautiful songs composed by Padma Newsome during his 2005 residency at Giardini La Mortella,' Hvass explains. 'It is a rich botanical paradise created by Lady Walton on the island of Ischia, off the Bay of Naples in Italy. Our imagery is an attempt at visualizing how we imagine the garden, in accordance with the music. Many of the creatures and plants in the imagery are taken from Padma's lyrics. It took us a very long time to draw this, as it was our first intricate forest illustration when we were still developing a style and learning how to do these kinds of illustrations.'

TITLE: Clogs, *Veil Waltz*
CLIENT: Brassland
SIZE: 30.4 x 30.4 cm (12 x 12 in.)
PRINTING PROCESS: Offset
INKS: CMYK
COMPS PRESENTED: 1
REVISIONS: 1 round
APPROVAL: Clogs
INVOLVEMENT WITH FINAL PRINTING: None

'Collage on a photo background,' Hvass states matter-of-factly. Of course, with family being so important to both designers, it should come as no surprise when we find out who took the photo. 'It is by Hans Kruse, who happens to be Sofie's Dad,' she says with a smile.

TITLE: Efterklang, *Parades*
CLIENT: Rumraket/Leaf
SIZE: 30.4 x 30.4 cm (12 x 12 in.)
PRINTING PROCESS: Offset
INKS: CMYK
COMPS PRESENTED: 4
REVISIONS: 8 rounds
APPROVAL: Efterklang
INVOLVEMENT WITH FINAL PRINTING: None

'This illustration was part of my bachelor project,' Hvass explains. 'It was an attempt at creating a little world,' she adds. A world where all of the inhabitants of Efterklang's songs could exist.

TITLE: Number0, *Parallel/Serial*
CLIENT: Rallye
SIZE: 30.4 x 30.4 cm (12 x 12 in.)
PRINTING PROCESS: Offset
INKS: CMYK
COMPS PRESENTED: 3
REVISIONS: 2 rounds
APPROVAL: Number0
INVOLVEMENT WITH FINAL PRINTING: None

Sometimes an image is not what it first appears, and when you have the talents of Hvass&Hannibal, combined with their willingness to merge the handmade and the digital, you can be in for a surprise. 'This artwork is actually made of fabric sewn together to form little collages,' Hvass explains. 'We then placed the collages behind a piece of glass which has been spray-painted. The end result is kind of a textural examination of the music.'

TITLE: Efterklang/Fundal, *Leaves: The Colour Of Falling*
CLIENT: Efterklang / Tambourhinoceros
SIZE: 30.4 x 30.4 cm (12 x 12 in.)
PRINTING PROCESS: Offset
INKS: CMYK
COMPS PRESENTED: 3
REVISIONS: 2 rounds
APPROVAL: Efterklang / Tambourhinoceros
INVOLVEMENT WITH FINAL PRINTING: None

'In the summer of 2015, the opera *Leaves – The Colour of Falling* was performed in the thousand-square-metre nuclear basement of the former Copenhagen Municipal Hospital,' Hvass explains. 'The opera was commissioned by Copenhagen Opera Festival, and the artwork was based on photographs from the opera.' The duo then added their own take, with 'painted strokes to emphasize the cultish atmosphere of the opera.'

INVISIBLE CREATURE

BAND OF BROTHERS

 One thing is immediately apparent when you view the work of Invisible Creature, and that is the absolute joy that they obviously have in creating imagery and illustrations. It is in every wash of colour or inked line, all of the little details, whether they are creating a space station straight from a sixties children's book, or joining bodies together in some macabre sci-fi mash-up. Brothers Don and Ryan Clark come by that enthusiasm honestly, often referencing their grandfather, Alfred Paulsen, who spent nearly three decades as an illustrator for NASA, as a huge influence. Combined with a father who was obsessed with woodworking, 'the desire to create, and the potential to do it with precision and imagination, was simply ingrained in us,' they explain. Early on, that creative drive would find success in both design and music. The brothers would come up through the California hardcore scene and eventually move to Seattle, where they would find massive success with both their design work and their metal band Demon Hunter. The Clarks may be the only designers featured here who have also signed recording contracts and sold hundreds of thousands of records. Years of balancing international touring with client needs eventually focused the brothers towards what they really desired, and they formed Invisible Creature. The studio allowed them to create products and pursue their illustration assignments, while still holding tight to their music packaging roots.

'When we began working in the music industry, the CD was king. Physical album sales were thriving,' Ryan Clark explains. 'Artists and labels were willing to invest in the packaging, and we were given a lot of freedom to explore the format. We were determined not only to push the limitations of CD packaging, but to quickly fill our portfolio with innovative design work,' he adds. 'For the first decade of our careers, the majority of our work was for record labels that really believed in the importance of excellent design. This gave us the opportunity to play with a range of styles and experiment with unique solutions. This was a heyday for us, when we could propose elaborate concepts, and album sales would sustain higher packaging costs.' It wasn't built to last, as the entire music industry would find out. 'As the digital revolution began to take effect, we saw these freedoms begin to wane. As physical music sales declined, labels were less willing to invest in complex packaging. Things like spot colours, special papers, die cuts, foils and custom components became too costly to justify. More often than not, we found ourselves limited to eight-page booklets with no special inclusions. A small handful of labels remained steadfast in their desire to push premium packaging despite industry changes, but these quickly became exceptions to the rule.'

Without sounding too nostalgic, the Clarks clearly hold on to the draw of the physical packaging. 'Not to overly romanticize it,' Ryan begins, 'but there's a certain permanence to physical packaging that warrants passion. Speaking as someone who has been working in the medium for nearly twenty years, it's difficult to muster up the same fervour for a digital-only marketplace. It's harder to invest in something that feels so fleeting. These days, as long as we're still working on a design that will see some sort of physical manifestation, it's worth the investment. If the future is completely devoid of physical packaging, I fear our enthusiasm for album artwork may dwindle.'

It has created a separate economic reality for each individual artist. 'The only way to gauge the value of physical packaging is by whether or not an artist's fans are receptive to it,' he explains. 'If the fans are willing to pay for physical product, that will allow it to exist. How many of them and how much they are willing to pay will dictate just how elaborate or involved that packaging can be,' Ryan continues. 'There are really only two driving forces that keep physical packaging alive: one, the demographic that has yet to catch up with the digital platform, and two, the collector or fan that wants to own something physical regardless of how or where they actually listen to the music. Eventually, everyone will catch up with the rest of us. When they do,' he worries, 'physical product will be driven solely by fringe collectors.'

These days, the Clarks don't linger around once a release is out in the marketplace. 'Early on in our careers,' Ryan explains, 'we were prone to follow along as our work was absorbed, but the longer we work in the field, the less exciting that is. Think of it as a band whose song plays on the radio. The first time it happens, they call all of their friends and celebrate. If it becomes normal to hear yourself on the radio, it eventually lacks that same lustre. Time jades the fortunate,' he smiles.

The duo carry on the tradition of stalwarts like Storm Thorgerson, P. R. Brown, Dirk Rudolph, Stefan Sagmeister, Vaughan Oliver, Peter Saville, Roger Dean, Reid Miles, Alex Steinweiss, and Frank Frazetta, while also bringing a bevy of influences to the table. 'Early on, we were heavily influenced by some of the guys mentioned above,' Clark explains. 'When you're getting started, it's hard not to emulate. As we progressed, I believe we started to look elsewhere for inspiration. It comes in the form of film and TV, fashion, fine art, advertising … so many different things. There is a quote by Antoine de Saint-Exupéry that says, "Perfection is achieved, not when there is nothing more to add, but when there is nothing left to take away." This is something that I gravitate towards more and more these days. It can be tempting to just keep adding, but I've found that my favourite album artwork is usually pretty lean. That's not to say it necessarily has to be minimal, but I try to be mindful of unnecessary decoration. I find that can be the quickest way to date your work.'

HOW CAN I FIX IT?

When taking on a music packaging assignment, or any assignment for that matter, Ryan finds that 'the best way to approach any piece of commercial art is to ask, "Where/what is the problem, and how can I fix it?" With album artwork the question is how to best execute a visual counterpart to the music. Depending on the vision (or lack thereof) from the artist, the solution could be a million different things. To make it even more subjective, there's really nothing to say whether or not an album's artwork has any definitively quantifiable value. It is, after all, a piece of art on the face of another piece of art.' Clark often asks, 'Who's to say that an album cover has anything to do with the success of an album?'

The brothers look for those projects where 'the designer may actually become an integral creative force within the album as a whole. You can surprise the audience, subvert them, perplex them, or even give them exactly what they'd expect. Depending on the project, and how adventurous the artist is, the "solutions" are limitless. We've been able to create album artwork that ranged from appropriate to bizarre, tasteful to unsettling,' he smiles. 'Luckily, after having designed hundreds of album packages, we still love it. We may be more selective these days, but there's something simultaneously comfortable and challenging about working on album artwork. It's nice to work in such familiar territory, and the right project (and client) can spark incredible ideas.'

'There's something particularly magical about a unanimously incredible album with incredible artwork,' adds Ryan. 'It's rare, as it requires excellence from two separate parties – but that's when it's perfect.'

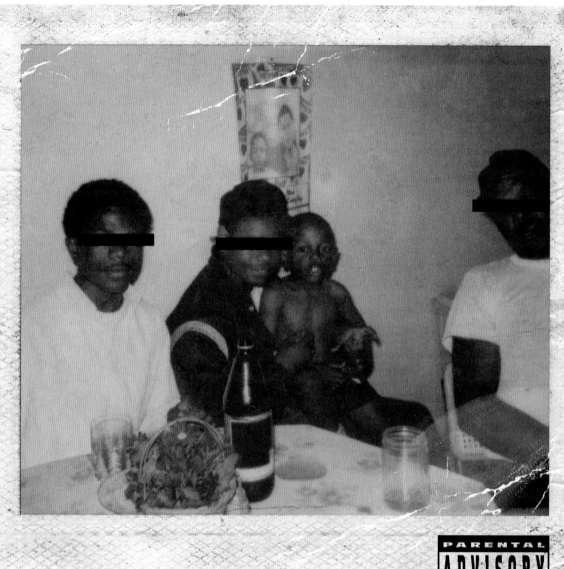

TITLE: Kendrick Lamar, *good kid, m.A.A.d city*

(Top) **TITLE**: Starflyer 59, *My Island*
(Middle) **TITLE**: Trip Lee, *Rise*
(Bottom) **TITLE**: August Burns Red, *Rescue & Restore*

TITLE: Foo Fighters, *Echoes, Silence, Patience & Grace*

TITLE: Norma Jean, *O'God, The Aftermath* (interior page)

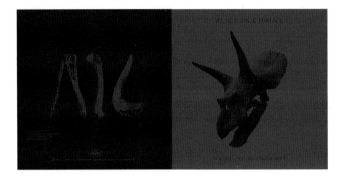

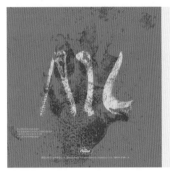 

(Above) TITLE: Young The Giant, *s/t*
(Left) TITLE: Alice In Chains, *The Devil Put Dinosaurs Here*

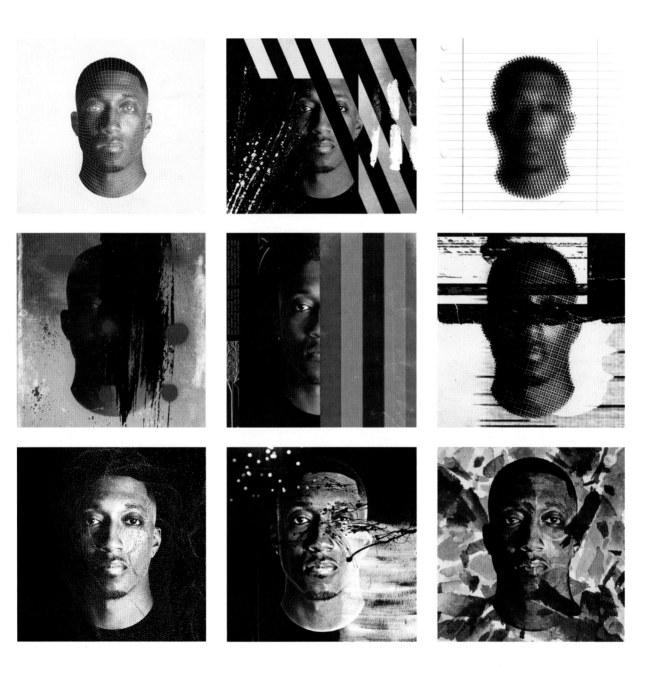

TITLE: Lecrae, *Anomaly*

TITLE: Kendrick Lamar, *good kid, m.A.A.d city*
CLIENT: Interscope Records
SIZE: 30.4 x 30.4 cm (12 x 12 in.)
PRINTING PROCESS: Offset
INKS: CMYK
COMPS PRESENTED: 5
REVISIONS: 2 rounds
APPROVAL: Interscope Records
INVOLVEMENT WITH FINAL PRINTING: None

'Kendrick was pretty involved with the overall concept of the album art – he knew exactly what he wanted to see from the beginning, which was refreshing,' Don Clark explains. 'There wasn't a ton of back and forth as he had picked out all of the Polaroid images himself and knew the order in which he wanted the viewer to see them. I look back at the concept for this album packaging and this was definitely very personal for him and I think it worked out perfectly. At the time that I was working on this, I obviously had no idea this album would sell the way it did and cement Kendrick as perhaps the greatest rapper alive. Honoured to work on it,' he adds.

TITLE: Starflyer 59, *My Island*
CLIENT: Tooth & Nail Records
SIZE: 30.4 x 30.4 cm (12 x 12 in.)
PRINTING PROCESS: Offset
INKS: CMYK
COMPS PRESENTED: 1
REVISIONS: None
APPROVAL: Starflyer 59
INVOLVEMENT WITH FINAL PRINTING: None

'We've worked with Jason Martin and Starflyer 59 for years and he's one of our favourite music clients,' Don Clark adds. 'He always gives us a small start of an idea then allows us to run wild with it. For this record, I really wanted to create it by hand and photograph the outcome. I used nails, red thread and scraps of found paper to create the typography and the background. The song titles and lyrics were created digitally in post. I love how this turned out – printed on uncoated stock paper and the interior unfolds into a small poster.'

TITLE: Trip Lee, *Rise*
CLIENT: Reach Records
SIZE: 30.4 x 30.4 cm (12 x 12 in.)
PRINTING PROCESS: Offset
INKS: CMYK + PMS 8025
COMPS PRESENTED: 5
REVISIONS: 2 rounds
APPROVAL: Reach Records
INVOLVEMENT WITH FINAL PRINTING: None

'Reach Records have always been a great client to work with,' Ryan Clark says. 'Long after labels started clamping down on physical cost per unit, Reach continued to invest in premium packaging. The artwork for Trip Lee's *Rise* features an O-card with metallic ink and embossing. Though not always a necessity, small additions like this often add to the value of the physical product.'

TITLE: August Burns Red, *Rescue & Restore*
CLIENT: Solid State Records
SIZE: 30.4 x 30.4 cm (12 x 12 in.)
PRINTING PROCESS: Offset
INKS: CMYK + PMS 8340
COMPS PRESENTED: 1
REVISIONS: None
APPROVAL: August Burns Red
INVOLVEMENT WITH FINAL PRINTING: None

'August Burns Red is one of my favourite artists to work with. To date, I have designed ten albums for the band,' Ryan Clark says. 'Despite being an extremely heavy and technical metal band, they never want their album artwork to follow any typical metal aesthetic. The design for this particular album was created by hand-drawing and painting each piece separately, then compositing and colouring in Photoshop.'

TITLE: Foo Fighters, *Echoes, Silence, Patience & Grace*
CLIENT: RCA
SIZE: 30.4 x 30.4 cm (12 x 12 in.)
PRINTING PROCESS: Offset
INKS: CMYK
COMPS PRESENTED: 5
REVISIONS: None
APPROVAL: Foo Fighters
INVOLVEMENT WITH FINAL PRINTING: None

'This was the record that really changed our "professional" lives,' Don Clark explains. 'Not only were the Foo Fighters one of our favourite bands of all time, Dave Grohl was punk rock royalty and I had been a fan since his first band, Scream. The band flew us down to their Studio 606 and we talked ideas and concepts for a few hours. Once we presented the "tube-bomb" it was the unanimous winner – and thankfully our favourite as well. There were many domestic and international singles in both CD and vinyl form that allowed us to create a ton of cohesive art for this album cycle. These types of projects come around once in a lifetime and we're thankful that it turned out the way that it did.'

TITLE: Norma Jean, *O'God, The Aftermath*
CLIENT: Solid State Records
SIZE: 30.4 x 30.4 cm (12 x 12 in.)
PRINTING PROCESS: Offset
INKS: CMYK
COMPS PRESENTED: 4
REVISIONS: Many
APPROVAL: Norma Jean
INVOLVEMENT WITH FINAL PRINTING: None

'This project was one arduous process after another,' Ryan Clark says with a grin. 'From the elaborately messy-type treatments to the insane photo compositing to the band's final approval, it certainly felt like the odds were stacked against this artwork ever seeing the light of day. It may very well be the longest I've ever worked on any one album. In the end, this artwork resulted in our first Grammy nomination, which was a nice silver lining to what otherwise seemed like one big uphill battle.'

TITLE: Alice In Chains, *The Devil Put Dinosaurs Here*
CLIENT: Capitol Records
SIZE: 30.4 x 30.4 cm (12 x 12 in.)
PRINTING PROCESS: Offset
INKS: CMYK
COMPS PRESENTED: 12
REVISIONS: None
APPROVAL: Alice In Chains
INVOLVEMENT WITH FINAL PRINTING: None

'Had Alice In Chains not been one of my all-time favourite bands, I certainly would've dropped this job midway through,' Ryan Clark laughs. 'The final album cover that you see here is the first thing I sent the band after the initial round of sketches. They approved the design fairly quickly, and that was that. After about a month of radio silence, the band had gotten cold feet about the design for a number of reasons. Long story short, I went back to the drawing board, submitting two to three covers at a time. Before returning to the original, I spent weeks and provided eleven different covers. Though the process was frustrating, I was glad that we ended up back at square one because I knew that was the way it should be.'

TITLE: Young The Giant, *s/t*
CLIENT: Roadrunner Records
SIZE: 12 x 12 cm (4.7 x 4.7 in.)
PRINTING PROCESS: Offset
INKS: CMYK
COMPS PRESENTED: 3
REVISIONS: None
APPROVAL: Roadrunner Records
INVOLVEMENT WITH FINAL PRINTING: None

'Self-titled albums are always the hardest to create art for,' Don Clark explains. 'Many times the trickiest part is finding that initial spark of an idea, especially if the band doesn't necessarily know where they want to go. For this album, we just started playing around with shapes on the page and slowly the style and concept presented itself – a combination of found art and textures. The concept here was essentially a vague coming-of-age story, especially as this was a young band at the time, and on a brand-new major label.'

TITLE: Lecrae, *Anomaly*
CLIENT: Reach Records
SIZE: 30.4 x 30.4 cm (12 x 12 in.)
PRINTING PROCESS: Offset
INKS: CMYK + spot varnish
COMPS PRESENTED: 3
REVISIONS: None
APPROVAL: Reach Records
INVOLVEMENT WITH FINAL PRINTING: None

'Lecrae is another one of my favourite artists to work with,' Don Clark says. 'Not only is he a friend, but he also gives me the freedom to interpret his art into visual art and I love that. This was a big album for him and I wanted to make sure we got it just right. Lecrae sorta operates on an island and doesn't necessarily fit into any category or style and I've always respected that – something I feel IC does as well. He's an anomaly and I wanted the art to show that he's distinct – and his style, talent and voice flourish in many different forms, colours and textures.'

MORNING BREATH

SKATEPUNKS GROWN UP, KIND OF

 In the mid-nineties Doug Cunningham and Jason Noto found themselves working side by side at Think Skateboards in San Francisco. Finding that their collaborations were often the most exciting projects that they were working on, the duo quickly took note of their creative connection. By 2002, they were carving out a studio in Brooklyn and fast making a name for themselves as Morning Breath. Their fun and energetic graphics found their way onto skateboards and snowboards and posters and apparel and even massive murals, while they added an edgy and textured quality to their work for the music industry. As the years moved forward, those styles merged as one, creating one of the most distinctive styles in music packaging today.

'As music has become more available in downloadable/streaming formats, the packaging has become less important for the industry,' observes the duo (so intertwined are Noto and Cunningham that they ask to be quoted as one). 'From a financial standpoint, the budget for creating the artwork has been in a steady decline and the budgets have become smaller. The amount spent on elaborate photoshoots, and/or special packaging having pretty much dwindled. But, while some of that work has gone away, there is the exception of vinyl releases and speciality packaging. The percentage of artists doing speciality packaging is pretty small, but some pretty innovative packages are still being produced. There will always be this audience that want something physical to purchase from their favourite bands, and creating something that offers something special and creative is still a great way to connect with fans.'

'When we create a full physical package/campaign, we are invested not only in the cover, but also in how the whole package works as a coherent piece. This forces you to dig deeper and to wrap your head around more than just a cover, often resulting in a more in-depth cover design as a result.' This dedication to every little corner of their packaging is what truly sets Morning Breath apart. While their general design chops are clear when the record sleeve is in your hands, further investigation allows you to really appreciate the intertwined graphics in the QBert release, invites you to interact with the stickers on the Brand New album, read through the intense booklet for the Grammy-nominated AFI record, and chuckle at the joys running all over the many Queens of the Stone Age releases.

START AT THE BACK OF THE MAGAZINE

Their love of album art is linked more closely to innovators from the past than any recognizable style in their own work. 'There are two designers at the top of our list when it comes to recognizing their title as masters of album artwork,' Morning Breath adds. 'One would be Storm Thorgerson ... It seems that just about every iconic classic rock album of the seventies had come out of his studio; images that defined that generation's rock music. The other is Reid Miles, for Blue Note Records, which he single-handedly gave the aesthetic that is now universally associated with jazz music. Both these men have done something with music-based artwork that no other designer has been able to accomplish.'

When it comes to their own way of working and aesthetics, they admit that, 'while we have many influences on our work, the most impactful would probably be the designers who created the small ads in the back of magazines from the sixties/seventies.' They say this with a knowing smile, as it is most definitely true. It is their ability to take this 'everyman' style of images and advertisements – for everything from sea monkeys and toy soldiers to Twinkies and cheap

beer – and make them into something funny and cutting and modern and edgy that makes them so amazing. That imagery comes from a place that connects everyone in a very simple and blue-collar fashion, and Morning Breath retains that quality, while elevating the imagery to a higher plane.

That doesn't always mean that they are heavy-handed with clients as far as style is concerned. 'In most of the music packages we've designed, the primary goal is to have it feel right for the artist/music genre,' they explain. 'Sometimes that might mean that we put our personal aesthetic taste aside, and focus on what's right for the mood/feel of the album. What will resonate best with the fans?' This is what makes their illustrations for Queens of the Stone Age so delightful. It also gives them the skills to assemble a gorgeous selection of nine different sleeves for the Foo Fighters and their Sonic Highways series, slicing up a massive painting that combines all of the cities visited.

Those talents have allowed for 'many years when we were very much part of a privileged few that were given the opportunity to work with so many artists, and were really able to contribute to pop culture,' they add with a small smile. Those opportunities have come in different shapes and sizes: 'We have worked with all combinations: artist, labels, management, etc. Each has its own set of challenges,' he explains. Those challenges can include being asked to design for digital only. 'Our approach to getting the cover remains similar, but the overall experience is not as dedicated and sometimes not as thoughtful,' they lament. 'There can also be the compromises you have to make. Unlike our work in our personal art, or even the commercial campaigns we are commissioned to do, album art is primarily about the artist's vision, or a visual accompaniment to the music. At the end of the day, it is always more about them than it is about the artwork, so that balancing act can be difficult at times.' It is not luck, but talent and hustle that allows Morning Breath to navigate all of those concerns and consistently achieve breathtaking results.

'The most successful packages come about through a number of things,' they explain. 'For one, the artist needs to be good, respected. There needs to be chemistry between us and the artist or label, and there also needs to be trust. We have worked with many different personalities under many different circumstances. We always strive to do our best, but sometimes bad ideas by those that have final say don't end with the best results. Our personal favourites have always been working with an artist that truly respects what we do, likes our approach, and comes to the table with loose ideas, but trusts our interpretation of those ideas.' That trust in each other's talents often holds the key to happiness on all sides.

Sound City
REAL TO REEL

MAGNETIC **RECORDING TAPE**

*SPLICE FREE
*HIGH FIDELITY
*SUPERIOR QUALITY

1 INCH X 1800 FEET

606

88765-44992-1
606

TITLE: Various artists, *Sound City – Real to Reel*

(Clockwise from top left) **TITLE:** Foo Fighters, *Medium Rare*; **TITLE:** Foo Fighters, *Sonic Highways*
TITLE: Foo Fighters, *Songs From The Laundry Room*; **TITLE:** Foo Fighters, *Greatest Hits*

(Above and opposite) **TITLE:** DJ QBert, *Extraterrestria*

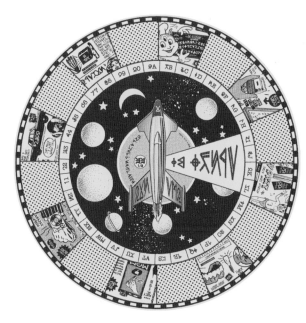

(Clockwise from top left) TITLE: Queens of the Stone Age, *Make It Wit Chu* (EP); TITLE: Queens of the Stone Age, *Make It Wit Chu* (7-inch)
TITLE: Queens of the Stone Age, *Make It Wit Chu* (single); TITLE: Queens of the Stone Age, *3's & 7's* (collected single and EP)

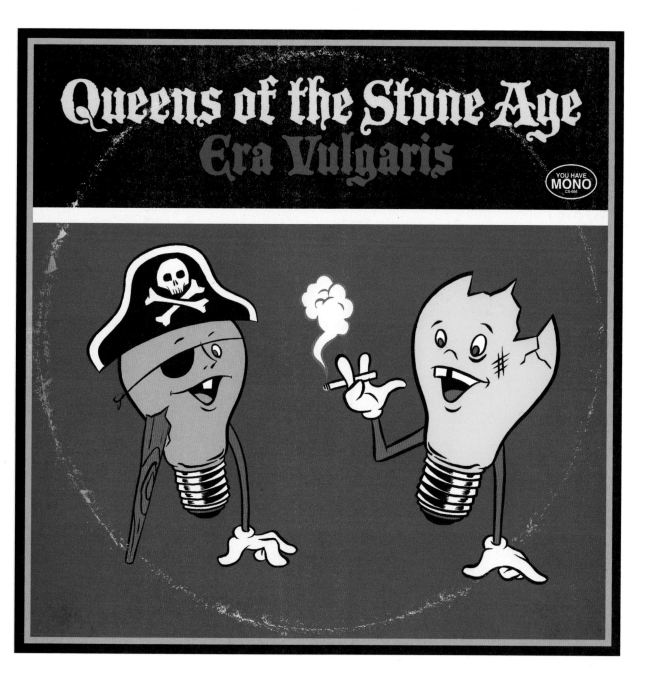

TITLE: Queens Of The Stone Age, *Era Vulgaris*

You'll Find All the Answers

Something Special... for Someone Special!

I am a Nightmare

Turn tin to gold. I want pure energy! Throw everything I own into the fire. I want to find a way. I want to throw up snakes. Do I have to die to see the other side? I am a nightmare and you are a miracle (we're growing out of the ground, it's kind of freaking me out.) I am a nightmare and you are a miracle. I am a nightmare and you are a miracle (we're growing out of the ground, it's kind of freaking me out.) I am a nightmare and you are a miracle. So come shake your Zen out. Give me pure energy! My heart is glowing fluorescent. I want you to possess it. I'm not a prophesy come true. I've just been goddamn mean to you. So what is this thing laced with? Please don't replace me. I surrender. Embrace me. Whatever we're faced with. I am a nightmare and you are a miracle (x4) Blessed be the lost at sea the rest, in peace, watch what they conceived end. Though I am messed up, no distress! I fall asleep holding your hand Among alien dunes, you are a pale vision of blue. And I'm my second self - the second thief so go save someone else. I am a nightmare and you are a miracle. (x4)

(Opposite) TITLE: Queens Of The Stone Age illustrations; (Top) TITLE: Brand New, *I Am A Nightmare* (front and accompanying materials)
(Bottom) TITLE: Lieutenant, *If I Kill This Thing We Are All Going To Eat For A Week* (front and back)

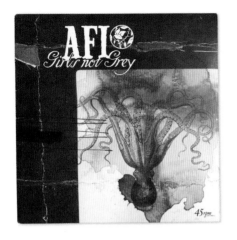

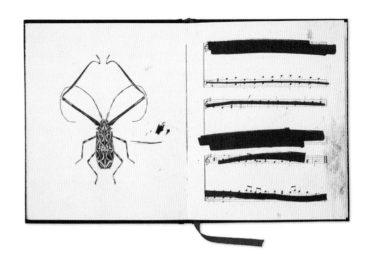

TITLE: AFI (various releases)

TITLE: Slayer, *Psychopathy Red*

TITLE: Various artists, *Sound City – Real to Reel*
CLIENT: Roswell Records/RCA
SIZE: 30.4 x 30.4 cm (12 x 12 in.)
PRINTING PROCESS: Offset
INKS: CMYK
COMPS PRESENTED: 5
REVISIONS: 1 round
APPROVAL: Dave Grohl
INVOLVEMENT WITH FINAL PRINTING: None

The official soundtrack to the documentary *Sound City* showcases highlights from the series. Foo Fighters frontman Dave Grohl founded the supergroup Sound City Players with many of the musicians who appear in the movie. Capturing many of the performances from their travels to different cities to soak up the local music scenes, the soundtrack was nominated for two Grammys. 'We had to go with a look that really captures the old-school recording techniques that Dave was showcasing as he visited important studios in each city. Once we saw these old reel-to-reel boxes that the recordings would be stored on for the master tapes, we knew exactly what we wanted to do,' explain Morning Breath. 'Getting to listen to these supergroups, with everyone from Paul McCartney to Stevie Nicks to Trent Reznor on there, was definitely a major bonus!'

TITLE: Foo Fighters, *Medium Rare*
CLIENT: Roswell Records/RCA
SIZE: 30.4 x 30.4 cm (12 x 12 in.)
PRINTING PROCESS: Offset
INKS: CMYK
COMPS PRESENTED: 1
REVISIONS: 2 rounds
APPROVAL: Foo Fighters
INVOLVEMENT WITH FINAL PRINTING: None

'Working on this RSD compilation release was so much fun!' exclaim the duo. 'I bought that meat at the supermarket on the way to work and then put it on the scanner and used the actual receipt on the back for the track list and finished that in a couple hours.'

TITLE: Foo Fighters, *Sonic Highways*
CLIENT: Roswell Records/RCA
SIZE: 30.4 x 30.4 cm (12 x 12 in.)
PRINTING PROCESS: Offset
INKS: CMYK + UV gloss and matte
COMPS PRESENTED: 1
REVISIONS: 3 rounds
APPROVAL: Foo Fighters
INVOLVEMENT WITH FINAL PRINTING: None

After *Sound City* Dave Grohl decided that he wanted to do something similar for the band's next album. They travelled to nine different cities and wrote and recorded a song in each, capturing the entire thing for a TV series. Illustrator Stephan Martinière was brought in to create this metropolis that combines all of the cities into one. 'A limited edition of the LP covers was released,' Morning Breath add. 'Eight cropped-in sections of the original, representing one of the cities, and the centre "infinity building" being the ninth. When presented side by side it acted as a large nine-piece puzzle of the cover art measuring 92 x 92 cm [36 x 36 in.].'

TITLE: Foo Fighters, *Songs From The Laundry Room*
CLIENT: Roswell Records/RCA
SIZE: 30.4 x 30.4 cm (12 x 12 in.)
PRINTING PROCESS: Offset
INKS: CMYK
COMPS PRESENTED: 2
REVISIONS: 2 rounds
APPROVAL: Foo Fighters
INVOLVEMENT WITH FINAL PRINTING: None

Preparing this EP for Record Store Day, Morning Breath knew they 'wanted to really highlight the fact that two of these tracks were demos of favourites from the Foo Fighters catalogue,' they explain. 'We were able to get images of the original master tapes as well as Dave Grohl's own tape case collection that the songs were culled from. Once we had those, we knew we couldn't go wrong with this look. The concept was to make the album art look like a vintage cassette tape, as Dave originally taped his first FF recordings on cassette all by himself before fully starting the band.' So they built in a J-card that wrapped halfway around the cover.

TITLE: Foo Fighters, *Greatest Hits*
CLIENT: Roswell Records/RCA
SIZE: 30.4 x 30.4 cm (12 x 12 in.)
PRINTING PROCESS: Offset
INKS: CMYK + UV + emboss
COMPS PRESENTED: 10
REVISIONS: 2 rounds
APPROVAL: Foo Fighters
INVOLVEMENT WITH FINAL PRINTING: None

'One of the concepts we really loved in the first presentation was one that played up the band name in a winking way,' explain Morning Breath. 'Most people don't know that the term relates to various UFOs or mysterious aerial phenomena seen in the skies over both the European and Pacific theatres of operations by Allied aircraft pilots in World War II.' The cover was originally hand-painted by Morning Breath with One Shot paint on fabricated sheet metal. Actual size 92 x 92 cm [36 x 36 in.]. 'The original painting is hanging in Dave Grohl's recording studio,' they add.

TITLE: Foo Fighters, *Wasting Light*
CLIENT: Roswell Records/RCA
SIZE: 30.4 x 30.4 cm (12 x 12 in.)
PRINTING PROCESS: Offset
INKS: 4 spot inks
COMPS PRESENTED: 8
REVISIONS: 5 rounds
APPROVAL: Foo Fighters
INVOLVEMENT WITH FINAL PRINTING: Press check

'*Wasting Light* was cool because we shot all the photos ourselves,' the pair explain. 'That was something that we had never done before. We also wanted it to be a test-print-looking package using only all Pantone printing, making fourth and fifth colours when they overlap.'

TITLE: AFI, *Girl's Not Grey*
CLIENT: DreamWorks Records
SIZE: 17.7 x 17.7 cm [7 x 7 in.]
PRINTING PROCESS: Offset
INKS: CMYK
COMPS PRESENTED: 1
REVISIONS: None
APPROVAL: AFI
INVOLVEMENT WITH FINAL PRINTING: None

'This one was a ton of work, as we had the intensive booklet and alternative packaging,' explain Morning Breath. 'AFI were stretching out both musically and visually,' they add. 'We started layering on textures and things started getting darker and darker, and everyone started getting happier and happier about where it was headed. Little did we know that *Sing The Sorrow* would end up with a Grammy nomination for limited-edition packaging.'

TITLE: Brand New, *I Am A Nightmare*
CLIENT: Procrastinate! Music Traitors
SIZE: 30.4 x 30.4 cm (12 x 12 in.)
PRINTING PROCESS: Offset
INKS: CMYK
COMPS PRESENTED: 3
REVISIONS: 3 rounds
APPROVAL: Brand New
INVOLVEMENT WITH FINAL PRINTING: None

'For the new Brand New single we knew that we wanted to have them break new ground visually,' the duo explain. 'We ended up making everything by hand using a collage style. It has an embossed cover, a sticker reveal on the forehead, comes with an engraved record, plus a die cut.' Not to be left out, they add that it, 'also came with these creepy prayer books with lyrics to the song which are just amazing.'

TITLE: DJ Qbert, *Extraterrestria*
CLIENT: Thud Rumble
SIZE: 30.4 x 30.4 cm (12 x 12 in.)
PRINTING PROCESS: Offset
INKS: 4 spot inks
COMPS PRESENTED: 1
REVISIONS: None
APPROVAL: DJ Qbert
INVOLVEMENT WITH FINAL PRINTING: Yes

'This is literally one of the craziest things we have ever worked on,' they say. 'Not only does it have multiple die cuts and reveals and various pieces, but you can even play the insert like a DJ using your phone. That print has a bluetooth module stuck inside, and we used conductive ink on the inside of the card in the shape of touch sensors. The conductive ink tracks run to the module, where the signals are sensed and turned into midi commands sent over to the iPhone using bluetooth. It is a ton of fun and totally rad!'

TITLE: Slayer, *Psychopathy Red*
CLIENT: American Recordings
SIZE: 30.4 x 30.4 cm (12 x 12 in.)
PRINTING PROCESS: Offset
INKS: CMYK
COMPS PRESENTED: 3
REVISIONS: 2 rounds
APPROVAL: Label Creative Director
INVOLVEMENT WITH FINAL PRINTING: None

'This is one of my favourite designs that we have done,' the Morning Breath boys say. 'The song is about a Russian serial killer. We made the whole thing using only words written in Russian and the record played backwards had messages from the Russian murderer. And it came in a string-tied envelope. Creepy!'

TITLE: Queens Of The Stone Age, *Era Vulgaris*
CLIENT: Ipecac Recordings, Interscope Records, Rekords Rekords
SIZE: 30.4 x 30.4 cm (12 x 12 in.)
PRINTING PROCESS: Offset
INKS: CMYK
COMPS PRESENTED: 6
REVISIONS: 4 rounds
APPROVAL: Queens Of The Stone Ager
INVOLVEMENT WITH FINAL PRINTING: None

'This is the record that comes the closest to the personal work that we do,' the duo say. 'Drawing from everything we love about those cheap magazine ads filled with weird clip art in the sixties and seventies, and then our favourite junky cartoons and animation from the same era, we really went crazy on this one. When the dust finally cleared, we had created twelve characters that lived in this bizarre *Era Vulgaris* world.'

TITLE: Lieutenant, *If I Kill This Thing We're All Going To Eat For A Week*
CLIENT: Dine Alone Records
SIZE: 30.4 x 30.4 cm (12 x 12 in.)
PRINTING PROCESS: Offset
INKS: CMYK
COMPS PRESENTED: 6
REVISIONS: 3 rounds
APPROVAL: Nate Mendel
INVOLVEMENT WITH FINAL PRINTING: None

'We knew Nate Mendel from working with the Foo Fighters, where Nate plays bass,' the duo explain. 'When it was time for him to make an album on his own, he decided on the name Lieutenant, and when we listened to what he was working on we were blown away.' The designers got intensely involved in the organic process as they were designing the album cover, until that became the cover itself. 'We were fascinated with the look of our quick photos of working on our sketches,' they add. 'Once we finally got up the courage to show Nate how cool we thought they were he was totally behind heading in that direction for the actual cover art.'

PAULA SCHER

THE GROUND WE BUILD UPON

 Paula Scher is undeniably one of the most celebrated American designers of the last forty years, and rightly so. As a partner at Pentagram since 1991, she has created landmark designs for cultural institutions and global corporations with a skill and refinement that have become part of the visual language that we have all learnt to speak. She has been a restless creative, always pushing her skills and mode of problem solving. Somehow she has managed to master an obsessive style of painting, educate generations of designers, find herself honoured by every organization imaginable, write and also be the subject of books and television shows, and do it all while always giving back to the design community and being smart and charming at every turn. It's easy to forget that Scher had already had a celebrated career working for a decade as an in-house art director at CBS Records before any of this, but so much of what has made her so amazing as a creative was formed during those years. For me, and most likely for Scher, she will always be a record cover designer. 'I think the period that I grew up in in the record industry, which was phenomenally exciting, had to do with the amount of money attached to it as well as the music. It wasn't just the music; it was the amount of money in the music,' she adds. 'And one year was more profitable than the rest, until it crashed. So it was very high living. You didn't have a sense of it. You thought that was the way things were. Until they weren't.'

Where do you see differences in how designers today approach designing for the music industry versus when you started out?

I can't pretend like I know enough of them to actually know what they go through. I would make some assumptions. I think there's a lot less money to throw at a record album. When I worked at CBS Records, they would spend, say, three thousand dollars for a front and back cover illustration. And that's 1976 money, so that's probably close to twelve thousand now, and now I think they probably spend three thousand, if that. I think the value of the work dropped. I think it's a field for people who are starting out. In the time I worked there, there were people of all ages making those things. I don't think that could exist now.

The music industry back in that day was perceived the way we currently think about Apple and Google. I think technology companies replaced music companies in terms of power and influence. Music used to be the most important thing we exported except for guns. I'm serious. It sounds funny, but it was actually true. You have to understand what the power of those things was in those days; they were mammoth corporations. I worked for CBS. That was a behemoth in its day.

What are your feelings on the current vinyl boom and resurgence of large-format music packaging?

I find that amusing. Because it really talks about this other experience. It's completely impractical, but it talks about some missed experience that a consumer feels, that I find really charming. I think that there was a passion for the connection, some other kind of experience. It's funny with electronic media. You take these things for granted. It's like they're pumped into your situation whether you want them or not, in a way. They're just so readily available. And the idea of actually taking this time and space to listen to a record and look at a record cover, and sometimes read the lyrics, is what that is about. It's this other way of using time in relationship to the music that makes it great.

How important is it to present music with a physical representation?

It's a way of referring to it. If I listen to something on my iPhone, I love when one of my covers comes up. They still do. It's the brand of the music. So you know what sequence, you know what album you're looking at, because you make the visual relationship. It works with identity design marks. It's the same thing.

What were your favourite parts about working at CBS?

I liked that I got to make so many albums! It wasn't just like I was dedicating myself to one album for three or six months. I was working on a couple a week. And some of them didn't fly, some of them got rejected, some of them got changed into terrible things, some of them were terrific. But that I got to have that experience, which is really not an experience many designers have anymore. It's gone away.

When I started out, I worked in-house. I just learned so much and so fast from working on so many projects at a time.

I know, it was incredible. I started working in the music industry when I was about twenty-three. I was a senior art director when I was twenty-five. By the time I was thirty, I was already over the hill.

Also, you don't have time even to worry about being precious about a design. To a certain extent things just have to get done to the best of your abilities.

That's mostly what I was concerned with. I didn't even see any value. I did this poster back in the day for all these jazz albums I designed called *The Best of Jazz*. And it's collected by all these museums now, and I used to wrap Christmas presents in it. I don't even have any copies I saved. Things like that. You just didn't have any sense of that. You just made the stuff, and that was what was really fantastic.

BEN NEWMAN

IT'S NOT A SECRET
ANY LONGER

One of my favourite things to happen in the music industry over the last several years has been the Secret 7" project. It is something that has generated enough amazing design work that those sleeves alone could fill this book. One of my favourite sleeves from that mountain of magic is actually by a man best known for illustrating children's books. Ben Newman's take on Black Sabbath's *Age Of Reason* shouldn't work at all, yet it is jaw-droppingly amazing and note-perfect in every way. I thought he would be the perfect person to tell us a little more about how this all came about.

'The Secret 7" project is an annual event raising money for the War Child charity that provides much-needed assisstance in areas of the world experiencing or in the aftermath of conflict,' Newman explains. 'The project raises money by taking seven tracks from seven well-known musicians from around the world and pressing each track one-hundred times to seven-inch vinyl. Artists are then invited to create and interpret the tracks in their own visual language, resulting in a one-of-a-kind sleeve for every seven-inch.'

The process of purchasing these discs is filled with surprise, as the cover design literally has to convince the consumer to buy it. 'It totally flips the way we normally buy music,' Newman adds. 'The buyer is purchasing the record based solely on the cover design and it's actually the song and artist that is hidden from them. In most circumstances, you purchase a record for the music and if you like the cover art then that's a huge bonus,' he says. 'With the Secret 7" project, it's up to the cover image to sell the artist's music for charity, and I think this is what makes the project a lot of fun and really interesting.'

The project has attracted some of the most talented creatives in the world, and paired them with some of the most amazing songs ever recorded, so how does it feel to be included in such select company? 'It's a strange feeling,' Newman conceded. 'To me, it's just playing and amusing myself in my own bubble in the safe confines of my studio, so a lot of the time it's hard to imagine what will happen when you release it into the world.' He is quick to add that 'the best part about being included in the project was that I got to help raise some money for a very deserving and important charity.'

Once they have their song, each designer taps into a very different vein of inspiration. For Newman, he was already 'a big Melvins fan, so illustrating a cover design for a Black Sabbath song was ideal,' he says. 'The song has a very solid and chunky riff, and there is a simplicity and repetition that make the song very immediate. I wanted to create something very simple, repetitive and bold but odd and godlike. I had been practising origami from an old book I had as a child back then, and I think that definitely filtered through into the design,' he adds.

When he works on his normal illustration and design projects, even a few in the music industry, he still approaches them all in a similar fashion. 'Usually the artists are quite specific about an element in my work that has caught their eye, or they feel works with their sound,' he explains. 'That acts as a springboard for where I go next. I work with a musician called Bronnt Industries Kapital, and on his projects I am given the tracks from the album and creative control. These sorts of projects are uncommon,' he admits. 'I love working like this because I get to listen to the music for days while I do other things and eventually an idea hits me or a sketch suddenly evolves into the cover art. It is the organic approach to music projects that is the main difference compared to my usual work.'

When it finally comes time for the Secret 7" show, there is a weird pressure to garner a good reaction, especially with walls filled with amazing sleeves from your peers. 'There was only one copy of this cover made and it sold in the first few minutes of the exhibition opening, so I take that as a positive,' Newman says, with a small grin.

NON-FORMAT

TRANSATLANTIC DREAM TEAM

In what may be the best example of the new work environment afforded by the Internet age, the fact that Non-Format stretches their office from Norway to Minnesota somehow serves only to make their work more cohesive and to keep their voice in the marketplace loud and clear. With Kjell Ekhorn in Oslo and Jon Forss in St. Paul, the dynamic duo have managed to capture a wide client base that sees their imaginative typography and bold concepts gracing everything from magazine covers to dynamic sportswear campaigns to wildly inventive musical compositions. Where they have excelled is in building tight working relationships with clients. But whether in their new arrangement with the agency ANTI or with London-based record label Lo Recordings, Non-Format always brings an approach to the process that can only come from them.

'Music packaging has changed enormously over the course of my career,' explains Forss. 'When I got my first job as a graphic designer, the compact disc was a mere seven years old and was mostly packaged as shrunken versions of LP sleeves shoved into plastic jewel cases,' he laughs. 'By the time I was working on my own music packaging projects, in the mid-1990s, things had moved along a bit, thankfully. Studios like Farrow, Me Company and the Designers Republic were using CD packaging formats as the primary form of expression, rather than as an afterthought.' Fast-forward through a CD renaissance to the MP3 explosion and a digital takeover. One thing that was unexpected with this shift was how they adapted to digital being the main driver for sales. 'The primary image to represent an album or single can be just an image that is a few thousand pixels square. We assume that it'll be accompanied by an artist's name and the title written underneath, so we tend not to worry too much about cramming a load of text into such a small area,' he explains. 'Creating an image with a bit of impact at such a small scale is not all that easy, but they said that about the CD when it temporarily super-seded the comparatively huge LP sleeve,' Forss says. 'Limitations like this can be a fantastic way of encouraging creativity. Digital packshots are to the LP sleeve what tweets are to the novel, probably,' he laughs.

Forss is philosophical about where the current trends in physical packaging stand in the big picture. 'The return of LP packaging is interesting and I can completely understand the fascination for a newer generation who probably grew up with their parents' towers of CD jewel cases. There's something very satisfying about the twelve-inch square cardboard sleeve that will probably endure for a while, but technology has a way of moving things along,' he admits. 'This makes sense given that music has been around for thousands of years and music packaging represents only a fleeting moment in its history.' That moment may be passing for the firm as we speak. 'Now that we've partnered with ANTI in Norway,' Forss adds, 'we can't justify the time these kinds of projects demand. The opportunity for creative expression always significantly outweighed the fees.' What he does love is the freedom to experiment that music projects afford. 'If we don't have a lot of freedom to explore new ground then there seems little point in taking it on. That's why we've mostly worked for just a few small independent labels that have trusted us to do our thing,' he explains. 'Our most successful major label work has tended to be the result of the band wanting to work with us, rather than the label asking us to pitch in ideas.'

WHEN GETTING THE JOB IS SECONDARY

When asked about the past masters of the format Forss is quick to reply. 'For me it all starts with Hipgnosis,' he exclaims. 'Some of my all-time favourite pieces of packaging were created by them. I think they utterly transformed what an LP sleeve could be. They represent an era when people would sit and explore every detail of a sleeve while they listened to the music. Hipgnosis really knew how to appeal to my adolescent mind. Back in the early nineties I went for an interview at Stylorouge, one of the great music-packaging design firms of that time. I went in to show the creative director Rob O'Connor my portfolio of fairly mediocre design work and, as he was leafing through the pages, there was a knock at the door. In walked a middle-aged man brandishing some printouts of what looked like a reworking of Pink Floyd's *Dark Side Of The Moon* packaging. Rob introduced me to this man, who was, of course, Storm Thorgerson. I immediately knew the significance of meeting this man but I did my best not to freak out in his company and remained as calm as I could. Perhaps my nonchalance was a little overdone because I wasn't offered a job, but at least I got to meet one of my design heroes,' he says.

Pulling Ekhorn and Forss together is a love of Pop Art and Japanese graphic design. 'We could list a dozen Japanese designers and only really scratch the surface,' he adds. 'No one does emotional minimalism quite like the Japanese. We're also lifelong fans of David Bowie. Not just the music but his astonishing transformations from one era to the next. Bowie naturally leads me to Brian Eno's diary *A Year with Swollen Appendices*, which was enormously influential on my work, especially in the beginning. Kjell and I talk a lot via Skype and often the subject comes around to one or other of the many podcasts we've been listening to,' he explains. 'We've always been just as interested in what motivates people as we are in form or style. I think there's a bit of a misconception that Non-Format is mostly concerned with style, but we're far more interested in really getting to know what makes a client tick and what it is they're trying to achieve. Kjell's mother also has a saying that's had quite an influence on Non-Format over the years. She says, "There's nothing so bad it's not good for something." Wise words.'

'Music packaging is more of a personal expression than most other graphic design disciplines,' explains Forss. 'It's perhaps about as close as graphic design gets to being fine art. There are no real problems to solve – well, apart from perhaps satisfying the recording artist and the record label. Even the issue of legibility seems pretty irrelevant when it comes to music packaging. There aren't really any wrong answers; it's more about establishing some kind of visual connection to sound.' When figuring out how that can create something truly special, he adds that 'great music packaging just carries you off somewhere. It connects with you on an emotional level. It speaks to you, personally, in a way that less successful music packaging simply doesn't. Of course, if you love the music, the packaging somehow becomes elevated in stature. It's akin to transubstantiation. If some people can accept that a glass of wine can miraculously become the blood of a deity's offspring then I see no reason why a cluster of type and images shouldn't undergo a similar transformation when they get wrapped around a collection of recorded sounds.'

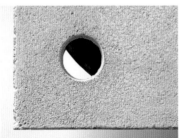  

TITLE: Peter Gabriel, *Sledgehammer*

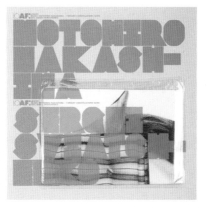

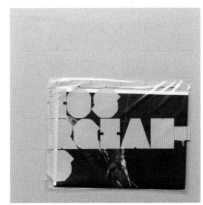

TITLE: Various artists, LoAF compilation

Luke

Vibert's

Volume — 3

Nuggets

(Above and opposite) TITLE: Luke Vibert, *Nuggets Vol. 3*

Hanne Hukkelberg
Rykestraße 68

TITLE: Hanne Hukkelberg, *Rykestrasse 68*

CLARION CALL
DOUBT
THIS MOMENTARY
RED LIGHTS
ACOLYTE
HALCYON
SUBMISSION
COUNTERPOINT
EPHEMERA
REMAIN

CHIMERIC

TITLE: Delphic, *Acolyte*

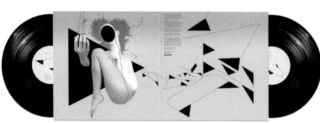

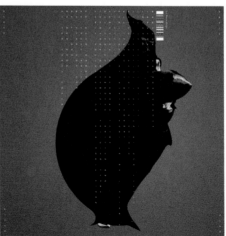

(Top left) TITLE: Black Devil Disco Club, *28 After*; (Top right, clockwise) TITLE: Black Devil Disco, Club *Eight Oh Eight* (back and front); TITLE: Black Devil Disco Club, *The Strange New World Of Bernard Fevre* (back and front); (Middle) TITLE: Black Devil Disco Club, *Circus* (front, interior and back); (Left) TITLE: Black Devil Disco Club, *Black Moon White Sun* (front and back)

(Above) **TITLE:** The Chap, *Mega Breakfast*
(Top right) **TITLE:** The Chap, *Well Done Europe*
(Right) **TITLE:** The Chap, *We Are The Best*
(Below) **TITLE:** The Chap, *We Are Nobody*
(Bottom) **TITLE:** The Chap, *The Show Must Go*

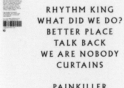

RHYTHM KING
WHAT DID WE DO?
BETTER PLACE
TALK BACK
WE ARE NOBODY
CURTAINS

PAINKILLER
RUNNING WITH ME
HANDS FREE
LOOK AT THE GIRL
THIS IS SICK

TITLE: Peter Gabriel, *Sledgehammer*
CLIENT: Secret 7"
SIZE: 20.3 x 20.3 cm (8 x 8 in.)
PRINTING PROCESS: Custom
INKS: Concrete
COMPS PRESENTED: None
REVISIONS: None
APPROVAL: None
INVOLVEMENT WITH FINAL PRINTING: None

'Secret 7" is an annual event that combines music and art for a good cause. We were invited to create one of seven hundred seven-inch single sleeves and chose Peter Gabriel's 1986 hit single *Sledgehammer*,' explains Jon Forss. 'We requested the vinyl seven-inch single to be sent to us so we could encase it in a specially made concrete sleeve.' Engineered and constructed by Rodney Forss, 'four holes reveal the edges of the record to reassure the owner that it's actually in there,' Jon says, adding that 'the piece was accompanied by a note that reads: "The greatest show of strength is non-violence."'

TITLE: Various artists, LoAF compilation
CLIENT: Lo Recordings
SIZE: 30.4 x 30.4 cm (12 x 12 in.)
PRINTING PROCESS: Digital and silk-screen
INKS: CMYK and various PMS colours
COMPS PRESENTED: 3
REVISIONS: None
APPROVAL: Lo Recordings
INVOLVEMENT WITH FINAL PRINTING: None

Creating packaging for compilations for the LoAF label, Non-Format had a three-inch [7.5 cm] or five-inch [13 cm] CD accompanied by an art print created by various contemporary artists and image-makers. These items are enclosed in sealed clear-plastic documents envelopes, attached to a grey pulp board that is cut to a twelve-inch LP format and then silk-screen-overprinted with the names of the recording and visual artists. In 2007 this project won a D&AD Yellow Pencil. In 2012 several items from this series were added to the permanent collection of the Smithsonian Cooper Hewitt National Design Museum in New York.

TITLE: Luke Vibert, *Nuggets Vol. 3*
CLIENT: Lo Recordings
SIZE: 30.4 x 30.4 cm (12 x 12 in.)
PRINTING PROCESS: Offset
INKS: CMYK
COMPS PRESENTED: One
REVISIONS: None
APPROVAL: Lo Recordings
INVOLVEMENT WITH FINAL PRINTING: None

'Gatefold LP packaging for Luke Vibert's third collection of production music from the archives of Bruton Music,' explains Forss. 'The archive was founded in London in 1977.' He adds that 'this packaging was nominated for a Tokyo Type Directors Club Prize.'

TITLE: Hanne Hukkelberg, *Rykestrasse 68*
CLIENT: Propeller Recordings
SIZE: 13.9 x 12.4 cm (5.5 x 4.9 in.)
PRINTING PROCESS: Offset
INKS: CMYK and PMS gold
COMPS PRESENTED: 3
REVISIONS: 3 rounds
APPROVAL: Propeller Recordings
INVOLVEMENT WITH FINAL PRINTING: None

Combining two of the incredible studios in this collection, Non-Format created the typographic composition for the front cover, 'and then we passed it on to New York-based designer & illustrator Mario Hugo, who created the delicate cover illustration using Indian ink stains'.

TITLE: Delphic, *Acolyte*
CLIENT: Polydor
SIZE: 30.4 x 30.4 cm (12 x 12 in.)
PRINTING PROCESS: Offset
INKS: CMYK
COMPS PRESENTED: Several
REVISIONS: Several rounds
APPROVAL: Polydor, Delphic
INVOLVEMENT WITH FINAL PRINTING: None

Working from an original photograph from Jake Walters, Forss recalls how Non-Format 'created the image of the band, as well as the band logotype'.

TITLE: Black Devil Disco Club, *28 After*
CLIENT: Lo Recordings
SIZE: 30.4 x 30.4 cm (12 x 12 in.)
PRINTING PROCESS: Offset
INKS: CMYK
COMPS PRESENTED: Several
REVISIONS: 3 rounds
APPROVAL: Lo Recordings,
Black Devil Disco Club
INVOLVEMENT WITH FINAL PRINTING: None

TITLE: Black Devil Disco Club,
Eight Oh Eight
CLIENT: Lo Recordings
SIZE: 30.4 x 30.4 cm (12 x 12 in.)
PRINTING PROCESS: Offset
INKS: CMYK
COMPS PRESENTED: 3
REVISIONS: 3 rounds
APPROVAL: Lo Recordings,
Black Devil Disco Club
INVOLVEMENT WITH FINAL PRINTING: None

TITLE: Black Devil Disco Club, *The Strange New World Of Bernard Fevre*
CLIENT: Lo Recordings
SIZE: 30.4 x 30.4 cm (12 x 12 in.)
PRINTING PROCESS: Offset
INKS: CMYK
COMPS PRESENTED: 3
REVISIONS: 3 rounds
APPROVAL: Lo Recordings, Black Devil Disco Club
INVOLVEMENT WITH FINAL PRINTING: None

TITLE: Black Devil Disco Club, *Circus*
CLIENT: Lo Recordings
SIZE: 30.4 x 30.4 cm (12 x 12 in.)
PRINTING PROCESS: Offset
INKS: CMYK
COMPS PRESENTED: 3
REVISIONS: 3 rounds
APPROVAL: Lo Recordings, Black Devil Disco Club
INVOLVEMENT WITH FINAL PRINTING: None

TITLE: Black Devil Disco Club, *Black Moon White Sun*
CLIENT: Lo Recordings
SIZE: 30.4 x 30.4 cm (12 x 12 in.)
PRINTING PROCESS: Offset
INKS: CMYK
COMPS PRESENTED: 3
REVISIONS: 3 rounds
APPROVAL: Lo Recordings, Black Devil Disco Club
INVOLVEMENT WITH FINAL PRINTING: None

'In 1978 Bernard Fevre, aka Black Devil Disco Club, released an obscure yet highly influential self-titled album,' Forss explains. 'His follow-up album, released in 2006 and aptly titled *28 After*, features photography by Jake Walters and an early example of our custom super-bold typefaces. We went on to design all of BDDC's follow-up albums, some featuring more of Walters's photography and some featuring illustrations by Géraldine Georges.'

TITLE: The Chap, *Mega Breakfast*
CLIENT: Lo Recordings
SIZE: 30.4 x 30.4 cm (12 x 12 in.)
PRINTING PROCESS: Offset
INKS: CMYK
COMPS PRESENTED: One
REVISIONS: None
APPROVAL: Lo Recordings, The Chap
INVOLVEMENT WITH FINAL PRINTING: None

TITLE: The Chap, *Well Done Europe*
CLIENT: Lo Recordings
SIZE: 30.4 x 30.4 cm (12 x 12 in.)
PRINTING PROCESS: Offset
INKS: CMYK
COMPS PRESENTED: One
REVISIONS: None
APPROVAL: Lo Recordings, The Chap
INVOLVEMENT WITH FINAL PRINTING: None

TITLE: The Chap, *The Show Must Go*
CLIENT: Lo Recordings
SIZE: 30.4 x 30.4 cm (12 x 12 in.)
PRINTING PROCESS: Offset
INKS: CMYK
COMPS PRESENTED: 3
REVISIONS: None
APPROVAL: Lo Recordings, The Chap
INVOLVEMENT WITH FINAL PRINTING: None

TITLE: The Chap, *We Are The Best*
CLIENT: Lo Recordings
SIZE: 14 x 13 cm (5.5 x 5 in.)
PRINTING PROCESS: Offset
INKS: CMYK
COMPS PRESENTED: 3
REVISIONS: None
APPROVAL: Lo Recordings, The Chap
INVOLVEMENT WITH FINAL PRINTING: None

TITLE: The Chap, *We Are Nobody*
CLIENT: Lo Recordings
SIZE: 30.4 x 30.4 cm (12 x 12 in.)
PRINTING PROCESS: Offset
INKS: CMYK
COMPS PRESENTED: One
REVISIONS: 3 rounds
APPROVAL: Lo Recordings, The Chap
INVOLVEMENT WITH FINAL PRINTING: None

'So far,' Forss explains, 'we've designed the packaging for all of The Chap's seven studio albums. The first five albums featured various illustrative or photographic interpretations of animals, ending with their greatest hits album *We Are The Best*, which featured our half-human, half-dog monstrosity which was our homage to David Bowie's *Diamond Dogs* album cover,' he says. 'For the follow-up album, *We Are Nobody*, we anthropomorphized a condom. For their latest album, *The Show Must Go*, we created a dystopian Hockney-esque image of a lifeless figure floating in a swimming pool.' Non-Format continue to help the band push themselves, as true believers in their talent. 'The Chap remain one of the best unknown bands in the world,' Forss laments.

DARREN OORLOFF

NEW KID IN TOWN

 Sometimes, the most important person in your career is the person that just sat down next to you. Such was the case with Darren Oorloff when Samuel Johnson arrived from London to spend a year working in a co-working studio in Melbourne. Johnson was working on various album covers and admired the logo work being done by Oorloff. As he hired Oorloff to help him out with small details on various jobs, he also began feeding him little opportunities to design covers for various clients. Johnson then headed back to London, and Oorloff, just a few years past graduating from school, continued the work he was doing, and started a rapid ascent towards being one of the most crucial visual voices in dance music today. 'I think at the start I was just doing whatever came my way. It was just fine-tuning my skills. I think it's only very recently that I found my own style and my own niche. While working at Sam's studio I was mostly replicating his style, but then when I was on my own, I just started doing my own thing and creating my own style. I also shifted from a lot of indie bands to the electronic music side of things. So I think that's where I channelled into. We ended up in two totally different worlds, but I learned a lot of early skills from him, and just how to deal with the music industry.'

Oorloff's visually arresting style and type manipulation is a unique mix of Illustrator, Photoshop, outsourced 3D constructions and what he can only settle on as collage. He often finds that the struggle is in making something still look ethereal and surreal. 'If you look at the originals, it's just getting the light, and getting the reflections right, and trying to make it look as realistic as possible. But I think it's also important for me that I don't want it to be too realistic. There always needs to be this element, this otherworldly feel or something. It's accessible but just out of reach. I think that's what's really fascinating to me,' he explains.

He relishes the reaction his images create. 'That's the biggest kick I get. I look at so much artwork, especially with Instagram and Tumblr – everybody's trying to make art. And my mission is to make it so people can't decode what I've done. That's what makes things interesting. If I look at something and I'm, like, "I don't know how they've done it," then I'm really impressed,' he says. Oorloff also wonders whether this is fair or not, 'but I think I'm finding that everyone's very reliant on the conceptual side of things currently. I'll be going to exhibitions where there may be someone that has put some sand on a piece of paper. And I think people are losing their technical skills. People aren't really spending that much time, and are heavily relying on this conceptual style. I don't know, I like looking at work, like paintings, that people have put hours into, and they've taken a lifetime to refine and get those skills.' It is that sense of detail and the obvious time put into his own work that quickly separates Oorloff from the pack.

KEEPING EVERYTHING RELEVANT

For Oorloff and his electronic music clients 'everything starts off with digital as the priority, and then flows into a physical piece as a secondary thing.' Because it is usually a large digital campaign, he is 'always conscious of how it's going to flow as a series, because everybody wants it to look cohesive. With digital, for instance, I need to make a Spotify banner or a Facebook cover or some sort of representation for the website, maybe a tour poster. So I'm always conscious of the image as a series anyway.' That's not to say that he doesn't love the physical side of things. 'I think people like to have something that's tangible, something that they can hold and they can show off. As a fan who wants to support the artists, you've got to go out and buy the records. I think it's important, and there is a place for it.'

He is still trying to figure out the social media aspect of this industry as it relates to his own work. 'Instagram has been a blessing and a curse,' he admits. He found the lure of online praise could distort his goals. 'It just got to this weird stage where I felt like, "Who am I designing for?" So I had to just rethink the way I posted things

on Instagram. I'm not that naturally good at social media,' he laughs. He has started using Snapchat videos and other tools to get instant reactions to work. 'I just find that decision-making's so much faster if you have somebody to bounce off.'

Oorloff is also expanding his visual references, recently falling under the spell of Rosław Szaybo, and also 'really pushing into this whole retro-futurism thing, combined with a lot of techno posters from the nineties'. He also loves Mat Maitland from Big Active, quickly dubbing him 'the king of collage'. He is quick to add that he tries to travel as much as he can and absorb the little cultural nuances here and there. 'I don't want to get pigeonholed into any particular style, so I'm just looking to absorb things from everywhere and make them look good together. Plus, the seventies retro-futurist sci-fi art, which I've been into for a long time. Sorayama is great. Shusei Nagaoka is incredible. I also go to a lot of gigs, and I often feel like I have a creative pool and when that gets depleted I fill it up by either going for a skate or going for a run. I need to exert myself in some way to get that. It's almost like a form of meditation,' he adds.

Working in music, 'you're an artist working with another artist,' Oorloff explains. So when you have a musician, they put so much time and so much love and effort into this record – way more time than I'd spend on a cover. Working with other artists, they're really involved and it needs to represent their art and represent their vision. It's quite a lot of responsibility, because I feel like I want to do their art justice. And that's what makes it more fulfilling as well.' Oorloff finds himself with a huge mix of music clients, from major label releases to tiny club nights, all with one consistent thread. 'For me,' he explains, 'of the things that I consider before I start a project, first and foremost is that it's got to be relevant to now, or what's happening in the environment. Because people are trying to make things viral now, it needs to be something that's going to go across all the blogs and get as many hits as possible. So it's a new way to think about things. And then at the same time, it needs to be timeless. If it is successful, then it's going to be put into print, and then when it's put into print it's around forever. So it's got to be relevant but also timeless. A lot of the stuff I do is pretty high-impact. I like the thought of it jumping off a shelf. I want people's eye to go straight there and be, "What is this?" Maybe it's not an artist they know, but I want them to pick up the record and look at it and just be, like, "OK, what's this about?" I try to put a lot of energy into it so that it stands out.' That work is more than paying off.

Lucianblomkamp

... of what I don't understand   3. Nothing (Ft. Rromarin)
...rawling ———————————   4. Still No (Ft. Trim) ———

TITLE: Lucianblomkamp, *Sick Of What I Don't Understand*

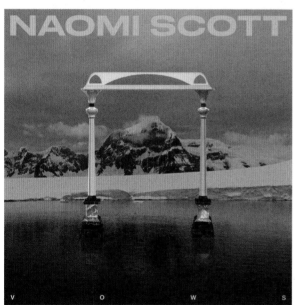

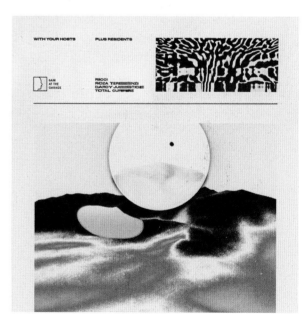

(Clockwise from top left) TITLE: Sluggers, *Anthem*; TITLE: REEKÄRLB, *Twilight Realm*
TITLE: Lucid, *Resident Mix*; TITLE: Naomi Scott, *Vows*

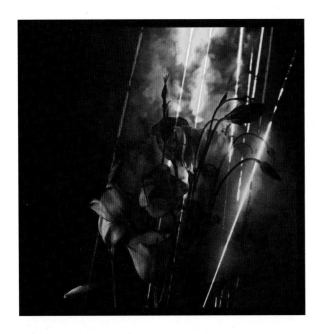

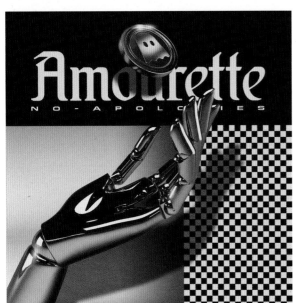

(Clockwise from top left) TITLE *Smoke in the Mirror*; TITLE DJ J-Heat, *New Jersey Transit Systems*
TITLE Crossfaith, *Freedom*; TITLE Amourette, *No Apologies*

TITLE Sam Setton, *My City*

TITLE: Lucianblomkamp, *Sick Of What I Don't Understand*
CLIENT: Huw Nolan, Good Manners
SIZE: 30.4 x 30.4 cm (12 x 12 in.)
PRINTING PROCESS: Offset
INKS: CMYK
COMPS PRESENTED: 1
REVISIONS: None
APPROVAL: Huw Nolan, Hugh Mclure
INVOLVEMENT WITH FINAL PRINTING: Pre-press

'Lucianblomkamp's *Sick Of What I Don't Understand* is an album that is spread across three separate releases,' says Oorloff. 'Each of the releases follows the idea of Lucian's evolving state leading up to its conception.' That evolution meant that part one is represented by fire, in which Oorloff brilliantly manipulates the imagery and type to project the 'slowly releasing anger and confusion contained within Lucian'.

TITLE: Sluggers, *Anthem* EP
CLIENT: Rudy Montejo, SMG, Fools Gold
SIZE: 30.4 x 30.4 cm (12 x 12 in.)
PRINTING PROCESS: Offset
INKS: CMYK
COMPS PRESENTED: 1
REVISIONS: None
APPROVAL: Rudy Montejo, Sam Peter
INVOLVEMENT WITH FINAL PRINTING: None

Working with Wacomka, Oorloff was brought in to design 'an alternate cover variation for Sluggers' *Anthem* EP, one that is exploring themes of duality through typography and shattered glass,' he says. The resulting exploration is one of the most bracing typographic images of the past decade.

TITLE: REEKÄRLB, *Twilight Realm*
CLIENT: Charles Breton
SIZE: 30.4 x 30.4 cm (12 x 12 in.)
PRINTING PROCESS: Offset
INKS: CMYK
COMPS PRESENTED: 1
REVISIONS: None
APPROVAL: Charles Breton
INVOLVEMENT WITH FINAL PRINTING: Pre-press

'French producer REEKÄRLB creates cinematic soundscapes paired with synth vocals,' Oorloff explains. 'The requirements for this cover were to be a vast, spacious landscape, whilst maintaining a degree of warmth and approachability.' The solution showcases an incredible combination of his 3D skills, along with his photo manipulation, to create a one-in-a-million viewpoint.

TITLE: Naomi Scott, *Vows*
CLIENT: Jordan Spence, When Nobody's Watching
SIZE: 30.4 x 30.4 cm (12 x 12 in.)
PRINTING PROCESS: Offset
INKS: CMYK
COMPS PRESENTED: 1
REVISIONS: None
APPROVAL: Jordan Spence
INVOLVEMENT WITH FINAL PRINTING: Pre-press

'Naomi Scott's *Vows* EP required an ethereal landscape with pop influences to match her sound,' explains Oorloff. To do this, he created that landscape from scratch, combining his unique talents to visually construct something mysterious, yet inviting.

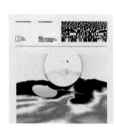

TITLE: Lucid, *Resident Mix*
CLIENT: Benny Rausa, Liam Alexander, 6am at the Garage
SIZE: 30.4 x 30.4 cm (12 x 12 in.)
PRINTING PROCESS: Offset
INKS: CMYK
COMPS PRESENTED: 1
REVISIONS: None
APPROVAL: Benny Rausa, Liam Alexander
INVOLVEMENT WITH FINAL PRINTING: Pre-press

'Lucid's *Resident Mix* presents talents that thread loose ideas of a loose time into a Lucid reality,' says Oorloff. In response, his design manipulates and twists every shape and texture available, while keeping a black-and-white palette that holds this reality together.

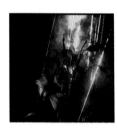

TITLE: Smoke in the Mirror, (Unlicensed Artwork)
CLIENT: Self
SIZE: 30.4 x 30.4 cm (12 x 12 in.)
PRINTING PROCESS: Offset
INKS: CMYK
COMPS PRESENTED: None
REVISIONS: None
APPROVAL: Self
INVOLVEMENT WITH FINAL PRINTING: None

This image of icy-looking roses and lasers comes from Oorloff's desire to communicate 'a war between nature and technology' in creating a visual presentation of the music within.

TITLE: DJ J-Heat, *New Jersey Transit Systems*
CLIENT: Alex Sushon, Night Slugs
SIZE: 30.4 x 30.4 cm (12 x 12 in.)
PRINTING PROCESS: Offset
INKS: CMYK
COMPS PRESENTED: 1
REVISIONS: None
APPROVAL: Alex Sushon, John William Lyons
INVOLVEMENT WITH FINAL PRINTING: Pre-press

For DJ J-Heat, Oorloff went in a different direction from his icy landscapes of robotic figures. He went right down to the subway, though still with his futuristic sheen. 'This cover was really inspired by the Jersey club sound,' he explains. 'Rugged, hollow and ghostly.'

TITLE: Amourette, *No Apologies*
CLIENT: Molly Smith, Ghostly International
SIZE: 30.4 x 30.4 cm (12 x 12 in.)
PRINTING PROCESS: Offset
INKS: CMYK
COMPS PRESENTED: 1
REVISIONS: None
APPROVAL: Molly Smith
INVOLVEMENT WITH FINAL PRINTING: Pre-press

One of the greatest qualities of Oorloff's work is that it can be inherently digital, yet with so much raw humanity. That made him perfect for Amourette's release. 'The requirements for the *No Apologies* cover were to be digital, with a retro-futuristic feel for warmth,' he explains. From the type to the position of the hand and the very act of catching the object, that feeling comes across at every shiny turn.

TITLE: Crossfaith, *Freedom*
CLIENT: Rew Kewbashi, Far East Entertainment, Sony Japan
SIZE: 30.4 x 30.4 cm (12 x 12 in.)
PRINTING PROCESS: Offset
INKS: CMYK
COMPS PRESENTED: 1
REVISIONS: None
APPROVAL: Rew Kewbashi, Kazuya Nakazawa
INVOLVEMENT WITH FINAL PRINTING: Pre-press

'Crossfaith's *Freedom* EP is inspired by a "Neo Tokyo" aesthetic style,' explains Oorloff. 'It follows a narrative in the music set in a dystopian future where the band goes in search of the idea of freedom in a world controlled by artificial intelligence.'

TITLE: Sam Setton, *My City*
CLIENT: Samuel Setton
SIZE: 30.4 x 30.4 cm (12 x 12 in.)
PRINTING PROCESS: Offset
INKS: CMYK
COMPS PRESENTED: 1
REVISIONS: None
APPROVAL: Samuel Setton
INVOLVEMENT WITH FINAL PRINTING: Pre-press

In one of his most evocative cover images, Oorloff depicts singer Sam Setton's journey, 'falling through the overwhelming sprawl of New York,' to create a sense of swimming hopelessly, yet also swirling in mysterious bliss. The end result is truly intoxicating.

LEIF PODHAJSKY

BEAUTY AND REPETITION

 All of the designers that are showcased in this book have created awe-inspiring, breakthrough solutions, but few have excited both the design community and consumers on the retail front in equal measure like Aussie Leif Podhajsky. His colourful psychedelic experiments and explorations play with the mind and the eye until the viewer is less certain about what they have seen, but definitely certain that they love being in that visual world. In that way, Podhajsky is probably the closest thing this generation has to its own Thorgerson – which is really high praise if you note how often Thorgerson is held up as the top of the mountain in this book. That Podhajsky wears that mantle with such grace and dignity and modesty makes him all the more deserving. Alarmingly, it is a career that almost didn't happen. Podhajsky found himself treading water as a graphic designer, before finally deciding that he had to strike out on his own for his mental and emotional sanity. It was lucky for all of us that he did. That move allowed him to begin forming the organic style that was at his fingertips when he gained broad exposure through his work with Tame Impala. Soon afterwards he was in high demand for the human connection inherent in his work, moving from Melbourne to London and then Berlin. The man who previously pushed pixels around emerged as the most emotionally analogue designer in the industry, every little swirl of colour cutting right through to the heart.

'I've been doing this for a number of years now,' Podhajsky begins, 'and when I started out in the music industry there was what seemed to be a slow decline around physical packaging and a move to more of the digital sphere.' He ponders that for a moment, before continuing, 'but as time has gone on, bespoke packaging has taken on a new life and found its place again in the music industry. There's a great thirst for limited editions, vinyl and anything that has a "collectors" feel. For me, this is great as I love designing with these in mind,' he adds. 'At present, there's a really interesting mix of engaging digital media and physical products, which is ideal as I think both have their place and help give scope and completeness to music projects.'

Podhajsky's work has such a deep wash of texture and detail, often mixed with his unique colour sense, that experiencing it with your own hands is optimal (especially when combined with some of his lovingly applied production twists). But his client base is often flirting with the mainstream, so digital applications can be just as important. 'My approach to designing for digital doesn't differ that much, as it's about communicating a message with the viewer, and this is the main rule I try and keep at the centre of my design,' he explains. 'Telling the story of the music, laying the foundation. Small things may change, like the size of the font you would use or making sure that the artwork also works on a small scale, but the overall approach is to focus on the music and create something that works across all mediums.' Speaking of all mediums, his clients' sales figures also mean that they sell their music across every availbale format. 'What surprises me', Podhajsky laughs, 'is that I still get asked to design CD's … it just shows how slow things actually move. I hear there's still a market for them somewhere.'

That drive for consumers to still experience music in a physical way is not lost on Podhajsky. 'There is a huge thirst and appreciation for it at the moment, and as humans I think we always have this connection with tangible objects,' he explains. 'Added to that, vinyl and collectors' editions only enhance the connection we have with music.' He has to smile when thinking about the naysayers when he first started out in the industry. 'I love the resurgence it's having after it was long foretold to be doomed. Although it's niche, physical packaging will always have a part to play in the marketplace.' He also relishes the new innovations in how music can be experienced. 'I feel like nowadays there are so many more interesting outlets for visual art and music to interloop, crossing boundaries of sound and vision.'

EVERYDAY INTERACTIONS
Podhajsky has become such a known commodity in part due to the broad sharing of his imagery online. His unique and evocative images have connected with people on an emotional level, to the point that they are invested in a different way. This modern marketplace, fuelled by technology, creates an interesting distance between the designer and the consumer, though. 'To be honest,' he admits, 'I feel a little removed from my work at times. I've gained a pretty good following on social media and done a lot of interviews, etc … but I miss real connection with people and my art,' he laments. 'The digital world has allowed me to be an independent artist and have my work seen all around the world. I sell prints online and post them out to far-flung destinations; I have clients in different continents, but unless you have community and everyday interactions, it can feel a bit distant and strange.' That has driven him to seek situations where he can see the one-to-one experience with his work. 'I'm going to try and have more exhibitions this year,' Podhajsky explains, 'as I love watching people interact with the work. It feels more real and special.'

Very clearly a disciple of Storm Thorgerson, Podhajsky's visual manipulation challenges his viewers, but he also invites them in his own unique fashion. He is also driven to share with others, so much so that he started his own site for curating those influences. 'I run a blog called Melt (visualmelt.com) with a bunch of other contributors,' he explains. 'I needed this space to detail the many influencers and creators that I feel too often get overlooked: Bas Jan Ader, Caspar David Friedrich, Magritte, Tolkien, Terence McKenna, Moebius, Bosch, Don Brautigam, Rousseau, Johfra, Hermann Hesse, Richard Brautigan, Hemingway, Henry Miller, Nick Cave, Captain Beefheart … and so many others.'

Podhajsky and the music industry are a perfect pair. 'I really like the collaboration,' he admits. 'I like being a part of music that inspires and that will live on forever.' While not fond of the deadlines the work can require, especially with the demands of major-label marketing schedules, he knows that the process is a partnership. 'It is a journey that we take together – this has a big influence on the work. Trying to create a campaign that fits everyone's ideas can be difficult, but it's often about compromise, but also knowing when to stick to your ideas and push for the best, clearest outcome,' he underlines. When it comes together, the packaging tells a story, 'taking the listener and viewer on a journey'. Podhajsky says he has 'always felt music and visual art go hand in hand, lifting each other to form a formidable combination that incites imagination and understanding. To me, as a visual artist, I've always been drawn to that connection. The interesting part is creating a piece of visual art which encapsulates an entire album, communicating its ideas, emotion and power in a single frame, but leaving enough room for interpretation and intrigue. Setting the tone is just as important as conveying the message. Hemingway did something similar in the way he wrote using words with a direct and simple structure to transmit emotion – the reader fills in the blanks with their own imagination. I've always loved that approach, letting the viewer form their own personal connection with the music and artwork but taking them on the first step.'

TITLE: Lykke Li, *Wounded Rhymes*

(Clockwise from top left) TITLE: Lykke Li, *Sadness Is A Blessing*; TITLE: Lykke Li, *I Follow Rivers*
TITLE: Shabazz Palaces, *Live At KEXP* (front); TITLE: Shabazz Palaces, *Live At KEXP* (back)

TITLE: Tame Impala, *Innerspeaker* (and related singles)

TITLE: Tame Impala, *Lonerism* (and related singles)

TITLE: The Horrors, *Higher*

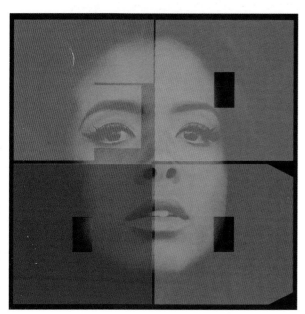
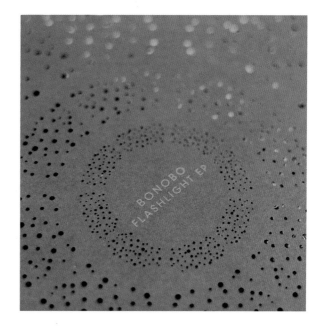

(Clockwise from top left) TITLE: All We Are, *s/t*; TITLE: Mount Kimbie, *Cold Spring Fault Less Youth*
TITLE: Bonobo, *Flashlight*; TITLE: Kelis, *Food*

(Above and opposite) TITLE: Of Monsters And Men, *Beneath The Skin*

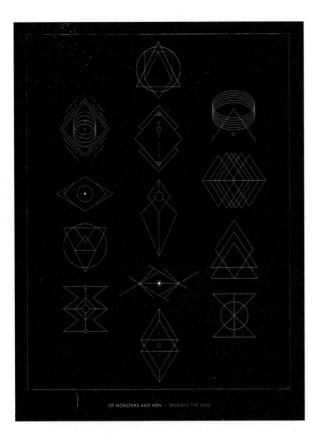

OF MONSTERS AND MEN - BENEATH THE SKIN

OF MONSTERS AND MEN - BENEATH THE SKIN

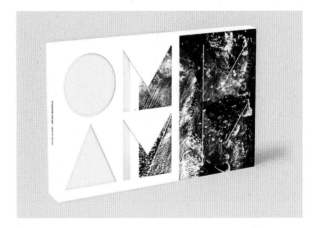

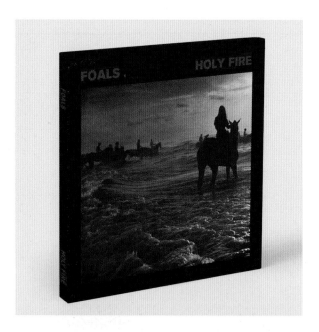

TITLE: Foals, *Holy Fire* (box set cover and related singles)

TITLE: Young Magic, *MELT* (and related singles)

TITLE: Lykke Li, *Wounded Rhymes*
CLIENT: Atlantic
SIZE: 30.4 x 30.4 cm (12 x 12 in.)
PRINTING PROCESS: Offset
INKS: CMYK
COMPS PRESENTED: 1
REVISIONS: Many rounds
APPROVAL: Lykke Li
INVOLVEMENT WITH FINAL PRINTING: Proofs

'I worked closely with Lykke and initially with David Girhammar, he creative partner,' explains Podhajsky. 'We spoke on Skype most mornings, orchestrating different approaches that Lykke wanted to explore. I then went to New York to finalize the layouts with her in person.' The project was aided immensely by original photos by Roger Deckker.

TITLE: Shabazz Palaces, *Live At KEXP*
CLIENT: Sub Pop Records
SIZE: 30.4 x 30.4 cm (12 x 12 in.)
PRINTING PROCESS: Offset
INKS: CMYK
COMPS PRESENTED: 1
REVISIONS: 3 rounds
APPROVAL: Sub Pop Records
INVOLVEMENT WITH FINAL PRINTING: Proofs

Sometimes, a designer's powers of persuasion are just as important as their concept. 'The original photo on this is by Jim Staley,' explains Podhajsky. 'I had to convince him about chopping up his photo, but once I explained the context he understood what I was trying to achieve,' he says. 'My idea for this piece was to recontextualize using collage and a crude cut-and-paste method to explore the themes of the music which has elements of African rhythms fused with new methods of sampling and cutting/chopping up old music and making new sounds from it. I wanted the focus not to be so much on the girl but the new pattern formed by slightly modifying elements of what we perceive as reality.'

TITLE: Tame Impala, *Innerspeaker*
CLIENT: Modular Recordings
SIZE: 30.4 x 30.4 cm (12 x 12 in.)
PRINTING PROCESS: Offset
INKS: CMYK
COMPS PRESENTED: 1
REVISIONS: Many rounds
APPROVAL: Kevin Parker
INVOLVEMENT WITH FINAL PRINTING: Proofs

'What can I say that hasn't already been said?' Podhajsky smiles. 'Kevin Parker, the main man behind Tame Impala, had a strong idea to create a sort of dreamy vortex, tinged with acid. I think this fits the music as perfectly as anything I've worked on.'

TITLE: Tame Impala, *Lonerism*
CLIENT: Modular Recordings
SIZE: 30.4 x 30.4 cm (12 x 12 in.)
PRINTING PROCESS: Offset
INKS: CMYK
COMPS PRESENTED: 1
REVISIONS: 12 rounds
APPROVAL: Kevin Parker / Modular
INVOLVEMENT WITH FINAL PRINTING: Proofs

'Kevin had these photos he had taken in Paris on a disposable camera and felt they captured the feeling of the album really well, being on the outside looking in. Being a sort of loner,' Podhajsky explains. 'The bars are the barrier between the viewer and the people pleasantly sitting in the sun having fun. I really associated with his idea and how the songs felt. I think a lot of people probably feel the same way, so I was interested in the universal feeling of being an outsider but showing this in a cryptic way that might not be obvious straight away. My job was to translate this into a full package and work up this story into the context of the album.'

TITLE: The Horrors, *Higher*
CLIENT: XL Recordings
SIZE: 30.4 x 30.4 cm (12 x 12 in.)
PRINTING PROCESS: Offset
INKS: CMYK
COMPS PRESENTED: 1
REVISIONS: 5 rounds
APPROVAL: Alison Fielding
INVOLVEMENT WITH FINAL PRINTING: None

Every once in a while someone brings in Podhajsky almost like an illustrator. In this instance, he says, he worked with Alison Fielding from Beggars Banquet and the band to come up with a set of marble artworks which would fit into their *Higher* box set. 'The idea was to keep the packaging quite simple in tones and layout with these more wild artworks poking through in parts as you explore the physical packaging.'

TITLE: All We Are, *s/t*
CLIENT: Double Six Recordings
SIZE: 30.4 x 30.4 cm (12 x 12 in.)
PRINTING PROCESS: Offset
INKS: CMYK
COMPS PRESENTED: 1
REVISIONS: 3 rounds
APPROVAL: All We Are
INVOLVEMENT WITH FINAL PRINTING: Proofs

'I met with the band and we really connected and I felt I understood what they wanted straight away,' Podhajsky explains. 'We wanted to convey a vulnerability but also a strength at the same time. I digitally painted this figure sitting on a chair and used different colours to convey a moment along with the messages of the album. I love how simple and complex this is,' he adds.

TITLE: Mount Kimbie, *Cold Spring
Fault Less Youth*
CLIENT: Warp Records
SIZE: 30.4 x 30.4 cm (12 x 12 in.)
PRINTING PROCESS: Offset
INKS: CMYK
COMPS PRESENTED: 1
REVISIONS: Many rounds
APPROVAL: Mount Kimbie, Warp Records
INVOLVEMENT WITH FINAL PRINTING: Proofs

Working with James Burton and Warp Records, Podhajsky found that
the band wanted to 'create artwork which was modern but also took
inspiration from old Blue Note jazz album covers. This is what I came
up with. I remember thinking it fit really well and was glad and surprised
when the band also loved it, especially as it was quite different from my
style at the time.'

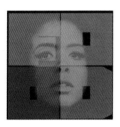

TITLE: Kelis, *Food*
CLIENT: Ninja Tune
SIZE: 30.4 x 30.4 cm (12 x 12 in.)
PRINTING PROCESS: Offset
INKS: CMYK
COMPS PRESENTED: 1
REVISIONS: Many rounds
APPROVAL: Kelis, Ninja Tune
INVOLVEMENT WITH FINAL PRINTING: Proofs

'Working closely with Kelis and Ninja Tune, this album was sort of a different
approach for Kelis,' Podhajsky explains. 'She wanted to explore a more
earthy, soulful sound and visual style.' The resulting cover, along with the
accompanying singles, provided a refreshing new look for the pop star.

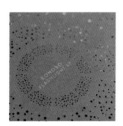

TITLE: Bonobo, *Flashlight*
CLIENT: Ninja Tune
SIZE: 30.4 x 30.4 cm (12 x 12 in.)
PRINTING PROCESS: Offset
INKS: CMYK
COMPS PRESENTED: 1
REVISIONS: 10 rounds
APPROVAL: Bonobo, Ninja Tune
INVOLVEMENT WITH FINAL PRINTING: Proofs

'We wanted to create something special for this vinyl release and I designed
this die-cut dot pattern which revealed this almost larva-like yellow and gold
artwork beneath, which shone through the holes like a light in the dark,'
explains Podhajsky. 'Working closely with Sean Preston from Ninja Tune,
we used new techniques in laser cutting that I didn't think would be
possible with such small holes,' he marvels. 'The sleeve is on matt stock
with the inner sleeve, which shines through, on supergloss. I really loved
this juxtaposition of texture, which helps highlight the concepts of light
and dark.'

TITLE: Of Monsters And Men,
Beneath The Skin
CLIENT: Republic Records
SIZE: 30.4 x 30.4 cm (12 x 12 in.)
PRINTING PROCESS: Offset
INKS: CMYK
COMPS PRESENTED: 1
REVISIONS: Many rounds
APPROVAL: Of Monsters And Men, Republic
INVOLVEMENT WITH FINAL PRINTING: Proofs

One would think creating a design around simplifying four letters would
be, well, simple. Podhajsky, however, turned it into an act of brilliance.
'Working closely with the band, we wanted to explore a super-simple and
graphical representation of their logo, with the artwork hidden within
the letters,' he explains. But once he was done with it, it was filled
with texture and depth, making the shapes that much more amazing.

TITLE: Foals, *Holy Fire*
CLIENT: Warner, Transgressive
SIZE: 30.4 x 30.4 cm (12 x 12 in.)
PRINTING PROCESS: Offset
INKS: CMYK
COMPS PRESENTED: 1
REVISIONS: Many rounds
APPROVAL: Foals, Warner Bros. Records
INVOLVEMENT WITH FINAL PRINTING: Wet proofs
and colour adjustments

'Yannis, from Foals, had found this image of these horses in the water
and wanted to explore this as a representation of the album,' Podhajsky
explains. Working from the original image by Thomas Nebbia, Podhajsky's
job was 'to crop and texture the photo to convey this sense of mystery
and intrigue – set the story in motion, so to speak'.

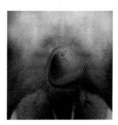

TITLE: Young Magic, *MELT*
CLIENT: Carpark
SIZE: 30.4 x 30.4 cm (12 x 12 in.)
PRINTING PROCESS: Offset
INKS: CMYK
COMPS PRESENTED: 1
REVISIONS: Many rounds
APPROVAL: Young Magic, Carpark
INVOLVEMENT WITH FINAL PRINTING: Proofs

'This cover is one of my favourites,' admits Podhajsky. 'I worked closely
with good friends Young Magic on this artwork. It was a really nice way
to work as I knew the band and the music really well prior to beginning
this journey. I think this really helped me form ways of working later on
in my career, how to work with musicians, how to translate the music
into a visual representation.'

BRIAN ROETTINGER

THE NEW VISUAL LANGUAGE

 How the skate-punk kid from Los Angeles became the most sought-after designer in the music industry is a true example of extreme talent finding its way to the top. Brian Roettinger graduated from CalArts in 2004 and quickly started helping his friends with their music projects, whether with posters or packaging or just getting a record pressed. In a funny way, he was always the person you would turn to to figure out how to get something done. Soon he was juggling a position at the Southern California Institute of Architecture with running his own Hand Held Heart record label and design firm, and his relationship with the band No Age was helping to produce some of the most interesting music packaging being done today. A Grammy nomination for No Age's *Nouns* record kicked everything into high gear and Roettinger knew he needed just to commit to his own pathway. What he couldn't possibly have known was that soon afterwards the biggest stars in the industry, from Jay-Z to Selena Gomez, would be joining the roster of indie stalwarts looking to bring his unique perspective to their projects. Not only is he now the designer behind some of the largest commercial records in the marketplace, but he is redefining the role of the designer in the music industry entirely. 'As I have done this longer, and for bigger artists, the role of a designer, and the general responsibilities of a designer, have changed dramatically in the sense that it's not just, "Oh, what's the album cover going to look like?" but "What is the rollout going to be? What's the campaign? What are we saying? What's the visual language? How does this translate across all media?"'

'My gateway into the music industry was not industry-related. I was doing stuff for smaller bands that weren't on major labels. So there rarely was an emphasis on innovation in terms of album packaging. We didn't think about social media or fan base or how many of these will we sell or what was the price point,' Roettinger explains. So much of that early work was about making something physical to document the music, that it is hard-wired into his current work. 'I hold so much weight in that process of making something physical, but a lot of bigger artists are not that invested in the tangible,' he adds. 'I notice Selena Gomez, she has millions of fans, but it doesn't necessarily mean those fans are super-psyched to buy some elaborate album packaging. In that sense, what's more important is what is the actual cover, what is the image, so in that sense it is more digital, because it's just purely about an image. But we do make tons of different versions of the albums, like limited ones, and box set ones that our fans buy, but it's not as important as the actual image itself.' He stresses that 'the weight the packaging plays really differs from artist to artist.' With Radiohead, they have the fan base that wants the tangible item. And I think that's actually changing, and it has changed in the last five years, with the resurgence of vinyl, and objects, people want to have tangible things, and that's never going to go away. So record labels and artists have started to see that, and they want to do cool packaging. They want to give them a reason to actually buy it.'

Roettinger stresses that 'no one wants to just spend ten dollars, twelve dollars and just get the songs with nothing, when they could just stream it and not have to pay. So giving them that extra bonus material, that is what feels special,' he adds. 'I think that has become a lot more of a commercial consideration than it ever has been, at least since the CD killed album packaging in the eighties.' It is that push that allows him to convince a massive artist that creating a sticker set for their release, or a crazy die-cut, or a more involved booklet or box set, is not only the cool thing to do, but absolutely necessary.

I AM EVERYWHERE

Few designers have the chance to see such high-profile releases roll out and experience the reaction on social media. 'Once anything is finished, and goes public, it's no longer the artist, or it's no longer my work; it's public, it's everyone else's,' Roettinger explains. 'But I do obsess, and I love all the versions that are reappropriations or bootlegs. There are tons of the Jay-Z ones where people make it a different number, like cross out the "44" and write "20", so it says "420", or they use different numbers, and they don't even have to do anything, they can just use the colour, put a little type on the top, and put a number at the bottom, and you're, like, "That's referencing the Jay-Z record." It's such a simple digital language, and it's easy to mimic, and that was the same with *Magna Carta*, in that people would have a black-and-white image, put some big black type, and then have it redacted, and it was easily bootleggable, easily recognizable, and I think that's when you know something is successful is when it is instantly recognizable.' Seeing these adaptations is not only gratifying, 'it also gives [the work] a lot more legs, it spreads the visual language,'

As Roettinger is influencing popular culture, his own work hearkens back to his favourites, such as Peter Saville, Hipgnosis and Barney Bubbles. Pretty much everything Hipgnosis did is phenomenal, and Factory Records is probably my favourite label of all time. Then Barney Bubbles is just so good.' He knows he is just calling out the classics but 'the consistency that they all had, I am just jealous,' he admits. The biggest influence on his work might very well be the unexpected. 'I am inspired by a lot of fine arts, which I think is obvious, but there's all sorts of things, from street typography to different types of writing to other cultures, typography, theatre, ballet, dance, sport. I hate to say that I'm inspired by everything, but I'm usually inspired by things that are unintentional,' he adds, before detailing his walk following a meeting in Times Square, 'where I saw this massive digital billboard, where the graphic that's supposed to be presented on it was missing, so it was just flashing all the error codes, and the sizes of the images, the dimensions, really big, and it was stunning, better than any other ad you could ever see!' he laughs. 'It was an error, but those are the things that I find so beautiful, because they had no intention of being visually compelling. Everything is so calculated, and designed, and fabricated, and painstakingly gone over that when something's just unintentional, and feels like, "Whoops!" – those are the beautiful moments.'

Roettinger is at the heart of a sea change in the industry. 'Artists have started to realize the value in having an art director overseeing everything, a person who understands what all this visual language is,' he explains. 'Before, they would split up all of the tasks, but now the general population is familiar with these artists as a brand, so just like any corporation or agency they have creative directors on staff, artists are starting to have that because they see the value.' That means getting his hands into a lot of areas. 'I like to see what the album cover looks like, then who is going to direct the music video, and what does the live show look like, how does that all come together as one cohesive statement?' he explains. 'I want to make sure that they all speak the same language. That they all carry the same tone and qualities and level of sophistication.' It's a challenge made greater 'with the way social media works now. With everything shared and in the public and so immediate, I find that there's so much competition, not between artist and artist, but just between seeing images,' he says. 'We could see millions of images a day that are disposable, so how do you create consistency within the clutter, and how do you make the artist jump out? That's my job now.'

TITLE: Jay-Z, *Magna Carta*

4:44

TITLE: Jay-Z, *4:44*

TITLE: Mark Ronson, *Uptown Special*

CAPSIZED
ROMA FADE
TRUTH LIES LOW
PUMA
CHEMICAL SWITCHES
LEFT HANDED KISSES
ARE YOU SERIOUS
SAINTS PRESERVUS
THE NEW SAINT JUDE
VALLEYS OF THE YOUNG
BELLEVUE
TRIMMED AND BURNING
VENETIAN BED MAKER
DYING BEDS
JACKSON BED MAKER
SHOULDER MOUNTAIN
PULASKI
CAPSIZED SOUND CITY

ANDREW BIRD
ARE YOU SERIOUS

(Top) TITLE: Andrew Bird, *Are You Serious*
(Bottom) TITLE: Duran Duran, *Paper Gods*

TITLE: Florence + The Machine, *How Big, How Blue, How Beautiful*

SISTERWORLD

...ECTION AND DESIGN BY BRIAN ROETTINGER
PHOTOGRAPHY BY ZEN SEKIZAWA
STYLING BY JENNIFER JOHNSON

TITLE: Liars, *Sisterworld*

NOUNS

TITLE: No Age, *Nouns*

TITLE: No Age (various releases)

TITLE: Jay-Z, *Magna Carta*
CLIENT: Roc Nation
SIZE: 30.4 x 30.4 cm (12 x 12 in.)
PRINTING PROCESS: Offset
INKS: CMYK
COMPS PRESENTED: 1
REVISIONS: 5 rounds
APPROVAL: Jay-Z
INVOLVEMENT WITH FINAL PRINTING: Proofs

As Roettinger explains it, the driving force behind this direction was really the redacted type and the photos of Ari Marcopoulos. 'The very black-and-white, 35-mm plain-shoot photographs that became this photo essay, where the photographs were essentially pointing towards the lyrical content, so there was a direct relationship to what Jay-Z was saying and the images that we were showing.'

TITLE: Jay-Z, *4:44*
CLIENT: Roc Nation
SIZE: 30.4 x 30.4 cm (12 x 12 in.)
PRINTING PROCESS: Offset
INKS: CMYK
COMPS PRESENTED: 1
REVISIONS: 5 rounds
APPROVAL: Jay-Z
INVOLVEMENT WITH FINAL PRINTING: Proofs

'For this release we really boiled it down to a few ingredients. We wanted something that could be immediate across any platform,' Roettinger explains. 'If it just becomes about a logotype, a title and a colour, we can take that colour, because we could own that colour; it's not like a colour like blue or red or green that is in the spectrum that people are familiar with. We can take ownership of that, we can take that colour, wrap a bus, or we can take that colour with no information and put it on a billboard.' That ownership of the colour started with the cover. 'Once people are familiar with it – "Oh yeah, that's the Jay-Z thing" – we can make merch that's just the colour of the shirt and we don't even have to say the name or title, we could just put something else. There were billboards that had no information in the beginning – just the colour. But then there were other billboards at the same time that were just the title with no information ... and then it started. It'd be three billboards in a row but then one billboard would say "4:44," and the others were blank but just the colour. It became this super-corporate takeover, whereby having this blank colour almost looks like you're erasing something that was there. It just felt like this blanking out of everything else and just being able to focus on this one element.'

TITLE: Mark Ronson, *Uptown Special*
CLIENT: RCA
SIZE: 30.4 x 30.4 cm (12 x 12 in.)
PRINTING PROCESS: Offset
INKS: CMYK
COMPS PRESENTED: Many
REVISIONS: Many rounds
APPROVAL: Mark Ronson
INVOLVEMENT WITH FINAL PRINTING: Proofs

'With Mark Ronson, I knew this had to be a very immediate, didactic, very graphic illustration or something. And he kept saying, "I want a logo, I want a logo," and we'd go back and forth about it,' Roettinger explains. 'He was sending me logos, like Red Hot Chili Peppers, or Rolling Stones, or Black Flag – some of the most iconic logos ever – and it's just, like, these are great and of course someone wants something that good,' he says. Roettinger started trying to redirect him with '"This is a cover, just stop thinking about a logo, blah, blah, blah," and then I just had to make something quickly, with photos and type, and as we were talking on the phone and discussing it I was making all these notes, and I was drawing speakers, records, and I was drawing turntables and wheels. I looked in my sketchbook and saw that all of these things are in the same circular format. I thought it should work really well if you blew it up, like a Roy Lichtenstein. It almost felt like it was from a newspaper, but it shouldn't be an illustration of a speaker or something. It should still have an element of abstraction, of some sort of super-pop visual language, I just did one version, really drew it up, and sent it to him, and he was, like, "This is it, wow, let's go for it," and it was really quick, and I should have just done what he asked at the start,' he recalls. 'Now, he uses it for everything and it's essentially his logo. Mark will say that he thinks the design actually helped the success of the song and the record, in that it was really globally acceptable and immediate.'

TITLE: Andrew Bird, *Are You Serious*
CLIENT: Loma Vista
SIZE: 30.4 x 30.4 cm (12 x 12 in.)
PRINTING PROCESS: Offset
INKS: CMYK
COMPS PRESENTED: 1
REVISIONS: None
APPROVAL: Andrew Bird
INVOLVEMENT WITH FINAL PRINTING: Proofs

When you know something is perfect, sometimes it is best to just go straight to the source. 'Andrew and I were going back and forth about stuff that felt aesthetically right and had a level of wit, a sense of humour, a use of language, and a use of imagery that felt, like, serious but funny,' Roettinger explains. Looking at a lot of John Baldessari's work they thought, 'This is great, maybe we could go in this world, and for me when something's so right on point, I'm very uncomfortable to just mimic. So we went straight to Baldessari, and Andrew and I met with him. I gave him all the song titles and he chose images that fit each title.' When making the box set he tried to format things so that it was 'very much how the physical object felt – almost like a Baldessari installation.'

TITLE: Duran Duran, *Paper Gods*
CLIENT: Warner Bros
SIZE: 30.4 x 30.4 cm (12 x 12 in.)
PRINTING PROCESS: Offset
INKS: CMYK
COMPS PRESENTED: 4
REVISIONS: 4 rounds
APPROVAL: Duran Duran
INVOLVEMENT WITH FINAL PRINTING: Proofs

How do you reinvent a band with such a rich visual history as Duran Duran? You create 'all these magnetic pieces that can be stuck to the cover so you could build the cover,' explains Roettinger. The magnets are direct references to past hits from the band.

TITLE: Florence + The Machine, *How Big, How Blue, How Beautiful*
CLIENT: Island Records
SIZE: 30.4 x 30.4 cm (12 x 12 in.)
PRINTING PROCESS: Offset
INKS: CMYK
COMPS PRESENTED: 1
REVISIONS: 3 rounds
APPROVAL: Florence + The Machine
INVOLVEMENT WITH FINAL PRINTING: Proofs

'The format of the book for this set was really special, just filled with wonderful images,' Roettinger says.

TITLE: Liars, *Sisterworld*
CLIENT: Liars
SIZE: 30.4 x 30.4 cm (12 x 12 in.)
PRINTING PROCESS: Offset
INKS: CMYK
COMPS PRESENTED: 1
REVISIONS: 3 rounds
APPROVAL: Liars
INVOLVEMENT WITH FINAL PRINTING: Proofs

For Liars's *Sisterworld* album, Roettinger explains, the design was dictated by the physical packaging. 'We were at my house, and wondering about creating this alternate universe that you can have a peep inside – How can we make images that were hidden, that you had to physically do something to see them? – and then that influenced the concertina/accordion fold,' he adds. The cover has a very personal touch for Brian. 'It's just the inside of my front door,' he explains. 'It's the speakeasy window in my front door, so it was perfect, it felt right aesthetically, and worked well small, but it also felt like there's something inside there.' The conversation quickly turned to 'What if there's a big ocean and forest, which was inspired by *Lord of the Flies*, where there is the potential to be in this world where no one else fits, except for themselves, which was how the band was feeling at the time.'

TITLE: No Age, *Nouns*
CLIENT: Sub Pop Records
SIZE: 30.4 x 30.4 cm (12 x 12 in.)
PRINTING PROCESS: Offset
INKS: CMYK
COMPS PRESENTED: 1
REVISIONS: 10 rounds
APPROVAL: No Age
INVOLVEMENT WITH FINAL PRINTING: Proofs

TITLE: No Age, *Everything In Between*
CLIENT: Sub Pop Records
SIZE: 30.4 x 30.4 cm (12 x 12 in.)
PRINTING PROCESS: Offset
INKS: CMYK
COMPS PRESENTED: 1
REVISIONS: 10 rounds
APPROVAL: No Age
INVOLVEMENT WITH FINAL PRINTING: Proofs

TITLE: No Age, *An Object*
CLIENT: Sub Pop Records
SIZE: 30.4 x 30.4 cm (12 x 12 in.)
PRINTING PROCESS: Offset
INKS: CMYK
COMPS PRESENTED: 1
REVISIONS: 10 rounds
APPROVAL: No Age
INVOLVEMENT WITH FINAL PRINTING: Proofs

'No Age is maybe the band I've worked with the longest. We have been friends for a long time, and have the same musical interests, and got into music the same way,' Roettinger explains. 'It's very collaborative, our process, being that they're just a two-piece. I become this anchor where if the two of them don't agree on something, I could usually break that. It's a healthy collaboration, in that over the years if all of us don't like something, then we don't do it,' he adds. 'With every record, we just have a dialogue and talk about ideas, and talk about the music, and talk about where this record could go visually, what did we do on the last one, what did we do on the one before that, why did we do it? Where are you guys at musically, where should this record be?' As much as the conversations seem to repeat, there is another quirk to their working process. 'I'd say for every record we've done, we've probably done a handful of different versions each time that were, like, "This is it, this is it, it's done, perfect, we're done, let's sleep on it," and we will come back the next day or two, and be, like, "Oh, what were we thinking?" All of us. We're pretty in sync in that way. Sometimes we start over, or sometimes we just change things, but it's a very different experience to all the other records I do,' he adds. 'They'll come to my studio, and we'll just share ideas and work on it. It's almost like I'm a third member in that way.'

SAM RYSER

LYNCHPIN ON MY LEATHER JACKET

 It's funny that one of the youngest designers in this collection should be far and away the most old-school in so many ways. Sam Ryser harkens back to a time when New York City, and most urban areas in the US, had been abandoned and left to artists and kids to run amok and explore and exploit. He is a lynchpin in an ever-growing underground punk scene that is taking back neighbourhoods and redefining what it means to interact with music and fashion and art. Much like so many of the seventies punk record labels that got their start by running stalls in the markets, Ryser has opened a shop inside a shipping container in an alleyway in Brooklyn. Surrounded by like-minded merchants, Dripper World is a collection of records, T-shirts, badges, posters, cassettes and a barrage of one-off items, many of which have Ryser's creative hands in them. In an odd way it serves as a temple of inspiration. Seeing all of it in person reminds shoppers that they too could make some of these things, and the entire operation feeds into Ryser's desire for the community to carve out their space in a city that is increasingly hoping to price them out. Within that scene Ryser is simply everywhere, whether playing in a band, illustrating a label's T-shirt, designing a cassette label or record sleeve, or making one of many zines in collaboration with others. I am sure he would be too humble to think about it in this way, but it is his creative sensibility that defines this scene and makes it the coolest-looking underground music scene in the entire world.

Ryser's punk rock lifestyle can have its drawbacks at times. 'I live in New York City and have been moving a lot recently,' he explains. 'Limitations on space and volume and my record player being dismantled and lost in the moving process have led me to a long stretch of listening to music mostly digitally,' he laments. 'I think that probably lumps me into the majority of people who don't care about physical pieces of music. Needless to say, the packaging element is just shy of eradication in this format. This makes packaging a record today all the more important to grab the potential listener's attention, whether it's going to exist on or off the Internet,' he says. 'Now, most bands have a Bandcamp, YouTube video, Spotify account, whatever AND a tape or record or all of the above. This combination and multitude of physical and digital platforms to draw the public into the world of your band is a massive change from the past, where two to three formats dominated the experience.'

'I design mostly for punk bands, like my own, who are more reluctant to take the kind of full digital dive that people in other genres have (free albums on the Internet, YouTube singles, U2 invading my privacy),' Ryser explains. 'Personally, I'm pretty technologically inept, and despite trying to learn I do ninety-nine per cent of my art old school,' he admits. 'If a band wants me to design a full record sleeve and insert, it will be scanned and touched up slightly, sized, formatted and sent over the Internet. But I have yet to do a band's website or do any actual composing digitally,' he explains. 'I would love to try either of those things, though,' he laughs.

SEEING IT ALL WITH HIS OWN EYES

Having his own store has given Ryser a lot of persepctive. 'Running a small shop, it's pretty clear to me that things that look like shit are valued a lot less than things that look great,' he says. 'Of course, you are speaking to someone who has a collection of empty soda cans ... but I think in terms of a broader public, it seems like a great band can be heard first and it won't matter to most people if their records or shirts look that cool. That being said, great art is always used as a selling point,' he adds. He also believes in adding as much value to the entire package as is possible, especially with added booklets and zines and posters, making the consumer truly excited to have made their purchase. 'The fact that you can hear anything on the Internet makes a record with nothing but vinyl inside a little disappointing,' he adds. Ryser is also a lover of music first and foremost and he will 'always pull a good-looking LP from the bin and take a chance on it if it looks great'.

DRAWING IT LIKE YOU LIVE IT

Ryser is forever in awe of the work of anarcho-pacifist artist and designer Gee Vaucher, best known in music circles for her work with the band Crass. When he is drawing and designing, he also brings to the table a fascination with 'hand-painted store signs; generic packaging imagery for disposable party supplies like balloons and tablecloths; canned beverages, especially old ones but some new ones; porcelain trinkets; school supply stores; business cards; T-shirts for schools or summer camps or crappy construction companies'. In a lot of ways, Ryser obsesses over the everyday designs that most people take for granted and often look past. Mixing the dismissed and discarded with a sharpened punk rock outlook brings about a potent, and personalized, mode of visual attack.

'I think a band's image can be the difference in them being understood or not,' Ryser adds. 'In a sense, you are contextualizing them, even if it is just for a shirt or something small.' His process takes all of that into account, creating an internal back and forth that produces unexpected results. 'Sometimes in my head I have to go, "OK, this band sounds like this, so this type of imagery is too similiar to their sound, this other style too random, this one is just random enough that it's intriguing, this font mixed in will draw you in and ground it." It's like a pinball hitting all the right bumpers,' he explains. 'Getting to do these projects is such a cool job,' he is quick to add. 'I love the problem-solving aspect, and figuring out how a band is presented makes for one of the best jobs there is out there.'

One of the drawbacks to working in an underground marketplace can be financial. Ryser also laughs that occasionally he gets a great commission and feels that flow of 'millions of ideas, and I feel like a genius', only to then sit down in front of a piece of paper and discover that he 'suddenly sucks at drawing and it is just agony to get those ideas out onto the sheet.' But all of that goes by the wayside 'when all the visual elements of the band or artist are cohesive and help to sculpt out and draw you into the world of the music. When those lines are blurred, nothing else matters and everything is perfect forever.'

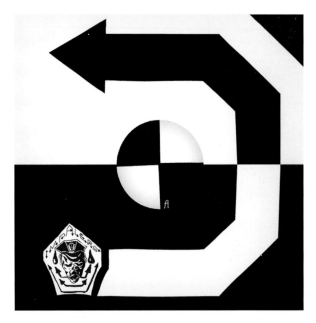

(Clockwise from top left) TITLE: Hoax, *s/t*; TITLE: Impalers, *Psychedelic Snutskaller*
TITLE: S.H.I.T, *Feeding Time*; TITLE: Mind Control, *s/t*

TITLE: Various artists, *Ground Zero NYC 2013 compilation*

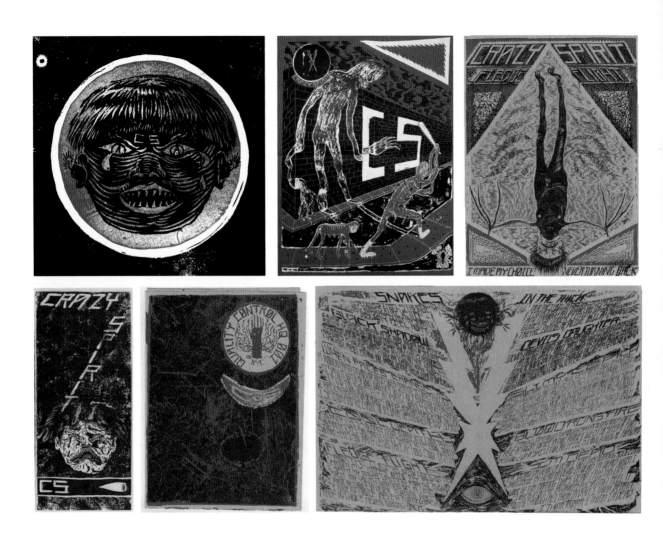

TITLE: Crazy Spirit, *Demo* (LP and various materials)

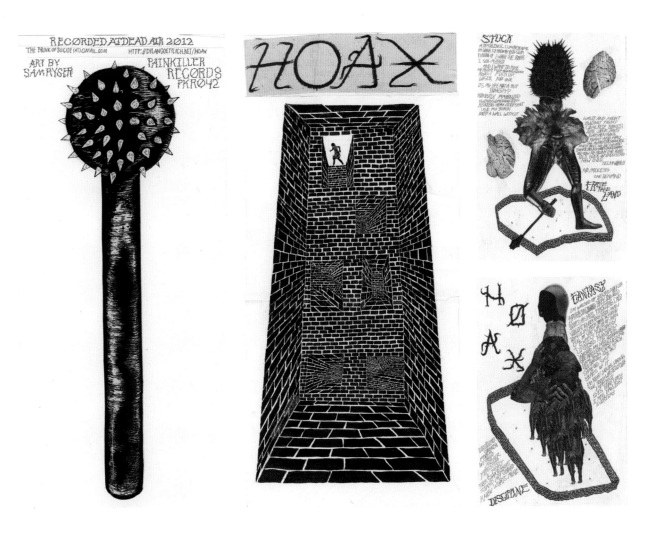

TITLE: Hoax, *s/t*

TITLE: Hoax, *s/t*
CLIENT: Hoax
SIZE: 30.4 x 30.4 cm (12 x 12 in.)
PRINTING PROCESS: Offset
INKS: Black
COMPS PRESENTED: 1
REVISIONS: None
APPROVAL: Hoax
INVOLVEMENT WITH FINAL PRINTING: None

Truly providing value for your money, Ryser explains that, 'for Hoax's album, they included a full-size poster for every song on the album by a different artist that they were friends with or involved with, including Cali DeWitt, Mark McCoy, Matt Adis, Shawn Filley, Sugi, Heather Benjamin, Emma Kohlmann, Guillem El Muro, Alex Heir, Colin Swanson-White, Jaybo Gardner and Tony Pasquarosa.'

TITLE: Impalers, *Psychedelic Snutskaller*
CLIENT: 540 Records
SIZE: 30.4 x 30.4 cm (12 x 12 in.)
PRINTING PROCESS: Offset, die-cut
INKS: Black
COMPS PRESENTED: 1
REVISIONS: None
APPROVAL: Impalers
INVOLVEMENT WITH FINAL PRINTING: None

'The head of 540 Records suggested that we do a die-cut cover, something similar to a promo copy of an old RnB single,' Ryser details. Diving head first into the process, he managed to capture that spirit perfectly, while still adding enough of his unique brand of weirdness to make it classic Ryser. After all of that, Ryser finds a unique bit in the final production that still delights him. 'My favourite part is that the inside of the cover is also printed,' he adds with a smile.

TITLE: Mind Control, *s/t*
CLIENT: Forward Records and Mind Control
SIZE: 30.4 x 30.4 cm (12 x 12 in.)
PRINTING PROCESS: Offset
INKS: CMYK
COMPS PRESENTED: 1
REVISIONS: 1 round
APPROVAL: Mind Control
INVOLVEMENT WITH FINAL PRINTING: None

'Mind control are from Duluth, and commissioned me for this asking for the theme of "mob mentality." I made a collograph print [stacked cut out shapes of cardstock paper rolled with ink and printed] for the cover and back cover, and took a relief print of some garbage for the centre labels,' Ryser details. 'The lettering on the cover is cut-out paper and the red streak is ripped-up paper,' he adds. After all of that one-of-a-kind hand work was complete, Ryser, 'realized I had accidentally copied a Rolling Stones cover design,' he adds with a smile and a shake of the head.

TITLE: S.H.I.T, *Feeding Time*
CLIENT: Static Shock Records
SIZE: 30.4 x 30.4 cm (12 x 12 in.)
PRINTING PROCESS: Screen-print
INKS: 2 spot inks
COMPS PRESENTED: 1
REVISIONS: None
APPROVAL: S.H.I.T
INVOLVEMENT WITH FINAL PRINTING: None

On occasion, Ryser's illustrations can be both playful and brutally direct. For the *Feeding Time* release from S.H.I.T he went immediately to dripping shit typography, surrounded by eager mouths. 'This was drawn with china marker and watercolor,' he adds, 'and there are shit-eating mouths on the labels too.'

TITLE: Various artists, *Ground Zero NYC 2013 compilation*
CLIENT: Toxic State Records
SIZE: 30.4 x 30.4 cm (12 x 12 in.)
PRINTING PROCESS: Screen-print, hand stamp, offset, risograph
INKS: Various
COMPS PRESENTED: 1
REVISIONS: 2 rounds
APPROVAL: Toxic State Records
INVOLVEMENT WITH FINAL PRINTING: Screen-printing

Much of Ryser's work is collaborative. 'The art for this record reflected the bands involved in the compilation,' he explains. 'I did the cover and back cover, Eugene Terry did the poster and there is a lyric booklet with a page for every band, drawn by a different band member. The cover of the booklet was drawn in charcoal by Henry Wood. Artists included Keegan Dakkar, Emil Bognar Nasdor, Mateo Cartagena, Nadine Rosario, Eugene Terry, Eric Hughes, Alex Heir, Shiva Addanki, Chi Orengo, to name a few.' Ryser 'chopped the original photo up for the centrefold so that it looked like broken glass was running through it. Ultimately it was decided that it was too confusing,' he adds, 'so now that version is hanging in someone's bedroom,' he laughs. For the screen-print, Ryser, 'drew the cover in red, and then we printed it in sky blue for the effect we wanted,' utilizing the unique controls available in the small-run printing process.

TITLE: Crazy Spirit, *Demo*
CLIENT: Quality Control, Toxic State Records
SIZE: 30.4 x 30.4 cm (12 x 12 in.)
PRINTING PROCESS: Offset
INKS: CMYK
COMPS PRESENTED: 1
REVISIONS: None
APPROVAL: Crazy Spirit
INVOLVEMENT WITH FINAL PRINTING: Originally screen-printed by hand by the group

'For the Quality Control release we printed the entire run of these by hand,' Ryser explains. 'With the covers printed on cardboard mailers we had to chop them all down to size by hand. I sent Ola stamps I had carved for the labels, which mostly fell apart in the mail,' he laments. 'In total, there were eight screen-prints per record, not including stamped covers and labels.' This is also a unique release in that this is the only Crazy Spirit record where Ryser was the only member of the band to make the artwork.

TITLE: Crazy Spirit cassettes
CLIENT: Toxic State Records
SIZE: 6.5 x 10.16 cm (2.56 x 4 in.)
PRINTING PROCESS: Screen-print
INKS: Various
COMPS PRESENTED: 1
REVISIONS: None
APPROVAL: Crazy Spirit
INVOLVEMENT WITH FINAL PRINTING: Helped with the screen-printing

'In Crazy Spirit each member takes care of a different part of the record,' Ryser explains. 'Whether it is carving a stamp for the centre label or drawing the insert. For this record I made the cover texture [which is different for each Crazy Spirit record] and red circle [also different for each release], and the poster. Henry Wood and Eugene Terry split up all the artwork for the twenty-page booklet, and we printed different colour schemes in the different presses.'

TITLE: Hoax, *s/t*
CLIENT: Painkiller Records
SIZE: 30.4 x 30.4 cm (12 x 12 in.)
PRINTING PROCESS: Offset
INKS: Black
COMPS PRESENTED: 1
REVISIONS: None
APPROVAL: Hoax
INVOLVEMENT WITH FINAL PRINTING: None

Perhaps my favourite way to see Ryser work is within the confines of black and white, stretching into his zine-making territory [Ryser teaches zine-making classes]. For this Hoax record his manic attention to ever shifting little details in his illustrations are evident, along with his unique handmade typography. All of it covering a folded LP cover, double-sided poster, and the usual labels. 'Absolutely everything here is collaged and hand drawn,' he is quick to add.

SPENCER DRATE & JUDITH SALAVETZ

JUST A COUPLE OF ROCKN'ROLLAS FOR LIFE

Marshall Crenshaw has been known for penning ear-candy tunes about quirky relationships, but it was in designing his landmark solo debut that one of the most prolific unions in album design history was formed. Spencer Drate had a knack for walking into high-profile jobs early in his career, whether working on ads for John Lennon or diving into Richard Hell and The Voidoids' *Blank Generation*, with the latter leading to a relationship with the iconic Sire Records. Soon after, while working on the Crenshaw album, Judith Salavetz asked if he might be interested in seeing what would happen if they worked together. Drate asked her to jump right in, and the rest is history. The duo would quickly find themselves working on projects for artists from Joan Jett to Bon Jovi, eventually amassing album covers for twenty-two inductees into the Rock and Roll Hall of Fame. Drate would follow his work for Billy Squier into the first-ever appearance by an album cover designer on MTV. Grammy nominations merged with exhibitions everywhere from the Louvre to MoMA, as the pair have also championed the form by writing numerous books and hosting exhibitions around the world. Some of their work for the likes of Talking Heads and The Velvet Underground would forever change the way the industry viewed design and production possibilities, making them the undisputed first couple of album cover design.

Where do you see differences in how designers today approach designing for the music industry versus when you started out?

SD: It is designing with the computer today, whereas a large period in my early music design life was a 'paste-up and mechanicals' era. The design approach is the same – a great concept with a great design! Most designers are NOT great type designers – the key to great design! Also, with the computer now you can do amazing things, composing and obtaining a 'clean' visual design. In my early days we dealt with 'traditional' retouchers; now Photoshop 'cleans' those images flawlessly. The problem I see in computer design is that some designers get too caught up in special effects and they lose the 'quality' of line in design, and photographers fall into this trap, also. The approach, in the end, as a designer is simple: you must have a great concept and design no matter what time period you are living in.

What are your feelings on the current vinyl boom and resurgence of large-format music packaging?

SD: Love it and have written articles on the vinyl area. My first book was *45 RPM* (2002), the first book on the history of the 45 [RPM]record picture sleeve! In the beginning of the vinyl discussion. Then after selling over 22,000 books worldwide we decided to author our *Five Hundred 45s* book, with a foreword by Lenny Kaye. Now we were in the middle of the vinyl explosion! A perfect book at a perfect time! The seventies was the most exciting LP packaging era, with die-cut albums galore, like Led Zeppelin's *Physical Graffiti*, which won a Grammy for best album packaging, Rod Stewart's 'whisky glass' album [*Sing It Again Rod*], J Geils's 'telephone' album [*Hotline*] and many more – the height of great LP design! I like the resurgence of vinyl and the large format, but I miss 'special packaging' in this area, as in the seventies. The 'special packaging' area in CDs was great – Spencer Drate, Judith Salavetz and Sylvia Reed designed a pro-only 'metal box' with CD and booklet for Lou Reed's *Magic and Loss* album, along with a 'peel-off bananas' CD package with booklet and CD for the Velvet Underground 1993 live

tour album; and Spencer Drate and Judith Salavetz designed a letterpress limited-edition CD of the Joseph Arthur *Let's Just Be* album, with booklet. I did not miss the LP in this era because we could use special materials, special effects and special printing techniques – a designer's dream. My co-design with Talking Heads for their *Fear Of Music* LP was Grammy-nominated for best album packaging in 1979 and is in the MoMA permanent collection, plus in a MoMA show this past year! This album had a special printed 'embossed' vinyl pattern on the album cover surface – one of the most iconic designed albums. In the end, I do hope the Vinyl LP does stay for music designers!

How important is it to present music with a physical representation?

SD: I feel people want to touch things and look at packaging, and if music packaging is well designed, people will want to keep it. I feel printing is so important. On computer there is only a 72 dpi visualization – not even close to 150 dpi at least in printing! Relating to books, we have authored twenty-one visually driven pop-culture books; printing in photo or art books is still big with readers. Rizzoli bookstore in NYC only deals with photo and art books and is successful. Printed matter is important to people.

How has selling music changed for you?

SD: This has not changed for me as a music designer. You are always presenting and hopefully executing great concept and design for the public.

Which designers are really exciting you currently in music packaging?

SD: Always has been: Stefan Sagmeister, Julian Alexander, Sean Mosher Smith, Brian Roettinger, Jeri Heiden, Vaughan Oliver, John Berg, John Pasche, Tom Recchion, Steve Byram, Peter Corriston, Roger Dean, Jamie Reed, Nigel Grierson, Stylorouge, John Warwicker, Storm Thorgerson, Peter Saville, Gabrielle Raumberger, Paula Scher, Kim Champagne.

HENRY OWINGS

START MAKING SENSE

One of the more interesting aspects of the reinvigorated vinyl market has been the return of deluxe box sets for reissued catalogue. Many labels specialize in this, and as that market has grown, many of them have come to Chunklet Graphic Control's Henry Owings to make sense of piles of audio and materials and turn them into something cohesive and spectacular. With his experience in releasing records on his own label, combined with his detailed archivist history, he is always the right designer for the job. This kind of box set work is almost a speciality industry in its own right, and I asked Henry to pull the curtain back for us a little bit.

'These jobs start up when I get an email. I get a call. I get a thumb drive. I get some text,' he begins. 'After that? It's really every man, woman, child and graphic designer for him/herself. My goal is to make sense out of so many divergent sources. My technical title is "art director" but oftentimes I find that a more fitting title is that of "puzzle solver" or "pixel janitor". Owings finds that these projects are generally label-driven. 'It's rare that I work directly with the artist,' he adds. 'I typically work with either the producer or the producer's assistant. I think it's best that there's a buffer between me and the artist.'

In debating how true to the era of the music inside he should stay, Owings often does so, 'but doing everything on a computer makes things go WAY faster. For instance, when I worked on the Hüsker Dü box set, I wanted it to feel like an early issue of *Forced Exposure* magazine, where the type was laid out mechanically and the images felt like they went through a photocopier. Did I use a photocopier? Yes, of course. But when it came to final execution, I had to bring it into the digital realm to finalize.' Owings looks at his computer 'the way a carpenter looks at a hammer or a screwdriver: it's a tool. In the early nineties, when I was very green to design, I was fortunate enough to watch Chris Bilheimer work at the REM office as he designed things for me,' he adds. 'I paid close attention to what he did, and his methodologies were (and continue to be) very influential to what I do.'

'One of the biggest problems I've had is that of quality material to work from,' he laments. 'The *Unwound* set is a good example. The label promised me tons of material to fill four boxes, but there just wasn't much to work with. So what did I do? I started shaking the trees. I know tons of photographers, and I asked them if they had any photos. When those avenues were exhausted, I then asked around even more,' he adds. Luckily, Jeffery Winterberg emerged with countless rolls of the band performing early in their career and he sent me negatives to scan.' He also has to deal with lots of images coming in web resolution, as he figures out how to make them work for large-scale print. 'It's a lot harder than it looks,' he admits. 'Basically, if it looks like I didn't do anything, I did my job.'

Every project like this has a dedicated team. Owings might handle ninety-five per cent of the design, but he might also 'hire a cartoonist to hand-illustrate some type (White Zombie, Scientists) or hire a high-end photo-retouch guy to resurrect the photos (Lee Hazlewood was a beast in that respect)'. He says he also knows that his job is 'made easy by producers that know what they want and trust me to do what I'm hired to do. When a producer has "a vision" it makes my job frightfully easy. If the producer is indecisive? It makes the project a nightmare. Luckily for me, that rarely happens,' he adds. 'Furthermore, I must give a big shout-out to the production people who make heads and/or tails out of what I provide them,' he says. 'As a guy that got his start working in the pre-press world, I try to make their job easy, but when I mess up (which can happen), they are super-vital to making sure that fuck-ups don't exist in the final product.' These projects often take years to assemble, but by the time they get to Owings, he generally has a few months to do his work. 'I just try to get my part done fast so they can get to selling records.'

'These projects rely on my history in publishing, writing, tour managing, and not just design,' he adds. 'Being a music nerd myself, I'm familiar with, if not downright obsessive about, a lot of the projects I work on. The collaborative facet of what I do is a lot of fun. And I've yet to be disappointed with the results.'

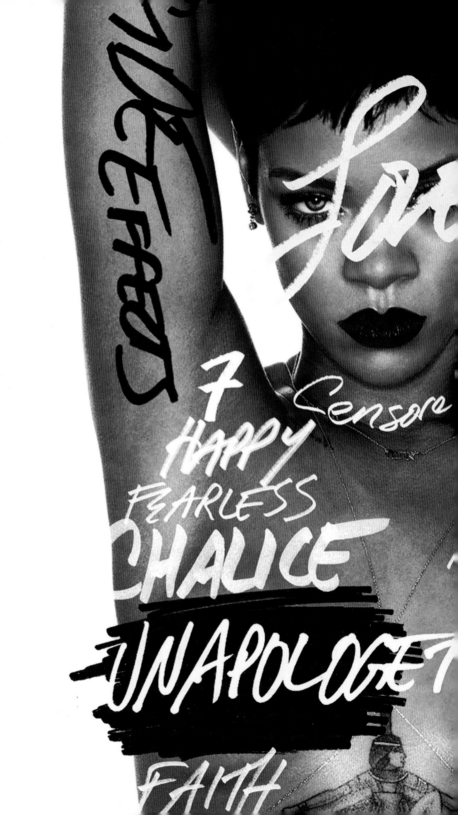

SCHULTZSCHULTZ

TWO WRONGS MAKE A RIGHT

 Marc Schütz and Ole Schulte founded Frankfurt-based agency Schultzschultz in 2007, after the two had met while working together at a small design firm. The smiles in their photo echo the playfulness in their naming of the agency. The duo make the very most of everything around them, including the likelihood that others will constantly mispronounce their names. Combining a love of both music and typography, they have quickly emerged as among the most engaging sleeve designers in the industry. Their ability to create something so cutting-edge and jaw-dropping out of just a few letterforms stands alone at the top of the mountain. I can't think of a studio that has compiled such incredible work as a stand-alone, much less the immense collection of awe-inspiring sleeves when taken as a whole. Not only are they incredible designers, but they are passionate about sharing those skills and inspiring others. That has led to their creating their own typeface designs, as well as teaching and speaking at the university level. If they empower the next wave of designers to be even half as talented and fun as they are, the world will instantly be a much better place.

'We've always wanted our music packaging to look great and stand out, because we consider the record sleeve to be a design object,' Schütz notes, but adds that there was a disruption to the artfulness of package design when 'smaller' became the norm. 'Fifteen years ago there were more CDs on the market, so we were also designing a lot of digipaks, which we didn't like because of the tiny format. Fortunately, with the rise of streaming and digital sales, digipaks are no longer relevant.'

They are quite happy that vinyl records are becoming collectables again, so their colourful, eclectic designs have room to groove, so to speak. 'Now a record collection is regarded as a design object by its owner, there's more focus on the record sleeve,' Schütz says. 'Most covers we design are released as physical objects, but we need to transfer the design to many different web formats for marketing. Since the design is no longer tied to a certain size, format or materiality, we try to make it work regardless of size and format.' Their bold work is tailor-made for these needs, working just as well on a record-store shelf as it does in a playlist on a streaming service. In some ways, that is just a nice by-product, as their hearts are clearly in the LP format.

Even though there are multiple factors in the release of the album, the actual object is still the main priority, according to Schütz. It is there that they can make the most of the format, and also bring along some creative bells and whistles via production techniques. 'We think that people who buy physical records like the authentic object, so we try to amplify the physical experience by adding special materials and finishes. We always try to visualize the music in the design,' he explains. 'Since we predominantly design for electronic music artists, most of our designs are abstract and influenced by op art, minimalism, suprematism and computer art, for example. And often they are just results of experimentation on the computer. Sometimes the experiments work and sometimes – even better – they fail.' Those happy accidents pay off nicely in their work. 'The abstract nature of the musical content gives us extreme creative freedom. We translate loudness, rhythm and repetition into bright colours, geometric shapes and optically confusing patterns, sharp contrasts and distorted typography … and that's really kind of fun to do.'

HERE I AM. LISTEN TO ME!

Because their designs have been so well received, the labels and artists trust them to do their thing – no drawn-out meetings or briefs required. 'Album cover design is much like a poster or book cover in a square format,' he explains. 'It has to attract people immediately, catch the eye and shout, "Here I am. Listen to me!" But it's much more than clickbait for the busy consumer. Schultzschultz's covers look as though they should be hanging in a gallery. 'You also have to consider that some people will put their favourite cover on a shelf or even frame it for some time. They usually don't do that with a magazine spread or a business card,' he says with a big smile.

With those goals in mind, they bring that playful sense of experimentation, along with cutting-edge typographic skills, and mix in a surprising amount of restraint. They know when one colour is enough to get the job done, and when a blitz of visual noise is needed. In the end, they are always looking to build something that will last, regardless of musical trends or visual whims. When all is said and done, their music packaging will be left standing.

According to Schütz, longevity speaks volumes. 'If you look at a record sleeve ten years later and still think it looks kind of cool, that's true success.'

TITLE: Ambivalent, *Daylights*

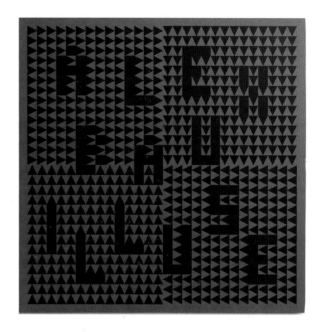

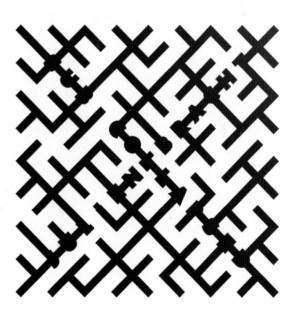

(Clockwise from top left) TITLE: Ilario Alicante, *Virgo Storm*; TITLE: Alex Bau, *Illuse*
TITLE: Julien Bracht, *Sub Collapsed*; TITLE: Sascha Dive, *Werewolf In The Woods*

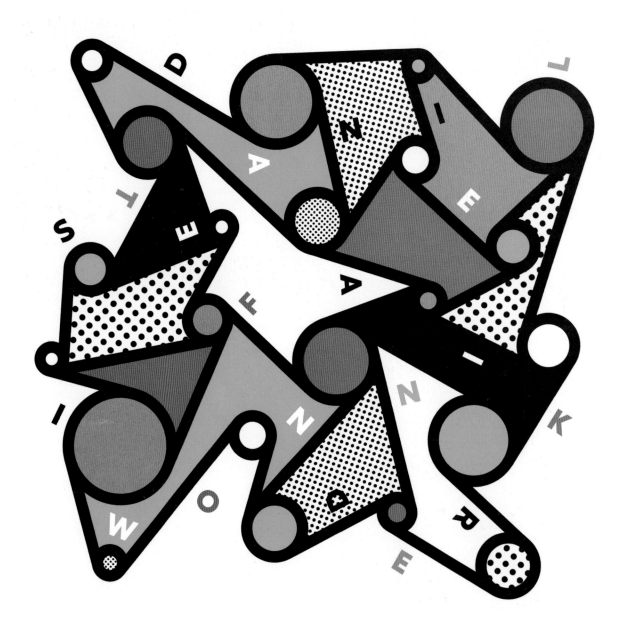

TITLE: Daniel Stefanik, *I Wonder*

TRESH ER DU NDOV SPIKE

(Clockwise from top left) TITLE: Mauro Picotto & Riccardo Ferri, *The Riff*; TITLE: Tim Green, *The Humming Syrup*
TITLE: Gregor Tresher and Petar Dundov, *Spike*

(Clockwise from top left) TITLE: Alan Fitzpatrick, *Truant*; TITLE: UNER, *Phamovi*
TITLE: wAFF, *Freeks*

VINCE WATSON · SPEAKER FREAKER
LC 11279 A SIDE
COR10011 ℗+© 2016 COCOON RECORDINGS
WRITTEN AND PRODUCED BY VINCE WATSON
PUBLISHED BY SPHERECOM MUSIC /
WESTBURY MUSIC LTD, LONDON.
DESIGN BY SCHULTZSCHULTZ.COM
MADE IN GERMANY

4260038314562

wordandsound

TITLE: Vince Watson/Frank Lorber, *Speaker Freaker / L'Obscure Objet Du Désir*

TITLE: Ambivalent, *Daylights*
CLIENT: Cocoon Recordings
SIZE: 30.4 x 30.4 cm (12 x 12 in.)
PRINTING PROCESS: Offset
INKS: CMYK
COMPS PRESENTED: 2
REVISIONS: None
APPROVAL: Cocoon Recordings
INVOLVEMENT WITH FINAL PRINTING: None

For US-born Berlin resident Kevin McHugh, who records as Ambivalent, Schütz felt that 'letters floating in the sky' would go perfectly with the monster bass-shaking techno inside. The type reacts almost as if the music is vibrating the cover from the interior.

TITLE: Ilario Alicante, *Virgo Storm*
CLIENT: Cocoon Recordings
SIZE: 30.4 x 30.4 cm (12 x 12 in.)
PRINTING PROCESS: Offset
INKS: Black
COMPS PRESENTED: 1
REVISIONS: None
APPROVAL: Cocoon Recordings
INVOLVEMENT WITH FINAL PRINTING: None

The Italian techno maestro provided heavy tracks for the *Virgo Storm* record, and in coming up with their ingenious black-and-white design that is filled with movement, Schütz explains that they drew heavily 'on weather maps for inspiration'.

TITLE: Alex Bau, *Illuse*
CLIENT: Cocoon Recordings
SIZE: 30.4 x 30.4 cm (12 x 12 in.)
PRINTING PROCESS: Offset
INKS: 2 spot inks
COMPS PRESENTED: 2
REVISIONS: None
APPROVAL: Cocoon Recordings
INVOLVEMENT WITH FINAL PRINTING: None

The subtle shifts in this design bring about an immense amount of tension, added to the spot-ink prinitng, which makes sense when Schütz explains that they wanted to convey 'harsh and cruel treatment' on the sleeve for *Illuse*.

TITLE: Sascha Dive, *Werewolf In The Woods*
CLIENT: Cocoon Recordings
SIZE: 30.4 x 30.4 cm (12 x 12 in.)
PRINTING PROCESS: Offset
INKS: CMYK
COMPS PRESENTED: 1
REVISIONS: None
APPROVAL: Cocoon Recordings
INVOLVEMENT WITH FINAL PRINTING: None

Creating an insanely awesome type-based solution, where so many designers would have had to rely on imagery for a title as evocative as *Werewolf In The Woods*, Schultzschultz instead convey 'aggression, a feeling of danger, spiky, bloody', all in two bold colours and a single manipulated font.

TITLE: Julien Bracht, *Sub Collapsed*
CLIENT: Cocoon Recordings
SIZE: 30.4 x 30.4 cm (12 x 12 in.)
PRINTING PROCESS: Offset
INKS: Black
COMPS PRESENTED: 1
REVISIONS: None
APPROVAL: Cocoon Recordings
INVOLVEMENT WITH FINAL PRINTING: None

Julien Bracht is one of the rising stars of the live techno scene, primarily down to his raw drum sound, which he often improvises on an acoustic set as he DJs. Playing the drums since he was six years old, it is when he locks in that the dance floor really fills up, so it makes total sense that Schultzschultz would 'bring the letters of this minimalistic design and merge with the graphic layer, locking everything together'.

TITLE: Daniel Stefanik, *I Wonder*
CLIENT: Cocoon Recordings
SIZE: 30.4 x 30.4 cm (12 x 12 in.)
PRINTING PROCESS: Offset
INKS: 4 spot inks
COMPS PRESENTED: 1
REVISIONS: None
APPROVAL: Cocoon Recordings
INVOLVEMENT WITH FINAL PRINTING: None

The Schultzschultz team had done some amazing one- and two-colour graphic solutions for Stefanik previously, but for *I Wonder* they decided to build a 'semi-illustrative, two-dimensional graphic and letter sculpture, and print it with four beautiful spot inks'.

TITLE: Mauro Picotto & Riccardo Ferri, *The Riff*
CLIENT: Cocoon Recordings
SIZE: 30.4 x 30.4 cm (12 x 12 in.)
PRINTING PROCESS: Offset
INKS: CMYK
COMPS PRESENTED: 1
REVISIONS: None
APPROVAL: Cocoon Recordings
INVOLVEMENT WITH FINAL PRINTING: None

Tackling this percolating track, the look of intersecting angles darting about makes perfect sense. Marc Schütz is quick to note that the sleeve has a heavy debt to 'early 20th-century Italian futurist poster design'.

TITLE: Tim Green, *The Humming Syrup*
CLIENT: Cocoon Recordings
SIZE: 30.4 x 30.4 cm (12 x 12 in.)
PRINTING PROCESS: Offset
INKS: CMYK
COMPS PRESENTED: 1
REVISIONS: None
APPROVAL: Cocoon Recordings
INVOLVEMENT WITH FINAL PRINTING: None

As part of a series of releases for London-based DJ/producer Tim Green, the studio developed a design where the type would wrap around a circular object in the middle of each sleeve. Schütz felt that 'syrup-like sound waves humming out from the middle' would be the perfect fit here.

TITLE: Gregor Tresher and Petar Dundov, *Spike*
CLIENT: Cocoon Recordings
SIZE: 30.4 x 30.4 cm (12 x 12 in.)
PRINTING PROCESS: Offset
INKS: CMYK
COMPS PRESENTED: 1
REVISIONS: None
APPROVAL: Cocoon Recordings
INVOLVEMENT WITH FINAL PRINTING: None

This record is essentially a massive techno freakout, leaving the listener mildly disoriented as they dance about the club, so the 'minimal typography has maximum impact' in how Schultzschultz manipulate it.

TITLE: Alan Fitzpatrick, *Truant*
CLIENT: Cocoon Recordings
SIZE: 30.4 x 30.4 cm (12 x 12 in.)
PRINTING PROCESS: Offset
INKS: CMYK
COMPS PRESENTED: 1
REVISIONS: 2 rounds
APPROVAL: Cocoon Recordings
INVOLVEMENT WITH FINAL PRINTING: None

Alan Fitzpatrick brings an insistent bass thump to *Truant* and Schultzschultz pick up on the music's tribal nature to create a perfect hybrid of techno house and Native American tapestry.

TITLE: UNER, *Phamovi*
CLIENT: Cocoon Recordings
SIZE: 30.4 x 30.4 cm (12 x 12 in.)
PRINTING PROCESS: Offset
INKS: CMYK
COMPS PRESENTED: 1
REVISIONS: None
APPROVAL: Cocoon Recordings
INVOLVEMENT WITH FINAL PRINTING: None

'The title is a combination of the first syllables of each track name that is contained on this record,' Schütz explains. 'We therefore also built the letters of this fragmentary title from graphic fragments.'

TITLE: wAFF, *Freeks*
CLIENT: Cocoon Recordings
SIZE: 30.4 x 30.4 cm (12 x 12 in.)
PRINTING PROCESS: Offset
INKS: CMYK
COMPS PRESENTED: 1
REVISIONS: None
APPROVAL: Cocoon Recordings
INVOLVEMENT WITH FINAL PRINTING: None

There is something inherently fun and mildly retro about the shuffling track here, and the studio's 'semi-illustrative freakish graphics on a simulated stone background' form a perfect fit.

TITLE: Vince Watson / Frank Lorber, *Speaker Freaker / L'Obscure Objet Du Désir*
CLIENT: Cocoon Recordings
SIZE: 30.4 x 30.4 cm (12 x 12 in.)
PRINTING PROCESS: Offset
INKS: 2 spot inks
COMPS PRESENTED: 1
REVISIONS: None
APPROVAL: Cocoon Recordings
INVOLVEMENT WITH FINAL PRINTING: None

In this design for a deep techno-house track, two spot inks seep into each other via overprint, like the music diving deep inside your conciousness.

SONNENZIMMER

SOUNDS OF THE SUNROOM

 There are few people in the world that I would rather sit down and talk about design and the creative process with than Nick Butcher and Nadine Nakanishi, the married duo behind the studio Sonnenzimmer (German for 'sunroom'). Seeing and, more importantly, hearing their minds at work can be a darting dance of push and pulls. They are razor-sharp yet compassionate and, more than anything, genuinely inquisitive. The results of their combined talents are creations that could only come from one place, awash in inviting colours, yet often placed in wildly challenging forms. When you discover that it is the end of a process in which one is often setting out new questions just as the other thought they had finally discovered the answer, you can see the layers forming that make their work so visually rewarding, and you understand that the two of them working together is inherent in that success. In many ways, their design work is akin to the way improvisational music works, when two players know each other well enough to play off of one another, yet their skills complement more than just overlap, quickly forming something completely unique and of the moment. Put simply, the work of Sonnenzimmer is quite simply music to the eyes.

Photographer, Troy Lehman

'It's has been fun and confusing to follow the tide of format changes that have influenced the industry for the last twenty years,' Butcher says. 'CDs went from being the gold standard to garbage in a fairly short timespan. I love that cassettes are making a comeback. Digital music is great for discovering new things, but makes things feel disposable/interchangeable, too. Streaming is just that: once it flows down the stream it's forgotten without a physical reminder.' Nodding her head, Nakanishi adds that 'It went from bulky presence to digitally intangible.' Butcher ponders that point and adds, 'I guess the standard now seems to be that the physical format is just a memento of our tactile past, while the digital presence and reach of music is the real showroom. Most physically engaged packaging seems to be reserved for vinyl fetishists at the moment, but there are always interesting things happening in the experimental music world. I just heard about a cassette packaged in a jar of water, for example!' he exclaims.

Nakanishi is quick to add that clients are drawn to them as designers of physical products, in line with their reputation in the printmaking world. 'When we get to do album work it is very much attached to the physical product,' she explains, so when that turns into the digital aspect 'it gets reverse-engineered.' Though she admits that they 'usually have ideas of what the moving image will be, working digitally still fits in with our improvised process,' she reveals.

The duo still ponder what exactly all of this means as far as the value of physical products in the current marketplace is concerned. 'It seems to be a stand-in for the status quo, says Nakanishi. She likens it to 'how it isn't a book until you have a book tour'. Butcher quickly adds that for him, 'if it isn't there to challenge your relation to physical items in general, it's probably just a beefed-up trophy thing.'

Once that product is out in the marketplace, Butcher feels like their reactions usually stop at the client. 'If they are happy with what we have produced, we're happy.' But Nakanishi is more keen to view it as a long game, and is willing to wait to see what might tip the scales. 'It is very delayed,' she explains. 'It can take up to three years to feel traction for the work, although sometimes it is faster. Sometimes we can see the feedback in terms of units sold, or distribution we can achieve. Blogs haven't really done much for us in the past five years. Traditional media is still pretty influential, surprisingly. A mention in *Pitchfork* can outdo our work of five years! A write-up in the *Chicago Tribune* can reach a lot of people,' she explains. Those outlets having an influence on sales can be both rewarding and frustrating.

A MAP OF THE STORM

Sonnenzimmer are students of design and innovation in print, and they are quick to acknowledge past masters such as Storm Thorgerson, with Nakanishi infuriated that a recent major piece on Pink Floyd in the *Guardian* failed to menton his contribution. Others, such as Yokoo Tadanori, Kim Hiorthøy, Stefan Marx and Ronny Hunger, elevate the form to the skies. As one would expect, they also bring to the table a diverse set of creative influences in their work, with Nakanishi referencing 'Robert Davidson (Eagle of the Dawn), Amy Sillman, the Chicago printmaking community, Dawn of Midi, Third Coast Percussion'; before Butcher adds, 'indigenous mapmaking, Steve Reich, my introverted friends who make solo electronic music, the endless awesomeness and boringness of techno, Niklaus Troxler and Jimi Hendrix.' Somewhere in that intriguing mix is the making of their genius.

When they are tasked with designing packaging for music, Nakanishi finds that they are 'allowed to go into the spatial qualities of the medium instead of being stuck in symbolism', before adding that it 'makes for a different kind of aesthetic atmosphere you can build on'. Butcher wonders if any image works with any kind of music. 'That's just the nature of pairing art and sound,' he suggests. 'There is an inherent forced connectivity we do as viewers/absorbers. That's the brilliance and curse. You can basically cram anything into the square or rectangle canvas provided by music packaging and it will speak. The question is what are you trying to say with it? Musicians seem to be genuinely open to the visual interpretation of their work, too,' he adds.

Nakanishi quickly agrees. 'They are very demanding in the best way. They know what it means to create your own aesthetic library, what it means to think about new work and make a body of work. The people we work with give us actual space to explore to find new things. They don't talk to us as mechanics but as peers that are equally creating work at the same time.' Butcher nods and relishes the musicians' 'willingness to go on a journey'. He does add that 'putting the band's name on the cover' can result in a long debate at times.

Butcher explains that their clients are 'mostly artists that are self-financing their releases. This usually gives us a lot of freedom, but not a huge budget,' before adding that 'working within constraints gives us new ideas.' Nakanishi is quick to point out that 'musicians have a real solidarity for the arts, and often we feel they are less confined to the self-imposed silos we put ourselves in. They understand music is the arrangement of shapes, and are confident in making art. It makes for better dialogue and less control.'

The pair find themselves excited about each new adventure a music-packaging design job can bring, and their unique set of skills has made for some of the most incredible CD and LP designs of the last decade. 'To be honest,' Butcher adds with a devilish smile, 'I'm looking forward to the next physical format.'

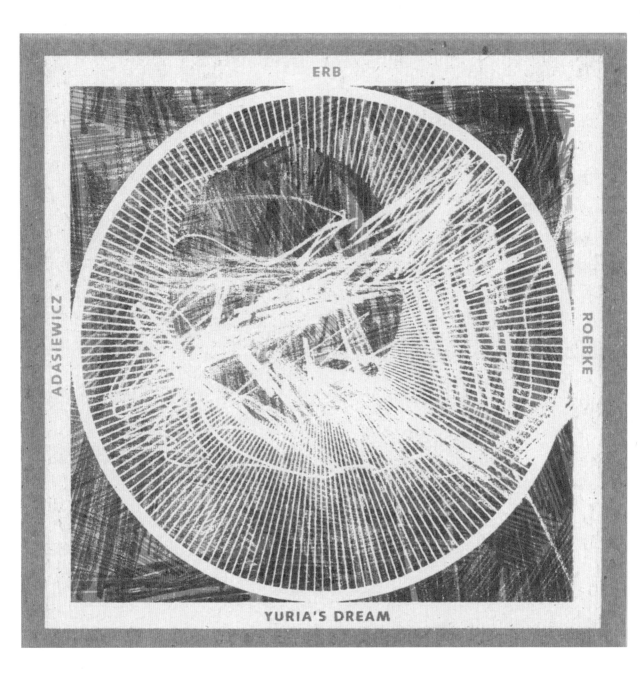

TITLE: Adasiewicz/Erb/Roebke, *Yuria's Dream*

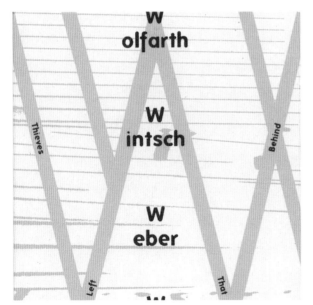

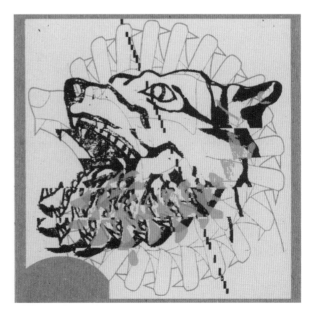

(Clockwise from top left) TITLE: Erb/Baker/Zerang, *s/t*; TITLE: Veto Exchange (various releases)
TITLE: The Urge Trio, *Live At The Hungry Brain*; TITLE: Wolfarth/Wintsch/Weber, *Thieves Left That Behind*

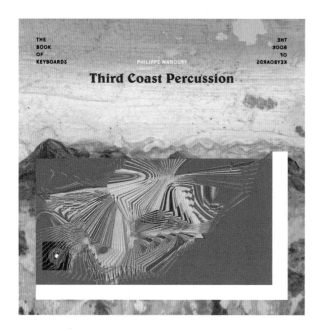

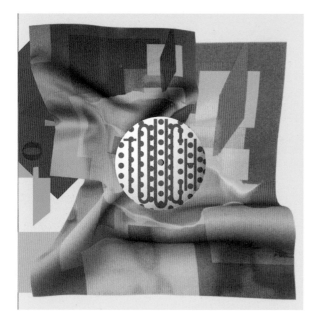

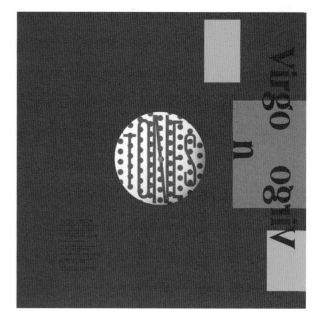

(Clockwise from top left) **TITLE:** Third Coast Percussion, *The Book Of Keyboards* (front); **TITLE:** Third Coast Percussion, *The Book Of Keyboards* (back) **TITLE:** Touch Tones, *Virgo on Virgo* (back); **TITLE:** Touch Tones, *Virgo on Virgo* (front)

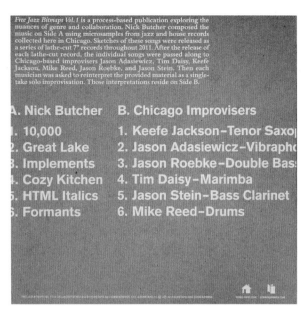

Nick Butcher, Keefe Jackson, Jason Adasiewicz,
Jason Roebke, Tim Daisy, Jason Stein, Mike Reed

Free Jazz Bitmaps Vol. 1 is a process-based publication exploring the nuances of genre and collaboration. Nick Butcher composed the music on Side A using microsamples from jazz and house records collected here in Chicago. Sketches of these songs were released as a series of lathe-cut 7" records throughout 2011. After the release of each lathe-cut record, the individual songs were passed along to Chicago-based improvisers Jason Adasiewicz, Tim Daisy, Keefe Jackson, Mike Reed, Jason Roebke, and Jason Stein. Then each musician was asked to reinterpret the provided material as a single-take solo improvisation. Those interpretations reside on Side B.

A. Nick Butcher

1. 10,000
2. Great Lake
3. Implements
4. Cozy Kitchen
5. HTML Italics
6. Formants

B. Chicago Improvisers

1. Keefe Jackson–Tenor Saxop
2. Jason Adasiewicz–Vibraph
3. Jason Roebke–Double Bass
4. Tim Daisy–Marimba
5. Jason Stein–Bass Clarinet
6. Mike Reed–Drums

TITLE: *Free Jazz Bitmaps, Vol. 1*

SONNENZIMMER

CHICAGO
U S A

SZ005
PUBLICATION
Round w Flat w Sound Collated
Printed June, 2014, Chicago
at Sonnenzimmer
First printing, edition of 250
Published by Sonnenzimmer, July, 2014
Music and art by Nick Butcher
& Nadine Nakanishi
All rights reserved. © 2014 Sonnenzimmer

POSTER
Round w Flat w Sound-Sphere
Tag Exact, 100 # cover, 5-color screen print
Printed at Sonnenzimmer, Chicago

Frontispiece: *Inflation*, video stills, 2014
Recorded May, 2014 in Chicago
at Sonnenzimmer

TRACK
Round w Flat w Sound
Flexi record, 33 RPM, 6 min.
Recorded May, 2014 in Chicago
at Harold Washington Library
and 36 S Wabash Ave.

This publication was produced on the occasion
of the exhibition *Cannonball Run III*
at Zeitgeist Gallery, Nashville, Tennessee, July, 2014.

This is # _____

Round
w Flat w
Sound

SZ005

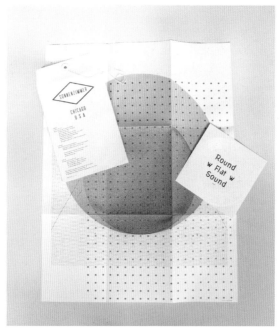

TITLE: *Round w Flat w Sound*

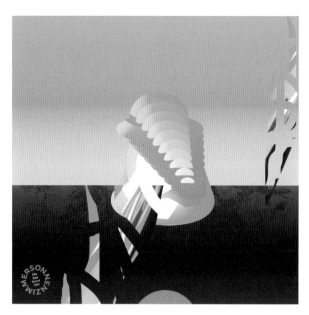
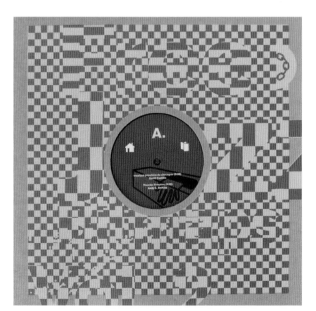
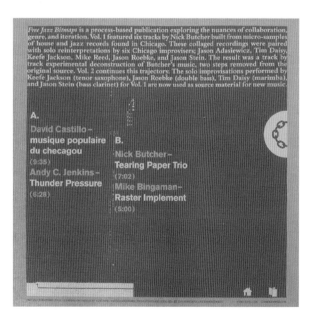

(Top) TITLE Sonnenzimmer, *The Sun Never Sets*
(Bottom) TITLE *Free Jazz Bitmaps, Vol. 2*

TITLE: Adasiewicz/Erb/Roebke, *Yuria's Dream*
CLIENT: Veto Records
SIZE: 12.7 x 12.7 cm (5 x 5 in.)
PRINTING PROCESS: Screen-printed
INKS: Cyan, magenta, yellow
COMPS PRESENTED: 1
REVISIONS: None
APPROVAL: Christoph Erb, Veto Records
INVOLVEMENT WITH FINAL PRINTING: Album sleeve screen-printed in-house

'At some point in your design career, you are beholden by the design gods to use a circle on the cover of an album,' Nakanishi laughs. 'This was our attempt, but we snuck in a square and a bunch of scribbles for good measure. Titled after Jason Roebke's delightfully poetic daughter, Yuria, we wanted the design to touch on the complexity and beauty of a child's mind.'

TITLE: Erb/Baker/Zerang, *s/t*
CLIENT: Veto Records
SIZE: 12.7 x 12.7 cm (5 x 5 in.)
PRINTING PROCESS: Screen-printed
INKS: White, blue, pink to purple split fountain, grey
COMPS PRESENTED: 1
REVISIONS: None
APPROVAL: Christoph Erb, Veto records
INVOLVEMENT WITH FINAL PRINTING: Album sleeve screen-printed in-house

Butcher explains that 'the only design prompt we received from Christoph Erb for this project was "fish". This led Nadine's idiosyncratic mind to gyotaku, the Japanese artform of making rubbings from fish. Looking back, I see the connection of printmaking and fish, but when she arrived at the studio with a perfectly good trout to smother with *sumi-e* ink, I was a bit perplexed. To this day, this is one of the most hands-on and simultaneously literal solutions we've used for creating an illustration.'

TITLE: The Urge Trio, *Live At The Hungry Brain*
CLIENT: Veto Records
SIZE: 12.7 x 12.7 cm (5 x 5 in.)
PRINTING PROCESS: Screen-printed
INKS: Grey, orange, black
COMPS PRESENTED: 1
REVISIONS: None
APPROVAL: Christoph Erb, Veto records
INVOLVEMENT WITH FINAL PRINTING: Album sleeve screen-printed in-house

'We continue to traverse the animal kingdom for possible cover models and landed on the German Shepherd,' the duo explain. 'The cover mixes digital and hand-drawn elements to convey a sense of urgency one might find when faced with a fulcrum and pivoting canine teeth.'

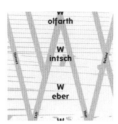

TITLE: Wolfarth/Wintsch/Weber, *Thieves Left That Behind*
CLIENT: Veto Records
SIZE: 12.7 x 12.7 cm (5 x 5 in.)
PRINTING PROCESS: Screen-printed
INKS: White, yellow, navy
COMPS PRESENTED: 1
REVISIONS: None
APPROVAL: Christoph Erb, Veto Records
INVOLVEMENT WITH FINAL PRINTING: Album sleeve screen-printed in-house

'This sleeve is dominated by a fairly straightforward typographic exploration of the musicians' last names, each starting with the letter W. The typeface used, Family, was soon after adopted by Dunkin' Donuts, which we credit this album for,' they say with a wry smile.

TITLE: Third Coast Percussion, *The Book of Keyboards*
CLIENT: New Focus Recordings
SIZE: 12.7 x 12.7 cm (5 x 5 in.)
PRINTING PROCESS: Screen-printed
INKS: CMYK
COMPS PRESENTED: 1
REVISIONS: 2 rounds
APPROVAL: Third Coast Percussion
INVOLVEMENT WITH FINAL PRINTING: Album sleeve screen-printed in-house

'This design was developed to work in tandem with a unique "no-glue" CD sleeve developed by Delicious Design League,' they explain. 'Offset-printed in Europe, screen-printed and die-cut in Chicago, the final package is as international as the music housed in the paper sleeve. For *The Book of Keyboards*, we took influence from an object close to our hearts, a small bell. Scavenged in a dusty second-hand shop in Schaffhausen, Switzerland this last year, the object depicts a small village in an alpine setting in a perfect patina. The improbable mix of image and sound that the object conjures has been a small inspiration since finding it. Many of the percussive sounds on *The Book of Keyboards*, metals especially, remind us of bells. In the recordings, we appreciate the arcane bell-like sounds traversing the lines of such modern compositions. The use of this small object in the artwork not only seemed appropriate, it was inevitable. Instead of focusing on the bell alone, we chose to isolate specific moments and pair those contemporary computer-generated graphics with our own landscape imagery culled from painting and found natural materials. The juxtaposition of hard-edge graphics, liquified vectors, and hand-painted marks captures the tensions of the music presented.'

TITLE: Touch Tones, *Virgo On Virgo*
CLIENT: The Quiet Life
SIZE: 30.4 x 30.4 cm (12 x 12 in.)
PRINTING PROCESS: Offset and screen-printed
INKS: CMYK (exterior), CMYK (interior), yellow and brown slip mat
COMPS PRESENTED: 1
REVISIONS: None
APPROVAL: Touch Tones
INVOLVEMENT WITH FINAL PRINTING: Slip mat screen-printed in-house

'Touch Tones consider themselves a "fake band" in that they don't play live and their songs were instigated in a recording studio environment,' Sonnenzimmer explain. 'We took the idea of "fake" and ran with it, blurring the lines between digital and analogue with the cover art. Built from digital graphics printed on silk, then photographed and integrated back into the digital realm.'

TITLE: *Free Jazz Bitmaps, Vol. 1*
CLIENT: Hometapes / Sonnenzimmer
SIZE: 30.4 x 30.4 cm (12 x 12 in.)
PRINTING PROCESS: Screen-printed
INKS: White (exterior); yellow, grey, green, blue (interior); blue (dust jacket)
COMPS PRESENTED: 1
REVISIONS: None
APPROVAL: Hometapes / Sonnenzimmer
INVOLVEMENT WITH FINAL PRINTING: Album materials all screen-printed in-house

'The Free Jazz Bitmaps series of releases was our first music-related publishing project at the studio,' they explain. 'Featuring original electronic music by Nick on Side A and a cast of talented Chicago-based improvisers on Side B, the series explored genre, iteration and collaboration. The album concept and design were both heavily influenced by Ornette Coleman's breakthrough album *Free Jazz: A Collective Improvisation*, which featured a die-cut cover revealing a portion of Jackson Pollock's painting *White Light*.'

Round
w Flat w
Sound

TITLE: *Round w Flat w Sound*
CLIENT: Sonnenzimmer
SIZE: 17.8 x 17.8 cm (7 x 7 in.)
PRINTING PROCESS: Screen-printed, foil-stamped
INKS: Purple (envelope); purple, blue to pink split fountain, green (poster), purple foil (flexi record)
COMPS PRESENTED: 1
REVISIONS: None
APPROVAL: Self
INVOLVEMENT WITH FINAL PRINTING: Album materials all screen-printed in-house

'*Round w Flat w Sound* was the first manifestation of the series of "meta-catalogues" we now publish for each of our exhibitions,' the duo explain. 'Instead of a straightforward cataloguing of the work produced, the meta-catalogues – coming in many forms, shapes and sizes – hope to expand upon the work in the form of an artists' book. It offers an affordable takeaway from the gallery experience. Produced on the occasion of a group show at Zeitgeist Gallery in Nashville, Tennessee, this piece features a flexi record of an original track by Sonnenzimmer (our first) that was featured in the exhibition.'

TITLE: *The Sun Never Sets*
CLIENT: Sonnenzimmer
SIZE: 30.4 x 30.4 cm (12 x 12 in.)
PRINTING PROCESS: Offset and screen-printed
INKS: CMYK (exterior), orange (dust jacket), purple (record)
COMPS PRESENTED: 1
REVISIONS: None
APPROVAL: Self
INVOLVEMENT WITH FINAL PRINTING: Album materials all screen-printed in-house

'*The Sun Never Sets* is our first non-exhibition-related album of original music as Sonnenzimmer,' they explain. 'The project was initiated through a commission by Intelligentsia Coffee in Chicago. We were approached to develop a concept for a large nine-storey public artwork for the façade of their Wicker Park location. Part of our pitch was to produce this LP featuring artwork and aural shapes that connected with the exterior work. Miraculously, they went for it! You gotta love Chicago,' they add with a smile.

TITLE: *Free Jazz Bitmaps, Vol. 2*
CLIENT: Hometapes / Sonnenzimmer
SIZE: 30.4 x 30.4 cm (12 x 12 in.)
PRINTING PROCESS: Screen-printed
INKS: Yellow and red
COMPS PRESENTED: 1
REVISIONS: None
APPROVAL: Hometapes / Sonnenzimmer
INVOLVEMENT WITH FINAL PRINTING: Album sleeve screen-printed in-house

'The follow-up to *Free Jazz Bitmaps, Vol. 1* was equally inspired by records of the past,' they add. 'This time, the functional and funky high-paced dance singles that Chicago made famous the world over through the development of house music. Designed to visually connect with *Vol. 1* and respectfully emulate the garish quality of the sleeves of some Chicago classics, this sleeve puts mustard and ketchup on the hot dog of house,' they say with a grin.

SUB POP ART DEPARTMENT

HERE TO SERVE YOU, THE ARTIST

 The history of Seattle's Sub Pop Records – from scrappy beginnings through the height of grunge and then countless reinventions – has been written elsewhere. One of the most important aspects of the label's success often flies under the radar, though: over two decades ago they did away with a cadre of local freelancers and brought in Jeff Kleinsmith to man the in-house art department, creating an important backbone and quality control for the label as it grew. That role has grown over the years so that Kleinsmith now operates as the creative director for the label. He has been complemented by the immense talents of many designers working alongside him, from the incredible Hank Trotter and Jesse LeDoux, to the current team of Dusty Summers, Sasha Barr and Bridget Beorse. The key to the success of the department has been the lengths they go to for their bands. 'I think we do way more for our bands than what we would for a freelance client,' Kleinsmith explains. 'That sounds weird, but Sub Pop bands are family – sometimes they are long-lost cousins who we don't know very well – but family nonetheless. It's open-ended. We don't ever enter into an agreement about how much time we will spend. Money never plays a role. We just work until they're happy.'

The time that the art department has been rocking and rolling has coincided exactly with the rise of the Internet, giving Kleinsmith a unique perspective on the changes in the music industry and how they apply to the design process. 'When I started this department twenty-three years ago, most mornings would start with turning on a hand waxer, firing up the analogue Xerox machine and drawing LP, CD and cassette templates by hand with a non-repro blue pen and a T-Square,' he laughs. Even though the office started with a computer, it was at the very beginning of the all-digital changeover, so much of the process was still down to FedEx and faxes and phone calls. Kleinsmith jokes, 'I would often have to wait for a band to get to the next city on tour so they could call me, and even then hardly any of them could speak the language of design.' Now, with all of those barriers to communication removed, and the general population more design-savvy than ever, he finds that he has 'bands texting and emailing me at all hours from all spots on tour. Plus, they know their way around computers and apps and they understand what I am doing, and how I am doing it.' He admits that 'sometimes there can be a bit of bump in the process, when artists specify which typeface they want, or send in a lo-res photo off of their phone and wonder why we can't turn it into a billboard, much less the record cover.'

All of this knowledge and connectivity is a huge bonus in so many areas, though. 'I really find that artists are involved in every single part of the process now – all aspects of the music business. It has returned to a DIY kind of mentality. More contact. More involvement,' he explains. 'In the end, it makes for more, and better, collaboration.' For Kleinsmith and the team this means that artists can better realize their vision for their release. 'I hear designers talk a lot about how the Internet has made them feel obsolete,' he ponders. 'I get that sometimes, but there is something really cool about how all of this has made things more collaborative than ever. I think some of my best designs have come from these kinds of collaborations with our bands.'

The department understands the digital world a lot of their releases live in, but their hearts remain in the physical products. 'We are still mostly releasing physical records with a digital version,' Kleinsmith explains. 'It's not as interesting as a design project if it's not going to end up in some kind of print shop. The design process and how we interact with the client is the same, and we're just as engaged and professional and all of that, but it's just not as fun without the physical end result,' he admits. 'It's like a road trip but you never stop for food,' he laughs. 'I want to mark up proofs with a Sharpie. I want to turn the prints in my hands to see the varnish layer catch light. I want to flick the paper edge to make sure it's 24pt. board, as spec'd. I like seeing what the physical manufacturing process does to something. And I really enjoy working with printers and manufacturers collaboratively to find the best ways to make a package work.'

That love of the packaging process, and the art department's continued close relationships with their printers and vendors is mirrored in the quality and care put into the final product. 'I think packaging will always play an important role in music,' Kleinsmith says. 'We are human, and as such we have a need to hold and touch something physical. As music packaging started to get smaller/digital in the mid-to-late nineties, the interest in giant colourful rock posters took off, but that has waned a bit and we've seen the comeback of the LP.' He ponders the cycles in packaging just in the time he has been designing. 'The popularity of particular package configurations has shifted and changed over the nearly three decades I've been doing this. It was tapes and LPs and then it was mostly just CDs, and now it's tapes and LPs and Deluxe LPs and digital and some CDs.' Once they have sent these labours of love out into the marketplace, they 'peek online every now and then to see what's happening out there, but for the most part I would rather just assume everyone loves everything we're doing,' he says.

STRONGER THAN YOU THINK

One of my favourite things about talking to Kleinsmith about design is that he is a person who always works to better what he considers his weaknesses. He doesn't shy away from them, but works long and hard at turning them into a secret strength, even if he is still insecure about them. 'I secretly wish I could draw! I often have ideas I could never realize as a designer,' he laments. 'I'm drawn to folks who can both design and illustrate (and especially use type).' He then wraps that around a 'love of the mid-century Polish film poster artists.' Then you add in 'seventies and eighties punk/post-punk graphics that were easily the most tangible and obvious influences on me. The visual aesthetic present there is really pleasing to me: simple, bold, immediate. The DIY-ness of it was inspiring to me in a way Frank Frazetta wasn't. As a young kid in a small town it made me feel like I could just start cutting junk out of old magazines for a mixtape or draw on old shirts.' After wrapping all of that together, he replaces traditional drawing with a wild combination of all of these: Polish film posters, mid-century illustrators and raw punk rock – to winning effect!

He admits that 'it's rare that one of our bands is searching for one of our particular styles. We each happen to have a design/illustration style that we generally keep in the closet while we collaborate on their project with them. We're usually being provided some materials that need to be included. Often it's a disparate collection of family ephemera or magazine photos or something. Sometimes bands started working with a freelance illustrator or photographer ... the lack of design industry experience that person brings can be really refreshing, weird and exciting. Bands as clients aren't that different than regular people as clients. It always comes down to personality more than what genre or discipline they come from. The difference is that I love music, so music clients are the best.'

TITLE: Flight Of The Conchords, *I Told You I Was Freaky*

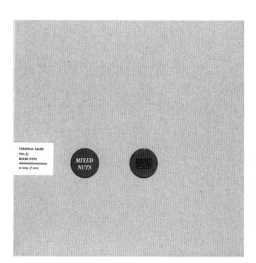

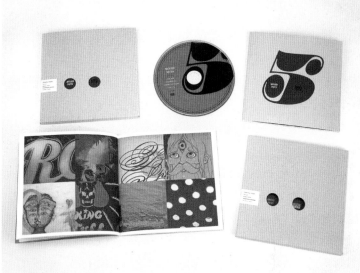

(Top) TITLE: Sub Pop, *Terminal Sales Volume 5: Mixed Nuts*
(Bottom) TITLE: Sub Pop, *Terminal Sales Vol. 4: Please to Enjoy!*

(Left) TITLE: Mass Gothic, *Loser*
(Below) TITLE: Wolf Parade, *Apologies To The Queen Mary* (deluxe edition)

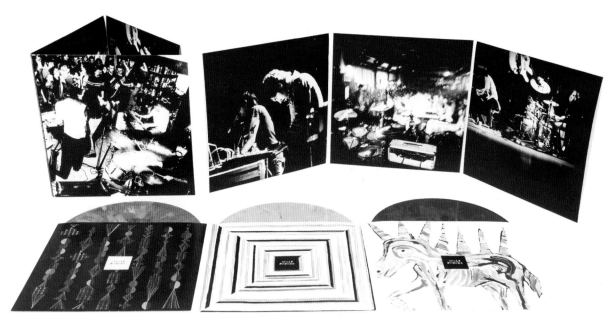

TITLE: Sleater-Kinney, *Live In Paris*

(Above, left) TITLE: Mudhoney, *On Top! – KEXP Presents Mudhoney Live On Top Of The Space Needle*
(Above, right) TITLE: Iron & Wine, *Beast Epic*
(Left) TITLE: Father John Misty, *Pure Comedy*
(Opposite, top) TITLE: Father John Misty, *I Love You, Honeybear*
(Opposite, bottom) TITLE: Beachwood Sparks, *The Tarnished Gold*

TITLE: Flight of the Conchords, *I Told You I was Freaky*
CLIENT: Sub Pop/HBO
SIZE: 30.4 x 30.4 cm (12 x 12 in.)
PRINTING PROCESS: Offset
INKS: CMYK
COMPS PRESENTED: 3
REVISIONS: 5 rounds
APPROVAL: Flight of the Conchords
INVOLVEMENT WITH FINAL PRINTING: Proofs

For the second Flight Of The Conchords LP, the band wanted to reference Seals and Crofts's 1972 *Summer Breeze* LP, 'so I wanted to hire an illustrator who could pull that off,' explains Jeff Kleinsmith. 'John Baizley was the man for the job. He works completely by hand so the revision process was arduous for the poor guy. From there we took his illos and expanded them into a pretty elaborate package. There is a die-cut and embossed front cover revealing portions of the art from the inner gatefold. The LP and CD sleeves have some amazing photography from Brian Tamborello.'

TITLE: Sub Pop, *Terminal Sales Volume 5: Mixed Nuts*
CLIENT: Sub Pop
SIZE: 30.4 x 30.4 cm (12 x 12 in.)
PRINTING PROCESS: Offset
INKS: CMYK
COMPS PRESENTED: 1
REVISIONS: 2 rounds
APPROVAL: Sub Pop
INVOLVEMENT WITH FINAL PRINTING: Proofs

Kleinsmith explains that 'the outer sleeve is made with a grey packing board and has a hand-applied paper decal containing band/song/label info.' Working with Sasha Barr they created 'three die-cut circles revealing text details from the twenty-four-page perfect-bound booklet inside. The booklet contains photos and band info, while the logo-patterned custom dust sleeve holds the actual disc,' he adds.

TITLE: Sub Pop, *Terminal Sales Vol. 4: Please to Enjoy!*
CLIENT: Sub Pop
SIZE: 30.4 x 30.4 cm (12 x 12 in.)
PRINTING PROCESS: Offset, emboss
INKS: CMYK
COMPS PRESENTED: 1
REVISIONS: 2 rounds
APPROVAL: Sub Pop
INVOLVEMENT WITH FINAL PRINTING: Proofs

'We decided to break the bank with this one! (Not really),' jokes Jeff Kleinsmith. Working with Sasha Barr they 'housed inside the embossed industrial cardboard packaging nineteen cards (one for each band) with band info/photo on one side and a unique illustration on the other. Also included is a 15-by-20-inch [38 x 50 cm] foldout poster with text by Chris Jacobs on one side and an art print on the other.'

TITLE: Mass Gothic, *Loser*
CLIENT: Sub Pop
SIZE: 30.4 x 30.4 cm (12 x 12 in.)
PRINTING PROCESS: Offset
INKS: CMYK
COMPS PRESENTED: 5
REVISIONS: 3 rounds
APPROVAL: Mass Gothic
INVOLVEMENT WITH FINAL PRINTING: Proofs

'The art is a collaboration collage using illustrations from Sub Pop artist Chad VanGaalen and photo elements from the band,' explains Dusty Summers. 'The idea was to have something that felt not dissimilar to The Beatles' *Revolver* but to also have a voice and feel all its own. Chad has a very distinct visual style that he uses for all of his own covers, and while we really wanted to use him for the cover, I felt it was important to try to get him to do something that felt special to Mass Gothic. By limiting him to black and white à la *Revolver*, we were able to get something wholly unique that also lent itself to fall right into the collaged elements.'

TITLE: Wolf Parade, *Apologies To The Queen Mary* Deluxe Edition
CLIENT: Sub Pop
SIZE: 30.4 x 30.4 cm (12 x 12 in.)
PRINTING PROCESS: Offset
INKS: CMYK
COMPS PRESENTED: 3
REVISIONS: 2 rounds
APPROVAL: Wolf Parade
INVOLVEMENT WITH FINAL PRINTING: Proofsxx

'For the tenth anniversary deluxe reissues of their Sub Pop debut album, Wolf Parade wanted to use the original elements within the package but come up with a new cover,' explains Dusty Summers. 'Focusing on a live photo from one of their first tours in order to capture the frantic feel of their early live shows did the job, and the original artwork of the both the full-length album and the supporting EP releases is used on the interior gatefolds with cropping and colour changes.'

TITLE: Sleater-Kinney, *Live In Paris*
CLIENT: Sub Pop
SIZE: 30.4 x 30.4 cm (12 x 12 in.)
PRINTING PROCESS: Offset
INKS: CMYK
COMPS PRESENTED: 4
REVISIONS: 4 rounds
APPROVAL: Sleater-Kinney
INVOLVEMENT WITH FINAL PRINTING: Proofs

'For their first-ever live album, Sleater-Kinney wanted a classic bootleg LP,' explains Jeff Kleinsmith. 'My mind went right to my Zeppelin and Floyd bootlegs I bought as a kid. I like the multiple Xeroxed band-photo collage look. I decided to hand-glue a photocopied sheet to each side of a prefab LP jacket. No credits. No song info. Legal, barcode and logo are all on a sticker on the (shitty) plastic sleeve. Of course, the cassette obviously had to look like it was recorded at home on a store-bought cassette,' he smiles.

TITLE: Mudhoney, *On Top! – KEXP Presents Mudhoney Live On Top Of The Space Needle*
CLIENT: Sub Pop
SIZE: 30.4 x 30.4 cm (12 x 12 in.)
PRINTING PROCESS: Offset
INKS: CMYK
COMPS PRESENTED: 1
REVISIONS: 3 rounds
APPROVAL: Mudhoney
INVOLVEMENT WITH FINAL PRINTING: Proofs

'This is a KEXP recording of Mudhoney live on top of the Space Needle, a feat that had never previously been attempted,' explains Jeff Kleinsmith. 'For the cover art I wanted an abstract version of the Space Needle, something you might see created around the time it was built [1962]. Edwin Fotheringham and I have been collaborating for decades, so I feel like we don't need a lot of words to get to the right place. I added a stylized band image, and some type design, and boom! Sonic Boom! Inside are stunning photos from Morgen Schuler of the band in action in front of a cloudless Seattle skyline and glistening Elliott Bay.'

TITLE: Iron & Wine, *Beast Epic*
CLIENT: Sub Pop
SIZE: 30.4 x 30.4 cm (12 x 12 in.)
PRINTING PROCESS: Offset
INKS: CMYK
COMPS PRESENTED: 7
REVISIONS: 2 rounds
APPROVAL: Sam Beam
INVOLVEMENT WITH FINAL PRINTING: Proofs

'For the first time in a while, Sam Beam (Iron & Wine) wanted to use art not created by himself,' Dusty Summers explains. 'We approached a few different artists that focused on embroidery. In fact, there were a number of pieces that were taken to final. The one we actually used, by Sara Barnes, hit the right tone with a loose quality that really gives it a sense of movement and shows the imperfection of the craft. The cover art is complemented by hand-stitched typography by Fort Lonesome from Austin. Rather than throw a bunch of bells and whistles at the package, we opted to do a few tricks that would complement the iconic artwork, printing it on a linen paper and adding thread stitching to the booklet,' he adds.

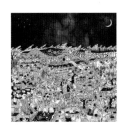

TITLE: Father John Misty, *Pure Comedy*
CLIENT: Sub Pop
SIZE: 30.4 x 30.4 cm (12 x 12 in.)
PRINTING PROCESS: Offset
INKS: CMYK, spot inks, foils
COMPS PRESENTED: 5
REVISIONS: 3 rounds
APPROVAL: Father John Misty
INVOLVEMENT WITH FINAL PRINTING: Proofs

'For Father John Misty's album *Pure Comedy*, we gave UK editorial illustrator Ed Steed the music from the album and let him do his thing,' explains Sasha Barr. 'He came back to us with two densely illustrated scenes bringing to life the album's themes of progress, technology, fame, politics, social media and human nature. We then added a die-cut top-loading outer sleeve, four different watercolour sky backgrounds with spot foils, foldout poster, clear plastic slipcase, and a holographic tarot card also featuring one of Ed's illustrations.'

TITLE: Father John Misty, *I Love You, Honeybear*
CLIENT: Sub Pop
SIZE: 30.4 x 30.4 cm (12 x 12 in.)
PRINTING PROCESS: Offset
INKS: CMYK
COMPS PRESENTED: 3
REVISIONS: 3 rounds
APPROVAL: Father John Misty
INVOLVEMENT WITH FINAL PRINTING: Proofs

'For this album, Josh (Father John Misty) worked directly with LA-based watercolour artist Stacey Rozich to produce the art for the outside cover and inside gatefold spread,' explains Sasha Barr. 'The two worked closely together, starting with Josh's initial ideas of representing the duelling sides of the Father John Misty character – a man with a chequered past and the new man having met the love of his life – as well as the very specific idea of Josh painted as a Renaissance cherub baby. Stacey took Josh's initial direction and fleshed it out in her trademark style. Josh and I then worked closely with our LP jacket manufacturer, Stoughton Printing, to come up with a way to turn Stacey's art into a deluxe double LP pop-up-style package, complete with an embedded MIDI player that plays the title track when opened. Unfortunately, we found the initial run of the deluxe double LP had warped the actual vinyl, so with some retooling we were able to make a final, unwarped product.'

TITLE: Beachwood Sparks, *The Tarnished Gold*
CLIENT: Sub Pop
SIZE: 30.4 x 30.4 cm (12 x 12 in.)
PRINTING PROCESS: Offset
INKS: CMYK and spot foil
COMPS PRESENTED: 3
REVISIONS: 3 rounds
APPROVAL: Beachwood Sparks
INVOLVEMENT WITH FINAL PRINTING: Proofs

'*The Tarnished Gold* is the third LP from California-based alt-country-surf band Beachwood Sparks,' explains Sasha Barr. 'Inspired by classic seventies Americana album covers and surf films, the band and I worked out a simple text-based cover using spot gold foil and a rainbow-coloured inside gatefold, with photos by Kathleen Nicholson and Neal Casal.'

BEN TOUSLEY

SOPHISTICATED WELL BEYOND HIS YEARS

 Little did Ben Tousley know that when he was approached by the band Grizzly Bear to design their *Yellow House* album, he was about to become one of the most celebrated designers in the music industry and would usher in a sense of refinement in the form that had been sorely lacking. He was then just eighteen years old, and it would have been easy to have been overwhelmed by the attention, but Tousley managed to balance continuing his studies with lending his skills to artists that he loved. By the time he graduated from Indiana University, it was safe to say that his portfolio was better not only than any student portfolio I had ever seen, but than ninety-nine per cent of the professional portfolios out there. Moving to New York, he worked with the brilliant Stephen Doyle at Doyle Partners, quickly making his mark with book covers and retail, as well as forming a fruitful creative partnership with Stephen Colbert, all the while continuing to dazzle with his music packaging. Not yet out of his twenties, Tousley had over a decade of intense industry experience when the calling to start up his own shop finally proved to be too strong. If this is what his first ten years look like, I can barely wait to see what magic the next ten produce.

'I came of age in the time of elaborate CD packages,' Tousley explains. 'With the beginning of the Internet and streaming it was kind of interesting wondering if the importance of album art would be threatened. And I think there was maybe a short period where it did dwindle a bit.' That was the fallow period that Tousley was entering into as a designer. However, he quickly saw that certain artists still embraced packaging, and those were the artists he had a connection with. He also saw consumers being re-educated about the need for visuals to go with their listening experience. 'Now, with our handheld devices always in our pockets, and imagery being king, I think it's still as important as ever,' he adds. That need for eye-catching imagery has pushed the acts that might have played it safe in the past to be more adventurous. 'It's been fun to watch the big billboard acts embrace a more artistic and creative approach to music packaging and branding,' he says. 'I hope it continues.'

'Luckily, most of the projects I've worked on have been printed packages. However, with that said I still always try to consider how the covers will appear on digital platforms,' Tousley adds. 'I like to make something that will look iconic and recognizable at a small size, which is where most people are first hearing music these days, and then be rich enough to be enjoyed when it's printed on a record.'

FROM RECORD STORE TO RECORD DESIGNER
Tousley came into designing for the music industry honestly; in fact, in the most honest way that you can. 'My first job was working for a record store in Indianapolis called Luna, which I think I got because I went in so often to buy things,' he laughs. He has never lost that love of the physical side of a release either. 'I'm a big fan of having an actual package to flip through while I sit and listen to the record,' he explains. 'I also do a lot of streaming and buying digitally these days, but when a record comes out that I really love, I try to get a copy and it's always worth it to see how the artists wanted to expand on it.'

One of the things that make Tousley stand out is the close relationship he ends up having with many of the artists that he works with. He is nearly an extra member of the band for Grizzly Bear at this point, and can be found at shows or even in the recording studio with some of his artists. There is one job in the music industry that he has yet to experience, though. 'I'd love to sell merch with the bands!' he exclaims. 'Going to the shows is one of my favourite experiences,' he adds. Tousley also can't help but keep tabs on the releases after they make their way into the marketplace. 'I do like to check and see the records in stores, publications or gently used bargain bins,' he admits. 'Lately I've been getting new work from the same labels,' he adds. 'But I almost always eventually get to work directly with the artists, which I think is invaluable and kind of essential. When I end up doing a lot of work

on a record with feedback from the artist filtered via managers on top of the label, it can be a frustrating process,' he explains. 'Not only in it feeling inefficient, but also because I find the end result to be less exciting than it could have been had there been a more engaging discussion at the beginning.'

As a designer with an immaculate sense of style inherent in his work, it is little surprise that he looks back to designers like Storm Thorgerson, Stanley Donwood, Peter Saville and Vaughan Oliver. Tousley also makes sure to connect directly with the project in front of him in the most basic but essential manner possible. 'The music and the people behind it are the primary influences,' he explains. 'Also, I don't like to do the same thing twice, so it's important for me to try and understand the context of an album – who made it and what influenced them,' he adds. He then expands the influences that can colour the project. 'Outside of that, I turn to artwork, films, literature and anything else that could then spark some kind of interesting connection. It's kind of like a game of telephone from there,' he laughs, 'and it's fun to see what works and how far you can link it.'

With an unusual career arc (given his early start in music packaging) eventually taking him into the hallowed halls of Mucca Design, Pentagram and Doyle Partners, Tousley has a unique perspective on the differences between working in music and other industries at the highest levels. 'Music packaging definitely has a bit more room for playfulness,' Tousley explains. 'And it should, I think. What I like about working with music is the intangible feelings it can conjure in a listener, and somehow trying to add to that experience,' he adds. 'Branding or book design work usually has more of a straightforward intention. That said, my favourite types of projects are the ones where the client is receptive to those ideas of playfulness and interpretation, as with the music projects.'

Already a decade in at such a young age, Tousley still has the euphoria of someone just entering the industry. 'I don't have anything I dislike about designing for the music industry,' he says. 'It's always been kind of a dream. It's an honour to be involved in any small way with records for some of my favourite musicians.' He also loves that these physical objects can possibly 'outlive us both and be shared with someone new down the road, which is a very wonderful feeling,' he says. 'I guess my favourite thing about music packaging is how undefined it is and how exciting that can be when you pair an image with an album. It's kind of open for interpretation,' he marvels. 'That said, the ones that have stood the test of time for me were iconic and created a world with the music I had not seen before. And that's not to say it wasn't a mundane image. I truly think it's the pairing of the image and the music that matters most.'

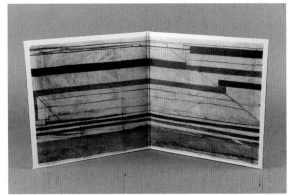

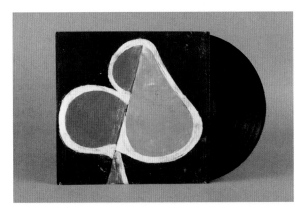

(This page and opposite) **TITLE**: Grizzly Bear, *Shields*

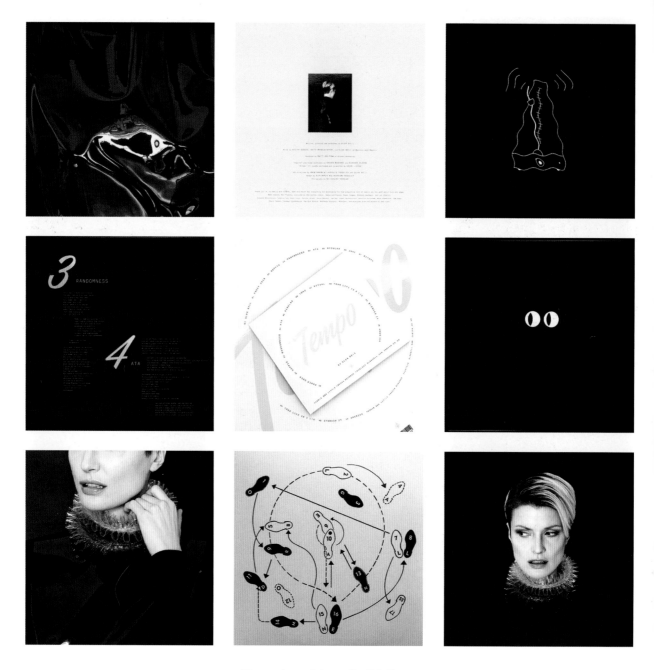

(Above and opposite) TITLE: Olga Bell, *Tempo*

TITLE: Grizzly Bear, *Mourning Sound*

(Clockwise from top left) TITLE: Grizzly Bear, *Painted Ruins*; TITLE: Grizzly Bear, *Four Cypresses*
TITLE: Grizzly Bear, *Two Weeks*; TITLE: Grizzly Bear, *Veckatimist*

(Clockwise from top left) TITLE: Sondre Lerche, *Please*; TITLE: Sondre Lerche, *Bad Law*
TITLE: Nico Muhly & Teitur, *Confessions* (front, back and related materials)

FLEET FOXES

I AM ALL THAT I NEED / ARROYO SECO / THUMBPRINT SCAR
CASSIUS, –
– NAIADS, CASSADIES
KEPT WOMAN
THIRD OF MAY / ODAIGAHARA
IF YOU NEED TO, KEEP TIME ON ME
MEARCSTAPA
ON ANOTHER OCEAN (JANUARY / JUNE)
FOOL'S ERRAND
I SHOULD SEE MEMPHIS
CRACK-UP

CRACK-UP

TITLE: Fleet Foxes, *Crack-Up*

TITLE: Grizzly Bear, *Shields*
CLIENT: Warp Records
SIZE: 30.4 x 30.4 cm (12 x 12 in.)
PRINTING PROCESS: Offset
INKS: CMYK
COMPS PRESENTED: 1
REVISIONS: None
APPROVAL: Grizzly Bear, Richard Diebenkorn Foundation
INVOLVEMENT WITH FINAL PRINTING: Proofs

Sometimes, a piece of art can inspire both the recording artist and the designer. 'Featuring *Blue Club* by Richard Diebenkorn, colour aquatint print from 1981, from his *Clubs and Spades* series, used with kind permission from the Richard Diebenkorn Foundation,' Tousley explains, 'the album's title was inspired by this series.'

TITLE: Olga Bell, *Tempo*
CLIENT: One Little Indian
SIZE: 30.4 x 30.4 cm (12 x 12 in.)
PRINTING PROCESS: Offset
INKS: Greyscale with baby-blue Pantone spot colour, double hits of high gloss
COMPS PRESENTED: 10
REVISIONS: 5 rounds
APPROVAL: Olga Bell
INVOLVEMENT WITH FINAL PRINTING: Proofs

'Olga and I collaborated with photographer Nicholas Prakas to create this image, in homage to the infamous Kit-Cat clocks from the 1930s,' Tousley explains. 'We wanted to make a modern and humorously, unsettling version of that iconic imagery. We manipulated Olga's eyes on the front cover to suggest them bouncing back and forth to the beat. Other images inside the album include the isolated eyes, melting surfaces, wobbly metronomes and Olga looking unsettled. Special double hits of high gloss feature over titles and the photography, creating a raised, shiny texture in physical copies.' Tousley is quick to add that 'this is one of my favourite projects I've worked on!'

TITLE: Grizzly Bear, *Mourning Sound*
CLIENT: RCA Records
SIZE: 30.4 x 30.4 cm (12 x 12 in.)
PRINTING PROCESS: Digital
INKS: N/A
COMPS PRESENTED: 3
REVISIONS: 2 rounds
APPROVAL: Grizzly Bear, Chyrum Lambert
INVOLVEMENT WITH FINAL PRINTING: N/A

In establishing a look for the singles around Grizzly Bear's *Painted Ruins* album, Tousley returned to the paintings of LA artist Chyrum Lambert. Once he had the perfect image, he drew the lettering with paint, markers, pen and pencil to get the desired effect.

TITLE: Grizzly Bear, *Painted Ruins*
CLIENT: RCA Records
SIZE: 30.4 x 30.4 cm (12 x 12 in.)
PRINTING PROCESS: Offset
INKS: CMYK
COMPS PRESENTED: 150
REVISIONS: 75 rounds
APPROVAL: Grizzly Bear, Chyrum Lambert
INVOLVEMENT WITH FINAL PRINTING: Proofs

'The process for finding the perfect artwork for this album was the most extensive yet,' Tousley admits. 'Final artwork is by contemporary Los Angeles artist Chyrum Lambert. After a lot of exploration, we agreed on this image and it was a short trip to the final product.' Once he had the design worked out, Tousley 'printed out the typography, distressed it by hand and then scanned it back so that it would better match the organic tone of the artwork.'

TITLE: Grizzly Bear, *Four Cypresses*
CLIENT: RCA Records
SIZE: 30.4 x 30.4 cm (12 x 12 in.)
PRINTING PROCESS: Digital
INKS: N/A
COMPS PRESENTED: 3
REVISIONS: 2 rounds
APPROVAL: Grizzly Bear, Chyrum Lambert
INVOLVEMENT WITH FINAL PRINTING: N/A

Continuing the series of digital singles covers featuring artwork from Chyrum Lambert and Tousley's unique typographic explorations.

TITLE: Grizzly Bear, *Veckatimest*
CLIENT: Warp Records
SIZE: 30.4 x 30.4 cm (12 x 12 in.)
PRINTING PROCESS: Offset
INKS: CMYK
COMPS PRESENTED: 10
REVISIONS: 5 rounds
APPROVAL: Grizzly Bear, William J. O'Brien
INVOLVEMENT WITH FINAL PRINTING: Proofs

'Beginning with artwork by William J. O'Brien,' Tousley explains, 'this campaign was fun because we received a huge amount of his beautiful drawings to choose from, eventually feeling this one represented the album best.' Once they settled on the image, Tousley designed the type 'to complement the artwork as well as the progression of the band from hushed folk act to a more confident, dynamic group. After I designed the titles, Amelia Bauer redrew them for a natural texture that would relate better to the artwork,' he adds.

TITLE: Grizzly Bear, *Two Weeks*
CLIENT: Warp Records
SIZE: 30.4 x 30.4 cm (12 x 12 in.)
PRINTING PROCESS: Offset
INKS: CMYK
COMPS PRESENTED: 10
REVISIONS: 5 rounds
APPROVAL: Grizzly Bear, William J. O'Brien
INVOLVEMENT WITH FINAL PRINTING: Proofs

'The is the cover for the lead single for the *Veckatimest* album,' Tousley explains. Again featuring artwork by William J. O'Brien, they chose this drawing, feeling that it best fitted with the celebratory tone of the song. 'With all of the supporting singles and releases for this album (there are maybe five related covers), we matched the same typography treatment to the *Veckatimest* album cover to create a unified campaign. After I designed the title, Amelia Bauer once again redrew it for a natural texture that would relate better to the artwork,' he adds.

TITLE: Sondre Lerche, *Please*
CLIENT: Yep Roc Records
SIZE: 30.4 x 30.4 cm (12 x 12 in.)
PRINTING PROCESS: Offset
INKS: CMYK
COMPS PRESENTED: 10
REVISIONS: 5 rounds
APPROVAL: Sondre Lerche, Lars Elling
INVOLVEMENT WITH FINAL PRINTING: None

'Sondre found this series of paintings by fellow Norwegian artist Lars Elling,' Tousley explains, 'which instantly felt like the complement to the album's theme of relationship breakdowns.' He adds further that 'Sondre and I had worked together on several records and projects prior to this, and this turned out to be my favourite.'

TITLE: Sondre Lerche, *Bad Law*
CLIENT: Yep Roc Records
SIZE: 30.4 x 30.4 cm (12 x 12 in.)
PRINTING PROCESS: Digital
INKS: N/A
COMPS PRESENTED: 10
REVISIONS: 5 rounds
APPROVAL: Sondre Lerche, Lars Elling
INVOLVEMENT WITH FINAL PRINTING: N/A

Keeping the series going, 'this is the cover for one of the main singles from *Please*, again with a painting by Lars Elling,' Tousley says. 'We actually made a cover for each of the ten songs on the album, with the same title treatment and a different painting from Elling.'

TITLE: Nico Muhly & Teitur, *Confessions*
CLIENT: Nonesuch Records
SIZE: 30.4 x 30.4 cm (12 x 12 in.)
PRINTING PROCESS: Offset
INKS: CMYK
COMPS PRESENTED: 2
REVISIONS: 1 round
APPROVAL: Nico Muhly & Teitur
INVOLVEMENT WITH FINAL PRINTING: Proofs

'The lyrics for this record are all based on YouTube comments to random videos that Nico and Teitur found,' Tousley explains. 'I loved the juxtaposition of the mundane lyrics and Nico's gorgeous orchestration, so I made the artwork by creating mundane objects found in the song subject and adding the text to them. The album cover is made with a letter board I bought and photographed for real light and shadow, with the supporting imagery made from fake receipts, fortune cookies, coffee stains, an ashtray and a fake "lost cat" flyer.'

TITLE: Fleet Foxes, *Crack-Up*
CLIENT: Nonesuch Records
SIZE: 30.4 x 30.4 cm (12 x 12 in.)
PRINTING PROCESS: Offset
INKS: CMYK
COMPS PRESENTED: 1
REVISIONS: None
APPROVAL: Robin Pecknold, Hiroshi Hamaya Estate
INVOLVEMENT WITH FINAL PRINTING: Proofs

'This is one of my favourite design collaborations,' Tousley admits. 'I'm a huge fan of Fleet Foxes and I worked on this directly with band leader Robin Pecknold over tea in my studio. He had a very clear vision already, using these photographs of Japanese landscape in the sixties by photographer Hiroshi Hamaya. I took his guidance and helped refine it with grids and typography.'

VISUAL DIALOGUE

THE FRAYED CORNERS OF HISTORY

Before he had even finished his studies at the University of Michigan, Fritz Klaetke had settled in as the head of his own design firm. Visual Dialogue was off to the races, and when he relocated to Boston, Klaetke quickly became an integral part of the creative fabric of the city – so much so that the studio created a successful gift shop to celebrate the city and its history. Carving out a reputation as one of the best firms in town, they soon reached out to claim national clients, while never losing a sense of their roots. It is the grounded approach that mixes so well with Klaetke's wash of refinement. When Visual Dialogue really hits the design mark, it often brings out Fritz's keen sense of modernism, along with his appreciation of the frayed corners of history. Few designers and clients have been paired as well as Klaetke and Smithsonian Folkways. It is no surprise that they have meshed so well, but the ability of Visual Dialogue to somehow refresh and reinvigorate these classic recordings to the level that they have is nothing short of breathtaking. If a decade ago you had predicted that one of the most important pieces of design for the music industry over the next ten years was going to be for a set of old Woody Guthrie songs, no one would have believed you. No one, that is, except Fritz Klaetke.

Photographer, Michael Piazza

'I think you could make a living designing music packaging back in the day, but it seems like those days are over,' laments Klaetke. Luckily for him, those kinds of jobs account for a fraction of his output at Visual Dialogue, but he admits there's a certain coolness attached to them. 'I still get a small thrill whenever I see a package I designed at a music store, but those days are few and far between. Now a review, with maybe a passing mention of the design, is the place I might most likely experience that.'

But he's no longer just designing album covers; he's creating entire packaging systems with historic reference on masters such as Woody Guthrie and Lead Belly for Smithsonian Folkways Recordings. Klaetke is carrying on a design tradition that started long before he was involved. 'As the non-profit record label of the Smithsonian Institution, the National Museum of the United States, it has a very different mission than most labels. We're preserving musical moments in time, not trying to sell the pop song of the moment,' he explains. 'Ronald Clyne was the designer who created more than five-hundred album covers for Folkways and defined the look of the label,' he gushes. 'Ever since I started working with them, I've looked to his work for inspiration and guidance.'

Combine that with the fact that his dad was an architect and that he grew up in a Mies van der Rohe house in Detroit; as he says, 'High modernism has always been an influence. I also try to take in as much interesting contemporary art as possible, whether that be at Art Basel Miami, local galleries or researching and creating street art for public art installations around Massachusetts.'

This modernist influence is nowhere more apparent than in the designs for Folkways, which feature careful overlays of typography on old photographs, and the use of one colour to create a striking juxtaposition that is simple yet brilliant. Klaetke says it's imperative to 'give music a visual reference point. That reference point then becomes part of our visual culture.'

STANDING THE TEST OF TIME

When designing anything, he says, 'I try to understand the parameters and limitations at the outset. Acknowledging the givens helps to focus the creative process. But design for music is perhaps more reliant on the pairing with the aural aspect to complete the experience.' Perhaps the biggest qualm with music package design is budget. 'I remember Vaughan Oliver lamenting the amount of money poured into music videos which, if successful, may be shown for a month or two, while a pittance is spent on a cover design, which can work for decades.'

When talking about what makes a cover design successful, Klaetke simply says, 'A design that seems inevitable, whether that be a sense of timelessness or capturing a specific moment in time.' In addition to running Visual Dialogue, Klaetke and his business and life partner, Susan Battista, opened a store in Faneuil Hall, called 1630, which celebrates Boston's past and present with products by local makers, vintage goods from around New England and products they've designed. 'As part of the overall experience, we quickly recognized how much of an impact music has on the interactions at the retail level – for better or for worse. The music we programmed for the shop features string or orchestral versions of contemporary songs by bands like Vitamin String Quartet (VSQ). It's been interesting to see how many people compliment the music, which at first listen suggests traditional classical music befitting the historic setting, but then they pick up on the modern tune, which plays off the old/new vibe of the shop,' he notes. 'This speaks to our philosophy that the best design works to help create a total experience touching multiple senses.'

He also finds that growing older in this business has afforded him some unexpected experiences, as well as even more surprising influences. 'I have to say that having a sixteen-year-old teenage daughter means I now know more about the latest top-forty pop hits than I ever have before,' he laughs. One of those defining experiences has been attending the Grammys, the US awards event that can forever etch your name in history. 'It's an amazing experience being surrounded by a diverse crowd all united by their love of music,' Klaetke explains. 'I remember being in line to pick up something and the guy in front of me was nominated for, I think, best rap song and the guy behind me was nominated for best classical composition. Later, when they called my name (crazy!), and after I had to string a few semi-coherent sentences together as an acceptance speech, I was sandwiched between Esperanza Spalding (best jazz vocal) and Brian Wilson (best historical album). Then the live show they put together is an impressive assemblage of the year in music. Put it on your bucket list,' he adds. We should all be so lucky as to cross off a bucket list item that includes rubbing shoulders with Brian Wilson.

THE
SMITHSONIAN
FOLKWAYS
COLLECTION

Smithsonian Folkways

LEAD
BELLY

TITLE: *Lead Belly: The Smithsonian Folkways Collection* (box set)

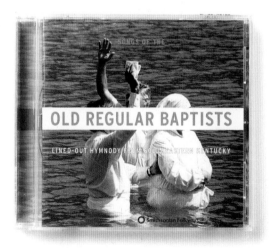

(Clockwise from top left)

TITLE: Various artists, *There Is No Eye: Music For Photographs*; **TITLE:** Pete Seeger, *Headlines & Footnotes: A Collection Of Topical Songs*
TITLE: *Songs Of The Old Regular Baptists: Lined-Out Hymnody From Southeastern Kentucky*; **TITLE:** Various artists, *Dark Holler: Old Love Songs And Ballads*

TITLE: Various artists, *Friends Of Old Time Music: The Folk Arrival 1961–1965* (box set)

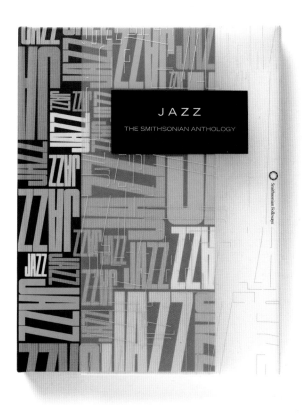

TITLE: *Jazz: The Smithsonian Anthology* (box set)

WOODY
AT
100

**THE WOODY GUTHRIE
CENTENNIAL COLLECTION**

Smithsonian Folkways

(Above and opposite) **TITLE:** *Woody At 100* (box set)

TITLE: *Lead Belly: The Smithsonian Folkways Collection*
CLIENT: Smithsonian Folkways
SIZE: 30.4 x 30.4 cm (12 x 12 in.)
PRINTING PROCESS: Offset
INKS: CMYK
COMPS PRESENTED: 5
REVISIONS: 3 rounds
APPROVAL: Smithsonian Folkways
INVOLVEMENT WITH FINAL PRINTING: Proofs

'This photo really captures Lead Belly for me,' Klaetke explains. 'The strength, the sorrow, the directness. If eyes are the windows to the soul …' he ponders. The powerful image houses a gritty one-hundred-and-forty-page book and five-disc design that treats its subject matter with reverence, while celebrating the rougher edges of the behind-the-scenes material.

TITLE: Various artists, *There Is No Eye: Music For Photographs*
CLIENT: Smithsonian Folkways
SIZE: 14 x 13 cm (5.5 x 5 in.)
PRINTING PROCESS: Offset
INKS: CMYK
COMPS PRESENTED: 1
REVISIONS: 2 rounds
APPROVAL: Smithsonian Folkways
INVOLVEMENT WITH FINAL PRINTING: Proofs

'John Cohen is truly a modern-day Renaissance man,' Klaetke explains. 'From his role in the folk revival as a member of the New Lost City Ramblers, to his poster designs reviving old wood types, to his recordings of traditional Andean music, to his film and photography work.' Compiling his photographs of other musicians into a book, 'this CD accompanies *There Is No Eye* and even features a photo of Woody Guthrie near the end of his life on the cover,' he adds.

TITLE: Pete Seeger, *Headlines & Footnotes: A Collection Of Topical Songs*
CLIENT: Smithsonian Folkways
SIZE: 14 x 13 cm (5.5 x 5 in.)
PRINTING PROCESS: Offset
INKS: CMYK
COMPS PRESENTED: 1
REVISIONS: 3 rounds
APPROVAL: Smithsonian Folkways
INVOLVEMENT WITH FINAL PRINTING: Proofs

'Printed on recycled cardboard at the request of Pete himself, *Headlines & Footnotes* features topical songs that still resonate today,' Klaetke explains, before adding with a wink, 'stay tuned for the definitive Pete Seeger box set from Folkways scheduled to be released next year.' The collection of previously released material, combined with live versions and studio outtakes serves both to fulfil the needs of diehard fans and inspire new ones.

TITLE: Various artists, *Dark Holler: Old Love Songs And Ballads*
CLIENT: Smithsonian Folkways
SIZE: 14 x 13 cm (5.5 x 5 in.)
PRINTING PROCESS: Offset
INKS: CMYK
COMPS PRESENTED: 1
REVISIONS: 2 rounds
APPROVAL: Smithsonian Folkways
INVOLVEMENT WITH FINAL PRINTING: Proofs

Sometimes in design the most important move you make is the move you don't make. Learning to stay out of the way of a great image is a skill that Klaetke has honed to a fine point, and there is no better example than here. 'When presented with an amazing image like the portrait of Dillard Chandler by John Cohen,' Klaetke says, 'the number one rule of design is "don't screw it up." Let the photo do the work and the type can take a back seat,' he adds with a smile.

TITLE: *Songs Of The Old Regular Baptists: Lined-Out Hymnody From Southeastern Kentucky*
CLIENT: Smithsonian Folkways
SIZE: 14 x 13 cm (5.5 x 5 in.)
PRINTING PROCESS: Offset
INKS: CMYK
COMPS PRESENTED: 1
REVISIONS: 3 rounds
APPROVAL: Smithsonian Folkways
INVOLVEMENT WITH FINAL PRINTING: Proofs

While working on the cover for this release, Klaetke was literally faced with a surprising problem. 'It's against the beliefs of the Old Regular Baptists, a religious sect in the Southern Appalachian Mountains, to allow their faces to be shown in photographs,' he explains. 'So putting the type in a stripe covering their faces solves the problem.'

TITLE: Various artists, *Friends Of Old Time Music: The Folk Arrival 1961 – 1965*
CLIENT: Smithsonian Folkways
SIZE: 15.2 x 31.1 cm (6 x 12.2 inches)
PRINTING PROCESS: Offset
INKS: CMYK
COMPS PRESENTED: 1
REVISIONS: 2 rounds
APPROVAL: Smithsonian Folkways
INVOLVEMENT WITH FINAL PRINTING: Proofs

'Recorded between 1961 and 1965 by a young Peter K. Siegel, *Friends of Old Time Music* brought the most influential traditional musicians to New York City for the first time, marking "the folk arrival". To show the array of musicians, we included photos by John Cohen, David Gahr, Alan Lomax, Robert Frank and others of all the performers featured in the collection,' Klaetke explains. To add to that feeling, the design pulls from the typography used in show posters of the era and evocative photos of the performers to wrap around a sixty-page book.

TITLE: *Jazz: The Smithsonian Anthology*
CLIENT: Smithsonian Folkways
SIZE: 15.2 x 31.1 cm (6 x 12.2 inches)
PRINTING PROCESS: Offset
INKS: CMYK
COMPS PRESENTED: 1
REVISIONS: 3 rounds
APPROVAL: Smithsonian Folkways
INVOLVEMENT WITH FINAL PRINTING: Proofs

Klaetke is on the record with his love for the work of Ronald Clyne, and a massive project where he could show that in a physical way was hard to resist. 'Paying homage to the classic Folkways *JAZZ* series of album covers designed by Ronald Clyne in the early 1950s, *JAZZ: The Smithsonian Anthology* uses the orignal type and colour palette reassembled into a new composition for the box-set format,' he explains. The design wraps around a two-hundred-page book housing six discs.

TITLE: *Woody At 100*
CLIENT: Smithsonian Folkways
SIZE: 30.4 x 30.4 cm (12 x 12 in.)
PRINTING PROCESS: Offset
INKS: CMYK
COMPS PRESENTED: 3
REVISIONS: 2 rounds
APPROVAL: Smithsonian Folkways
INVOLVEMENT WITH FINAL PRINTING: Proofs

'When creating the definitive box set for an American icon like Woody Guthrie, we wanted to avoid cliches and photos that have been seen a million times,' Klaetke explains. 'Luckily, we were able to find a passport photo of a young Woody that expressed his intelligence and impish nature. So we blew it up to life-size to confront the viewer directly – the same way his lyrics confront the listener,' he explains. With such a fresh, arresting cover, Visual Dialogue managed to reinvigorate an artist that everyone thought they had already seen everything from. The resulting one-hundred-and-fifty-page book and three-disc set would go on to win a Grammy for Best Box Set or Special Edition Package.

STIJN ANSEEL

KILLING VECTOR FIELD

The vast majority of the designers and studios featured in this book spend most of their time engaged with the music industry, accounting for most, if not all, of their most well-known portfolio pieces. But that doesn't mean that they are the only ones capable of designing a breathtaking sleeve for a musical artist, big or small. There are so many folks around the world that turn their talents to a record cover every now and again with stunning results. Stijn Anseel is certainly one of those, and I loved his work for De Portables so much that I couldn't resist shining a spotlight on it.

'I have known De Portables for years,' Anseel begins. 'I have worked on a few projects for them, handling the artwork for their other records as well.' Anseel designs for clients working in everything from publishing to education to chocolate bars. His work is crisp and graphic and terribly engaging. It is also a portfolio that you can see never being sullied by rock and roll. That makes his work on this album all the more fascinating, as it fits in perfectly with everything else he does yet seems like it is also from another planet.

'The packaging should be an extension of the music, translated into another artform, making the music tangible,' Anseel explains. 'When I am designing for a client in music, compared to my other clients it differs. There are no real boundaries when you design a record sleeve,' he says. 'It's also more of a hit-or-miss dynamic. You make something and the design just clicks with the band or it doesn't – you can't really predict it,' he adds, finding that he morphs into 'more of an artist for a client that is also an artist, but in a different discipline.' It requires getting on their creative wavelength and mindset. 'Making graphic design for more traditional clients is a much more rational process,' he says.

Inspiring this particular design was 'the title of the record, *The Killing Horizon*, which refers to a 19th-century German mathematician named Wilhelm Killing. Wikipedia says this: "A Killing horizon is a null hypersurface defined by the vanishing of the norm of a Killing vector field." It's pretty heavy stuff,' Anseel adds. 'There is a link to Einstein and his gravitational wave theory, which says that gravity is a distortion of space–time. And then there's Christopher Nolan's film *Interstellar*, where the main character uses gravity to physically communicate through time (the tesseract scene). In that scene time is visualized as these coloured strips … that was a direct inspiration,' he explains. Obviously needing a lot of thought and planning before he approached the work at hand, he also knew that everyone involved wanted 'that Optical Art trippy look'. Anseel is quick to add that he was coming at all of this parallel to the band. 'Those cosmic, sci-fi, pseudoscience references were also a big inspiration for the music. We share the same interest in these nerdy subjects,' he underlines, with a grin.

Working on an LP has given him an inside persepective on the deabte about vinyl versus digital formats. Anseel sees a renewed interest in authenticity among customers. 'Although LPs are sort of an anachronism, they seem to fill a certain gap in the market,' he observes. 'I simply like vinyl. It's big, straightforward. There's nothing like putting a needle on a record and hearing that crackling sound. It's all very analogue. As a band, it would be my preferred medium to publish my music on,' he adds. 'Let the marketing people worry about strategy.' It's obvious that he has finally come under the spell of rock and roll, as that last statement is spoken like a true musician.

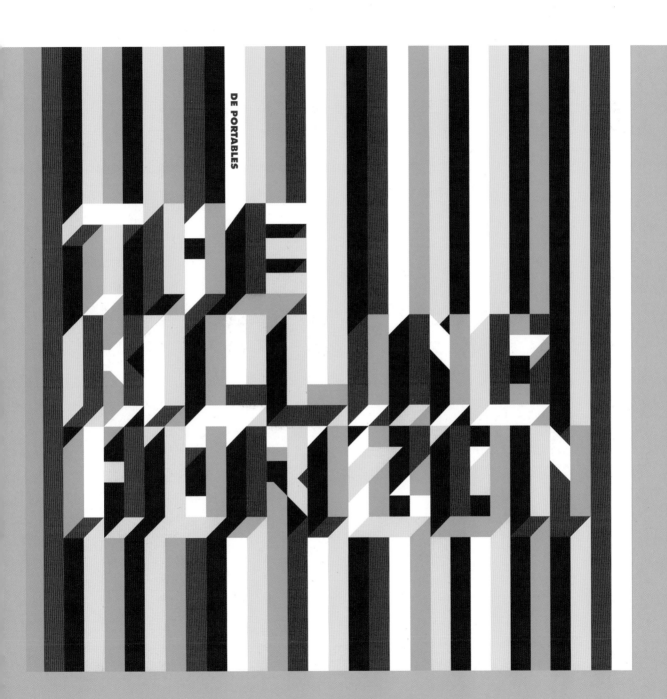

DE PORTABLES

THE MOVING HORIZON

AGI MORAWSKA

A BRAND YOU CAN TRUST

So much of working on music packaging is about relationships and trust. That can be your entry into doing this kind of work, whether you are friends with a musician or someone crazy enough to launch a record label. It is also how you keep doing this. Even if your studio grows in other directions, that bond will keep you both coming back to one another for every release. Such is the case with Agi Morawska. Her talents have taken her all the way to her position as a design director at Landor, one of the largest brand consultants in the world, but much like her need to get out on the open road on her motorcycle, she has never lost touch with her musical bonds.

'This is all about good ole' friendship,' Morawska explains, 'and the cultural legacy of Factory Records!' she adds with a big smile. 'My friend John Decicco was managing The Depreciation Guild, and John and the band wanted to find a long-term collaborator,' she says. 'I was lucky because my clients believe that having a relationship with a designer will allow them to create another dimension for their audience. Along with the music, gigs and interviews, we could create a visual tale, a world unfolding across singles, albums and posters, reflecting both the band and the music's journey,' she explains. 'I have been lucky enough to work on nearly all of the band's releases, posters and merchandise.'

Morawska is more in tune with the power of packaging than most, and she knows that when creating the physical packaging for a record, 'it should be an adventure, an experience. Like riding a motorcycle or woodworking, handling physical objects (vinyl records; a well-made, casebound book; a silk-screen poster) is not easier, faster or cheaper than consuming digital content, but it is – should be – infinitely more satisfying,' she says. 'It provides that sense of connection – you somehow feel it was made by people, for people, that it came to you from the band,' she explains. Never missing a chance to connect, she insists that the 'multiple elements in the vinyl packaging and the process of unpacking the record are an opportunity to tell a story, to send a consumer on a journey and set up little discoveries along the way.'

She was surprised to run into problems on these projects that she never faces in her day job. For instance, 'typesetting the Japanese cover versions, roughly knowing what the content is, is not the same as understanding each sign,' she explains. 'It still could say 'produced by forty specially trained Ecuadorian mountain llamas'. I secretly hope it does,' she says with a smile.

'For me, music packaging might be where design comes closest to art: you define and express the message, so perhaps the project even relies less on your prowess as a designer, rather reaching who you are as a human being,' she ponders. 'I used to create music and it's the same feeling – you have to allow yourself to become vulnerable. And if you ever felt that head rush and spine tingling while listening to a piece of music, you are really doing that project for yourself!' she adds.

'The great part of these projects is that they are populated by passionates, people who love music,' she explains. 'That love and excitement makes a project a thrill. It's a scout's summer camp of design projects.' And with that level of emotional investment, there is always the fear that you can be 'putting yourself in an emotional and creative freefall. It's terrifying.'

'In a world of quantity over quality, of immediate and mass-produced goods, we seek experiences – personal and authentic ones at that,' she outlines. It is why music packaging is so important, and why it might fly in the face of every marketing study or list of manufacturing and distribution analytics. 'I think similarly to printed matter, vinyl, with its mythology and mystique, has long ago crossed not only from basic to special goods, but further into the category of experiences.'

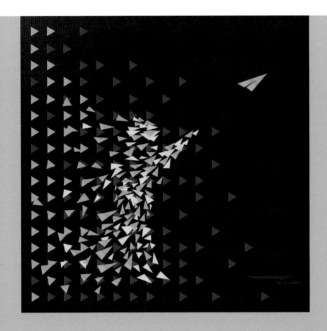

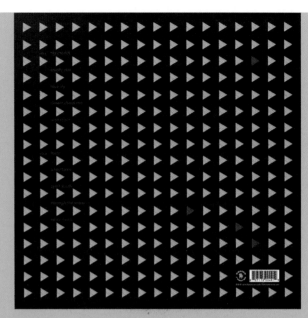

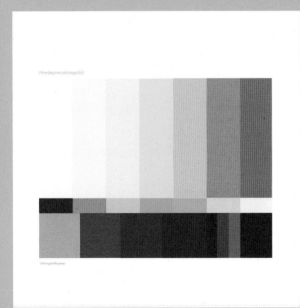

HEIKE-KARIN FÖLL

A WAVE OF CONNECTIONS

A lot of the packaging in this book has custom images created for the design: photographs, illustrations, logos, type solutions and sometimes even typefaces. But there is another way that record sleeves often find their perfect match. We have shown examples of designers using existing artwork and changing the context throughout, but I wanted to delve a little deeper into that dynamic with one of my favourite sleeves of the last few years; Christian Naujoks' *Wave*, featuring a painting by Heike-Karin Föll.

Both are highly regarded artists in their fields: Naujoks, with his music which seems to bridge so many genres, while tying them all together in a melancholy wash; Föll, with her abstract paintings and active brushwork and penchant for hiding little bits of collage. It should not have come as a surprise to me that they already knew one another, but it did.

'I met Heike during the Venice Biennale 2015,' Naujoks says. 'We knew each other before, but this meeting was by chance so we had lunch together, and we had a really extended and nice conversation. We talked about time, and how we both think it's really not linear,' he explains. This connection linked them closely as Naujoks considers this to be a 'major aspect of my music, especially with *Wave* – both aesthetically, time in music, but also in terms of life,' he stresses. 'So there was a bond. That's why I thought about Heike when it came to the cover. We met at a gallery show where some of Heike's works were being shown and we quickly agreed that her painting *Self Determined* would be the best choice,' he explains.

'Christian, along with Pete Kersten at Dial, Christian's record label, approached me about possibly using my painting on the cover. I felt that connection to Christian's work and agreed that it would be a good fit,' Föll explains. Her painting seemed almost ready-made for the project, with the colour wash of blue and the active line work. Even more so, you might be surprised to know that all of the type was already part of the painting, long before Naujoks had ever laid eyes on it.

'The approach to the visual aspect of making records is really specific with Dial,' Naujoks explains. 'Especially in terms of the relationship with contemporary art.' Specific to his album, he continues that 'with *Wave*, there are two very strong individual elements, the graphic design/typography by in-house designer Till Sperrle, and Heike's work on the front cover. So Heike's painting is not informed by the music at all, whereas Till's design of the back sleeve is really a response to the music,' he adds. 'I remember it was kind of a surprise for me when we first saw this design, but we immediately liked it a lot!' For Sperrle it is an everyday juggling act. 'I have worked with Dial for fourteen years now, so we are really experienced in this kind of collaborative work,' he says. 'It feels organic and works really well in general.'

The combination has been something that benefits all parties and makes the whole greater than the parts. And as the parts are pretty amazing on their own, that really says something. 'I love the aspect that my painting is circulating via this medium,' Föll is quick to add. 'Now a lot of people have already approached me from having seen my work on Christian's album cover. The fact, that the distribution reaches another audience than a show of my work might connect with makes this valid for me, as well as for my entire body of work.'

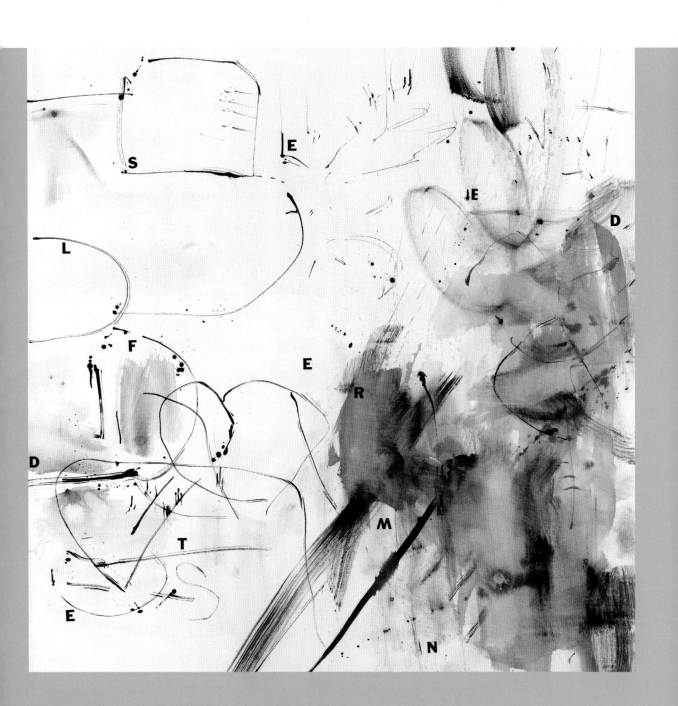

AFTERWORD

When I was starting the process of writing this book and assembling the collection of designers, I knew I would be getting the opportunity to talk to many of my music packaging heroes, both young and old. What I couldn't be prepared for was just how inspirational they would be. Many of the interviews made me challenge the very way that I have been designing for the past two decades. Torsten Posselt at FELD enthralled me with a detailed discussion of both his process and his philosophy when it comes to working on music projects. At the heart of his thinking was the pure joy that one gets when they open up a shrink-wrapped LP and put it on the turntable. Hearing those first notes as you ponder the sleeve and read the liner notes. Why should Posselt be denied that intense pleasure, just because he is designing the packaging? It turned out to be a very good question. While I don't think I will ever have the discipline to deny myself a listen to a record I am working on until it actually arrives sealed up and at my door, I do know that I will never lose that intense joy that comes with getting a new album in my hands. It's that feeling that drives everything this book seeks to capture.

On every page is a fascinating revelation, brought about by the bold and honest answers of the talented people assembled within. The DIY punk rock collaborations of Sam Ryser are not that far removed from the jazzy interplay of the duo that makes up Sonnenzimmer. Ben Tousley is loving every minute of working on Grizzly Bear's releases, but that doesn't mean that he isn't also going over a hundred rounds of looking at paintings with the band to find the right one. Brian Roettinger is literally rewriting the job description of a designer in the music industry. Bon Iver is ahead of the curve in inviting Eric Carlson out to his rural studio for days to get in a mental and visual jam session. Designers that are long since established, such as

Michael Cina and Jacob Escobedo, are digging deep into their personal loves and interests to somehow elevate their talents beyond the skyscraping levels they were already at. Oliver Hibert and Darren Oorloff are dipping back into past visual decades to find new and exciting voices and truly come into their own.

We were lucky enough to see the curtain pulled back on the massive process needed to complete two of the most ambitious projects the music industry has attempted in the last decade with the Paramount Records cases. And we also got to see the one-man band version, as Henry Owings wears forty-seven different hats to bring these wonderful box sets to the marketplace. Past masters of the form were not shy with their assessment of the state of the industry, which also led to my understanding as to how talented this new wave of designers truly are, doing so much with so few resources. From Mexico City to Copenhagen to Melbourne to Scottsdale, Arizona, creatives are working tirelessly to make something amazing to hold in our hands that does justice to the music within. For that, I will be forever thankful.

'There is art that's over-pretentious and over-symbolic.
And it's trying to pretend to be something way beyond what
it is – but I don't think we did that.'

'I heard a bit in the studio. I don't have much to say about music.
Usually I like it, and I just absorb it. I don't have much to say, and they
ain't let me say anything anyway. They say "For God's sake, Storm, do not
harm our song. Do not murder our tune." So I never say anything, really,
about the music. I just let it go over, really, I suppose. It's my job
to reinterpret it, really. So it doesn't really matter what I think, it matters
what comes out the other end. And with *Dark Side* it was very much about
the madness of the lyrics and about something that Rick said to me.
He said "Could we not have one of your funny pictures, Storm?" and I said
"What do you mean? That's what I do. Pictures. How about a change?"
I said "But I don't do graphics." He said "Well, why, is it a challenge?"'

— Storm Thorgerson

Hipgnosis founder Storm Thorgerson speaking about working on Pink Floyd's *Dark Side Of The Moon* album.

INDEX

ABOUT THE AUTHOR

John Foster is a world-renowned designer, author and speaker on design issues. His work has been published in numerous books and every major industry magazine, hangs in galleries across the globe and is part of the permanent collection of the Smithsonian. He is the proud recipient of a gold medal from the Art Directors Club. He is an international speaker, including numerous appearances at the largest design gathering in the world; The HOW Design Conference. Foster is the author of *New Masters of Poster Design* and *New Masters of Poster Design: Volume Two*; *Paper and Ink Workshop*; *1,000 Indie Posters*; *Dirty Fingernails: A One-Of-A-Kind Collection of Graphics Uniquely Designed By Hand*; *For Sale: Over 200 Innovative Solutions in Packaging Design*; *Maximum Page Design*; and is one of the authors of *Thou Shall Not Use Comic Sans*. He had the honour of penning the layout chapter of Debbie Millman's *Essential Principles of Graphic Design*, and has written columns for howdesign.com, brightestyoungthings.com and rockpaperink.com. He sits behind an enormous desk for drawing, painting and thinking and general computering. The goofiest foxhound, dachshund, and olde English bulldog to roam the land occupy the region directly below his feet.

Photographer: Lily Foster

ACKNOWLEDGMENTS

There were far too many instances where this book seemed as if it just wasn't going to happen. The driving forces from beginning to end were the designers you see featured here. They gave so much to the process and I can only hope that I have made them proud in the way that they are presented. I admire and love you all. James Evans was the first believer in this book and will forever be my champion. The next round is on me. Lucy York, Becky Ayre and Emily Potts all did their very best to make this book far better than I could have hoped. Your efforts did not go unnoticed. My family never stops filling me with love and joy, and I can't thank my wife Suzanne and my amazing daughter Lily enough for their patience through this process. So much love to both sets of my parents and my nine brothers and sisters (blended families are the best!) and my lifelong friends Bill Vierbuchen, Dave Bradbury, Chad Lafley and Rich Westbrook. Andrea Needle and Kim Fitts and everyone at Dream for providing a few fun hours in the week. Filippo Salvadori, Steve Wascovich and everyone at Superior Viaduct for releasing so much incredible music and allowing me to play a small part in it. You all are amazing.